Betty Isabel
6561

INTRODUCTION TO
PHOTOGRAPHY

INTRODUCTION TO
PHOTOGRAPHY

ROBERT B. RHODE

Associate Professor of Journalism
University of Colorado

&

FLOYD H. McCALL

Director, Color Photo Department
The Denver Post

THE MACMILLAN COMPANY
COLLIER-MACMILLAN LIMITED, LONDON

Seventh Printing, 1969

Library of Congress catalog card number: 65-15572

THE MACMILLAN COMPANY
COLLIER-MACMILLAN CANADA, LTD., TORONTO, ONTARIO

Printed in the United States of America

PREFACE

Not long ago we heard someone say, "Photography is a snap!" We enjoyed the play on words. Photography does involve the "snap" of the shutter and it does appear to be easy—deceptively so. But photography is not something to be mastered in one, or even ten, easy lessons.

Photography as a medium of communication or as an art—if one is willing to regard it as an art—would profit if more photographers were willing to subject themselves to discipline similar to that endured by the practitioners of the traditional creative arts. It is only through such voluntary submission to discipline that any means of expression can be mastered.

This book is intended as a beginner's guide to such discipline. It is not a handbook, a how-to-do-it manual. It is, we hope, a serious but not unreasonably difficult discussion of the how and why of photography: how it works and why it works as a truly remarkable means of expression in the hands of the informed and skilled. Both skill, born of disciplined practice, and information, born of consciously directed study, are essential. A photographer must know his medium thoroughly if he is to apply it successfully.

We are indebted to many persons who, over the years, have shared experiences and ideas with us. To list them all here and now is out of the question. But we are aware of our debt. We are especially indebted to the following for specific help with this book: Dave Buresh, photographer at the *Denver Post,* for many hours spent helping us print some of the photographs that appear in this book; Professor John Mitchell, School of Journalism, and Professor William Love, Department of Physics, University of Colorado, for critical, and therefore helpful, comments on portions of the manuscript.

R. B. R.
F. H. McC.

TABLE OF CONTENTS

Chapter   *Page*

1. WHAT IS PHOTOGRAPHY?   1
2. WHAT MAKES A PHOTOGRAPH?   11
3. COMPOSITION   32
4. DEVELOPING THE NEGATIVE   56
5. MAKING THE PRINT   69
6. THE NATURE OF LIGHT   85
7. THE LENS   100
8. LIGHT AS A LANGUAGE   129
9. LIGHTING WITH FLOOD AND FLASH   150
10. FILTERS FOR BLACK-AND-WHITE PHOTOGRAPHY   176
11. THE CHEMISTRY OF THE PHOTOGRAPHIC EMULSION   192
12. THE CHEMISTRY OF EXPOSURE AND DEVELOPMENT   204
13. COLOR AS WE SEE IT   222
14. COLOR AS WE PHOTOGRAPH IT   237
15. COLOR EXPOSURE AND FILTERING   250
    BIBLIOGRAPHY   264
    INDEX   271

LIST OF FIGURES

FIGURE   PAGE

 1. *Cutaway view of single-lens reflex camera*   13
 2. *Reflex camera with mirror in viewfinding position*   14
 3. *Reflex camera with mirror up in "exposing" position*   15
 4. *Depth by vertical location and overlapping figures*   38
 5. *Aspects of balance in stability*   48
 6. *Aspects of proximity and closure in stability*   49
 7. *The enlarger*   77
 8. *The spectrum of electromagnetic radiation*   88
 9. *Reflection and refraction of light*   92
10. *Prismatic refraction and dispersion*   95
11. *Converging or positive lens*   101
12. *Diverging or negative lens*   103
13. *Diagram of modern, high-speed lens*   104
14. *Image size and focal length*   109
15. *Long lens and telephoto lens compared*   115
16. *The retrofocus lens*   116
17. *Rollei camera with Mutar auxiliary lens attached*   119
18. *Aperture and depth of field*   126
19. *The characteristic curve*   137
20. *Effect of development time on gamma*   141
21. *Typical time-gamma curve*   142
22. *Honeywell Pentax 1°/21° Meter*   146
23. *The inverse square law*   166
24. *Filter effects*   181
25. *The polarizing filter*   185
26. *Silver bromide*   195
27. *Silver halide crystal lattice*   196
28. *Cross-section of photographic film*   203
29. *Photomicrographs of undeveloped and developed grains*   209
30. *Cross-section of color film*   242
31. *Color as reproduced by positive transparency*   245

Chapter 1
•
WHAT IS PHOTOGRAPHY?

Photography is so commonplace—more than 50 million persons in the United States alone shoot still or motion pictures—it seems perhaps a bit naive to ask, "What is photography?" This process, technique, art, hobby, or means of communication (and it is, at times, all these things) has become such a common thread in the fabric of our lives that we are unable, short of becoming hermits, to escape its effects and influences. Just because we tend to take such a commonplace element of life for granted, we also tend to assume we know what it is. But anyone who wants to use photography, or to be a photographer, must begin at the beginning with that simple question, "What is photography?"

Is photography an art or a mere mechanical process? Let's skirt that issue for the moment, with the promise to return to it a little later. Photography is an art *or* a process of producing images. But there are many ways of producing images; how is photography different? Photography produces images by the action of light on surfaces or substances that are light-sensitive. This seems a satisfactory, brief definition of what is essentially a simple, although somewhat miraculous and still not completely understood, application to human purpose of several chemical and physical laws. Light, a section of the spectrum of radiant energy, is reflected in varying amounts by objects around us. By catching this light, controlling its intensity, and directing it onto tiny grains of silver salts, we can create a change in those salts proportionate to the amount of light energy that struck each grain. Under chemical processing this change in the silver salts can be expanded until an image of the real objects is formed. Cameras, lenses, films, and all the chemicals and paraphernalia of the darkroom have but one major and primary purpose: they are all tools used in manipulating light and silver salts for the purpose of getting the two together in proper order to produce an image. But photography is more than tools and techniques. To end there is to end with the beginning.

Joseph-Nicéphore Niépce, whose experiments helped lay the basis for photography, conceived its function as merely "to copy Nature with the greatest fidelity." Niépce's partner in experimentation and invention, Louis Jacques Mandé Daguerre, said photography was "the process which gives Nature the ability to reproduce herself." Such were the views of two of photography's principal inventors, expressing the notion, since echoed

1

Story without words.

by others, that photography is a mirror of reality. There is some truth and value in this metaphorical definition, but we should be wary of accepting it literally.

Photography has also been called a language, and language, customarily taken to mean words and a method of combining words, is at best only an approximation of reality, never reality itself. A photograph, in many cases, may be a much closer approximation of the reality it attempts to recreate than words can give us; nevertheless, it is still not that reality itself. It is still only a photograph.

But the concept of photography as language opens an avenue for exploration. This would mean that photography is a medium of communication, a method of recording events and conveying messages, a system of

Picture possibilities are all around us.

making known viewpoints, ideas, and opinions about reality. In truth, events are being recorded throughout the world at this moment by the photographic method, and in a few hours you may be viewing some of this record in a newspaper or on a television screen or, in a few days, in a magazine or on a movie screen. Every day you are on the receiving end of a vast communication system, which includes photography as a message carrier, a system that would leave Niépce and Daguerre, could they witness it, incredulous. Today we view and accept as routine more information in pictorial form in one week than the average citizen of the first half of the nineteenth century, when Daguerre lived, viewed in a lifetime. Photography and its many offspring in the communications revolution of the last hundred years play a major role in the formation of the mental pictures of the world that people carry about in their heads. And many of our actions and reactions are based on our mental worlds, not on the real world. In the last hundred years these mental worlds, each one unique to each individual, have been immensely expanded and filled out with details that would have been unavailable without this worldwide communications revolution. In the last fifty years more and more of each mental world has been derived from pictures. The American's picture of the Wall, dividing East and West Berlin in 1964, was based more on the language of photography, transmitted by newspapers, magazines, movies, and television, than it was based on the language of words. To an extent impossible to measure accurately, our mental pictures of the society in which we live are created by photography.

Every photograph is really giving a report on something. It may be a report designed to serve a utilitarian purpose. It may be a report designed to serve an inspirational purpose. Or it may be a combination of the two.

If the utilitarian purpose predominates, the intent is to convey information such as place orientation or personality identification. Perhaps the photograph is a simple visual record of a place, a person, or an event; it could even be a rather complex record of all three. Mountains of photographs produced every year are intended to serve as memory aids; the album snapshots of the family reunion, of the children's birthdays, of the annual vacations represent an effort to preserve the moment. But there are more sophisticated aspects of the utilitarian purpose in photography. These aspects involve the accurate recording of events and objects in science, in engineering, in medicine, in architecture, in criminology, and in fashion, to name a few. Margaret Bourke-White, *Life* magazine staff

Emphasis with wide-angle lens and short distance between camera lens and subject.

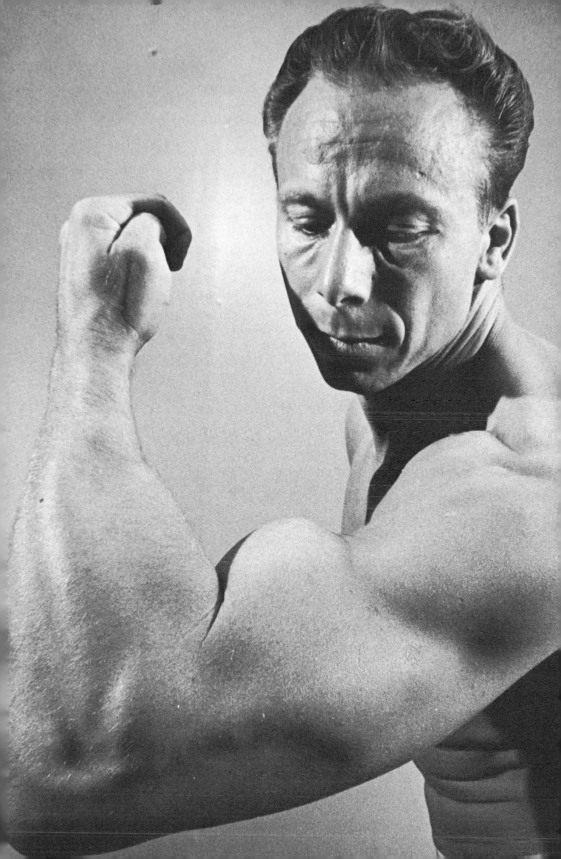

photographer, said "the little black box with a hole in it has become the chief recorder of history." This, of course, is the photojournalist's view of photography as a recorder of things as they are. The news photographer's journalistic reports of a given moment, or the photojournalist's documentaries, visual accounts of related moments fashioned into picture stories or picture essays, have wide diversity, ranging the gamut of human experience and human emotion.

Photography with inspirational purpose, with the intent to create esthetic and creative stimulation, remains a language or medium of communication. But this concept inevitably involves a question born with photography, an enduring question posed, among other places and other times, at the Virginia Museum of Fine Arts in 1959. When this museum displayed that year's "Photography in the Fine Arts" exhibit the motif was *Is photography art?* Paintings or drawings and photographs were grouped in pairs, based on similarities in mood and style, and museum visitors were asked to vote on the question. In a two-week period 549 voted yes and 49 voted no. One visitor marked his ballot, "Who cares?" Perhaps it is not really vital that we decide the issue. The value in considering the question at all lies, rather, in learning more about what photography is.

Art, it appears, has three roles to play, and a significant work of art performs all three. It provides self-expression for the artist, gives pleasure and/or stimulation to both artist and audience, and supplies a representation, an interpretation, or a criticism of life. Robert Frost probably summed all that up in one phrase when he said art should "strip life to form."

Life is a confusing spectacle under the best of circumstances, so surely a major contribution of art is the extraction of order, of some meaningful simplicity, from this confusion that surrounds us. The artist perceives some pattern, which, if extracted from the welter of experience, may provide a fresh interpretation to enrich and expand the experience of all who behold it. The work of art springs from life, but at the same time it is a world of its own, detached from the surrounding confusion. The work of art thus preserves a slice of life that might otherwise have dissolved in the constant flow and flux of reality.

A painter in producing his art can displace or simply leave out unwanted and distracting elements; he can rearrange to suit his perceived pattern of significance. The photographer is bound more closely to what exists, although there are techniques for eliminating or subduing the unwanted even in photography. But photography cannot, in its normal application, completely abandon the normal patterns, forms, and textures of reality. It is to a considerable degree, though not entirely, bound to them, and in this sense it does not usually create a world quite as much its own as a painting does; for a photograph is not, in the minds of its beholders, as separate from the real world as a painting. The photographer, then, cannot put as much of himself into a picture as the painter can.

However, if the objective is to record experience and if the greatness of a picture is to be measured by the vividness, the accuracy, and the

Unusual viewpoints can produce unusual pictures. The photographer was underwater when he took this picture of a swimming class for mothers and babies. (David Mathias, Staff Photographer, Denver *Post*)

immediacy with which experience is communicated, then the best photography stands preeminent. If, on the other hand, the objective is to record experience filtered through the personality of the artist, painting and other traditional fine arts seem to be the ideal media. A viewpoint that prefers one of these standards does not necessarily deny the value of the other. Nor are the two mutually exclusive: photographs can, and should ordinarily, represent something of a distillation of the photographer's personal view; and painting can be and often is vivid, accurate, and immediate. But photography, because of its nature, is stronger in one area, and painting is stronger in the other.

Whether photography is accepted as an art form or is not, it is the contention of the authors that a good photograph should have an effect of some sort *on* the beholder. It provides communication of information and/ or emotion, at the very least, and ideally does more: it also transmits a form of energy or emotional power from the photographer to the beholder —a heightening of vitality, an enhancement of the ability to live the abundant life.

Certainly any attempt to force photography to emulate traditionally accepted forms of fine art, such as oil painting, is an exercise in futility. Preoccupation with the production of pseudopaintings through photography leads nowhere, because this is contrary to the medium's basic characteristics. The painter's approach still persists to some extent in photography, but fortunately a majority of photographers have recognized the folly of using a camera to make a painting. This is not to say that photography's function is merely to copy nature. Photographic techniques are available to take the resulting picture far beyond the purely representational, and if the photographic worker believes such techniques provide him with a route to self-expression, who is to say him nay? It is only the effort to make a photograph look as though it were really a drawing or a painting that seems to lead to a dead end.

Two basic characteristics of photography clearly distinguish it from the other graphic arts; these are the nature of the image and the nature of the recording process.

The nature of the photographic image is simple enough in its broad outline and has only two major identifying elements: definition and tone. The photographic image is recognized generally by its acute definition of the subject, its remarkable delineation of fine detail. Less often is the image a deliberately blurred one. But in either case, there is seldom any difficulty at all in recognizing the reproduction as a photographic image. Subtle tone gradations, ranging in minute steps from white to black, are also typically photographic, although not all photographs contain the full tonal range of which photography is capable.

The photographic recording process also has two major characteristics: it is indiscriminate and it is instantaneous.

The film records all that is in front of the camera lens. The traditional artist with the paintbrush and palette can be selective; so can the photographer, but his job is more difficult in this respect, because he cannot simply order the lens to leave out a tree, a house, or other object. This all-inclusiveness of the photographic record can, of course, be either an advantage or a disadvantage, depending upon circumstances and image-recording purpose.

The same is true of the fact that recording the photographic image is, under usual circumstances, instantaneous. It is possible to catch the *now,* to capture the changing expression. This characteristic of photography is the major cause of those high-impact photos sometimes described as memorable accidents. Photography contains much of the accidental, but that is not the same thing as saying that most, or even a large percentage, of good photographs are the sole result of chance. Most good photographs are the result of craftsmanship coupled with the ability to see. The fact that photography is instantaneous creates certain disadvantages as well, for it means there is no stopping in the middle of an exposure; no changing of mind is possible. It also means each photograph is only one small slice of time, and this is never the full story of an event.

Combined, all these characteristics—the definition and tone of the image, the instantaneous and indiscriminate nature of the recording process—give a fine photograph a sense of authenticity, an illusion of reality. These characteristics appear to be the principal reasons why photography often seems to communicate something of the essence of an experience.

The photographer must recognize and accept these characteristics of his medium and put them to work whether his objective is utilitarian, inspirational, or a combination of both. He must develop the skill, or craftsmanship, needed to master these characteristics. And he must develop the ability to see beyond the commonplace, beyond the utilitarian purpose of the moment, which limits the seeing powers of most persons. He must see what there is before him that will make a photograph. Here is the imagination at work on observation; here is experience and knowledge at work on visual perception. Meaning born of recognition of the interrelationships of forms and patterns can be told in the photograph if the photographer first *sees* the forms and the patterns, separately and as parts of a greater whole. Then he must select from what he sees the most effective compositional elements available, which involves a decision about viewpoint, and he must select the most effective moment for the exposure, the moment when the elements of the composition have coelesced into a meaningful whole.

What is photography? It is a welding of craftsmanship—mastery of the controls that manipulate photography's characteristics—with mastery of seeing. The result can be a sharing of experience that permits the viewer as well as the photographer to live more deeply, to share in a fresh acknowledgement of wonder. The photographic image can be more comprehensible than reality itself.

Chapter 2

WHAT MAKES A PHOTOGRAPH?

The quality product depends—barring the happy accident—upon a beginning with the proper tools. The propriety of tools can only be gauged with reference to the task at hand. In photography the basic tool, the camera, comes in a riot of variety. The simple box camera is quite adequate for simple tasks and can produce results of surprisingly high quality in the hands of an expert who accepts the tool's limitations. Cameras of greater complexity give the photographer greater flexibility, although the final results may be disappointing if the craftsmanship of the tool user is unequal to the sophistication of his tool.

The simplest camera is the pinhole camera: a box that is light-tight except for a pinhole at one end, the end opposite the one at which the film is positioned. Some sort of flap is added so that light entering the pinhole can be controlled. All other cameras are merely refinements of this basic design. The two most important refinements, the ones that make the most important differences between cameras, involve substituting a lens with adjustable diaphragm for the pinhole and a shutter for the flap over the pinhole. The diaphragm controls the amount of light that passes through the lens by varying the size of the lens aperture.

The lens is usually the most costly single part of any camera. The simplest and cheapest camera has a lens made of only one or perhaps two pieces of glass; but a fine quality lens designed to produce a finely resolved image contains six or eight pieces of glass, all ground and polished to precise specifications and all assembled carefully and expensively into an intricate mount.

The story of the shutter is much the same. Shutters range from the very simple spring-actuated flap to bafflingly complex types. Complexity (and price) increase in proportion to the increase in the number of timings the shutter will provide. An intricate gear train is demanded for a shutter with automatic timings ranging from one full second down to 1/500 or even 1/1000 of a second. This type of shutter is usually mounted between the glass elements of the complex lens. Another shutter is the focal-plane type, located in the back of the camera just in front of the film. Focal-plane shutters are slotted curtains of cloth or metal that move across the film. Variations in the width of the slot and in the speed of the curtain's movement provide variations in exposure given the film.

The inexpensive camera is equipped with the simplest of lenses and shutters, designed to cope with only the average in picture-taking conditions. The lens is set for average focus (around 12 to 15 feet) and the fixed lens aperture is also an average (about $f/11$). The shutter speed is usually about 1/30 of a second. The box camera is simple, basically complete, but not designed to provide images of fine definition for maximum enlargement, nor images of small objects taken at close range, nor of rapidly moving subjects, nor of subjects in poor light. All these tasks require the more complex lens and the more complex shutter.

The professional photographer picks and chooses from among the more expensive cameras that provide a maximum degree of flexibility in focusing and exposure according to his own likes and dislikes, according to the photographic tasks he expects to encounter, and according to the price that seems reasonable to him.

THE 35-MM CAMERA

He may prefer the 35-mm camera, so called because it uses film that is 35 millimeters in width, the same width used in the production of the standard Hollywood motion picture. This classification includes many different cameras, but in general they have relatively high-speed lenses that permit picture-taking under poor light conditions without flash or flood lights and are relatively inconspicuous. They are thus the tools most often used if the objective is completely candid photographs. (So-called sub-miniature cameras, which are available in sizes smaller than a pack of cigarettes, provide the ultimate in undetected picture-taking. The film for these cameras is one-fourth to one-half the size of the 35-mm film.)

The 35-mm cameras are also popular among amateur and professional photographers alike for shooting color slides. They usually load with magazines or cassettes of film sufficient for 20 or 36 exposures, and each negative (or positive transparency) is about 1 by $1\frac{1}{2}$ inches. Lenses vary, of course, ranging from the very common $f/3.5$ to the ultrahigh-speed optics that reach $f/1$ and even beyond. Some of these cameras, usually the least expensive models, have a single, fixed lens; but many others are manufactured so that one lens can be removed and any one of two or perhaps as many as twelve others inserted in the camera body in place of the original lens. The purpose of all this is still the same—flexibility, to permit the photographer to get better pictures of the more difficult subjects, if his own craftsmanship is equal to the challenge.

THE REFLEX CAMERA

Some 35-mm cameras are equipped with rangefinders for focusing the lens. Others are made so that the user actually focuses the image projected by the lens; these are the single-lens reflex type. Single-lens reflex cameras, however, are not all 35-mm. The reflex design has been used for cameras producing negatives ranging in size from ¾ of an inch by 1 inch to 5 by 7 inches. Once the classic in this field was the Graflex, a massive black box

FIGURE 1

Cutaway view of a single-lens reflex camera, the Honeywell Pentax.

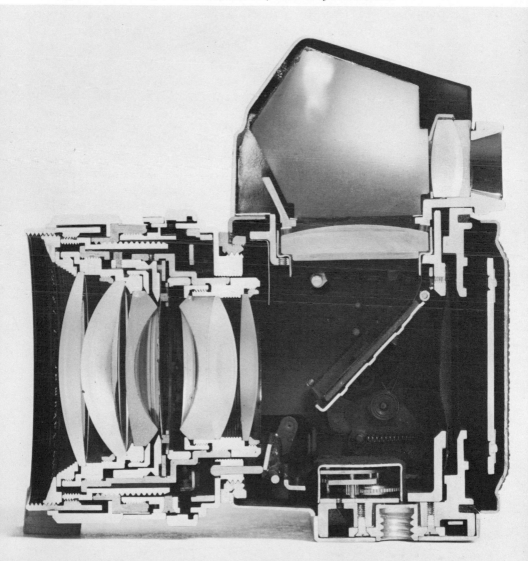

carried by press photographers in the early decades of this century, a box that "flipped its lid" when it was time to go into action.

The reflex principle involves a hooded ground glass in the top of the box, which the photographer inspects when focusing and viewfinding because the image of the subject appears on the glass. The image is transmitted to the ground glass by a mirror set at a 45-degree angle just behind the lens. When the photographer trips the shutter release to make the exposure, he also, by the same finger pressure, trips a mechanism that swings the mirror up out of the way; the image is then projected onto the

FIGURE 2
Reflex camera with mirror in viewfinding position.

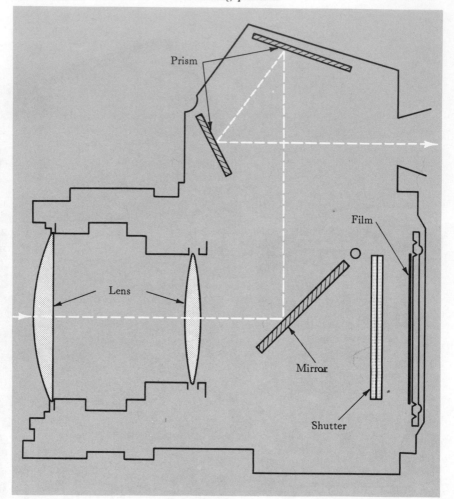

film. In the single-lens reflex camera the shutter is the curtain at the focal (or film) plane.

Many of the late model single-lens reflex cameras include an automatic mechanism that permits focusing and viewfinding on the ground glass with the lens diaphragm set at maximum opening; but at the instant before exposure the diaphragm stops itself down to the exposure aperture selected previously by the photographer. These are called automatic lenses. But not all lenses for these cameras are automatic; some have to be stopped down by hand after viewing and before exposure.

FIGURE 3

Reflex camera with mirror up in "exposing" position.

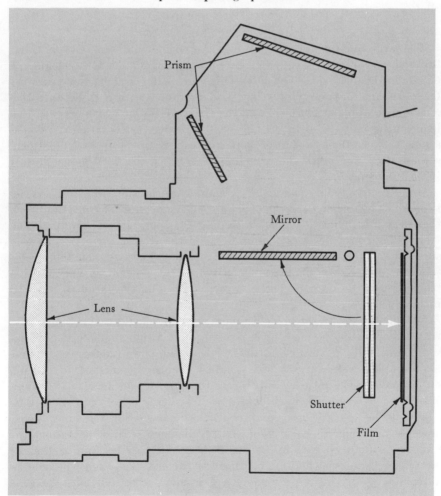

The same reflex principle is used in the top lens of the twin-lens cameras. The top lens, which has no shutter and no diaphragm (it is always "wide open"), is the one the photographer uses for focusing and viewfinding. The bottom lens is the taking lens, so it is equipped with a standard leaf-type, between-the-lens shutter and a diaphragm. The two lenses, the viewing lens on top, and the taking lens on the bottom, are mounted on the same lens board; when one is in focus, so is the other. Such twin-lens reflex cameras produce negatives usually $2\frac{1}{4}$ by $2\frac{1}{4}$ inches on film rolls that give 12 exposures per roll. These are generally compact, rugged cameras that provide something of a compromise between the 35-mm size and the large cameras.

LARGE FORMAT CAMERAS

The large cameras include not only the Graflex and similar types, but the bellows-equipped boxes that provide a rangefinder for focusing. A classic in this field is the Graphic, a brother of the Graflex. For years the Graphic came in two styles, as a Speed Graphic (with both between-the-lens and focal-plane shutters) and the Crown Graphic (with between-the-lens shutter only). But in the late 1950's Graflex Corporation developed a new between-the-lens shutter that could give speeds up to 1/1000 of a second; this eliminated the principal reason for the focal-plane shutter in these cameras.

Other relatively large and bulky cameras are the view and studio varieties, which are customarily used on a tripod and are intended for work that demands deliberate, time-consuming focusing and viewfinding. The view camera provides a maximum of adjustments for correction of perspective and thus lends itself admirably to such tasks as table-top, architectural, and scenic photography when a large negative (or positive transparency) is desired. These cameras take film sheets up to 8 by 10 inches in size.

Whichever camera the photographer selects, it should be one compatible with his operating methods and with his most frequent photographic assignments. Only general rules can be suggested, since photographers and photographic tasks vary so widely. Most photographers find it difficult but advisable to keep their heads before the dazzling spectacle of the range of equipment available. Each photographer should select only the equipment that he actually needs and avoid the nonessential, the superfluous, however handsome its chrome-plated blandishments. He must become intimately acquainted with his choice, whatever it may be. Setting the exposure, focusing, viewfinding, holding the camera steady must become as automatic as driving an automobile. Conscious attention must be concentrated on the problem of making the picture a good one and not on

Fashions change in cameras, too. Model on the right is demonstrating an 1890 Eastman Kodak camera. Model on the left demonstrates the 1965 Kodak Instamatic Camera with Kodapack Film Cartridge.

the manipulation of camera controls. Automation in cameras can relieve the photographer of much of the detail in mechanical manipulation of controls, but it cannot supply the imagination and understanding that go into effective picture-making.

THE EXPOSURE

Picture-making with photography always involves light; the word photography was derived from two Greek terms meaning light (photo) and writing (graphy). Control of the "writing" must involve control of the light.

The first step in light control is determining proper exposure. In scientific terms, exposure is the product of *intensity* of the light multiplied by *time* during which the light acts—$E = I \times T$. This is the *reciprocity law* of photochemistry. The intensity of the light is the reciprocal of the time: the greater the intensity the less the necessary time. It is also called the Bunsen-Roscoe law, after the men who collaborated in its discovery, Robert Bunsen, a German professor of chemistry at Heidelberg University, and Sir Henry Roscoe, an English chemist. According to this law, as long as the product of light intensity multiplied by time remains the same, the response of the light-sensitive emulsion is the same. If intensity is doubled and time halved, the product is unchanged. If intensity is 2 and time 4, the product is 8; if intensity is 4 and time 2, the product is still 8.

Actually, the light-sensitive photographic emulsion does not obey the reciprocity law exactly under all circumstances. The law holds, for all practical purposes, in the moderate or customary exposure range. However, if the intensity of the light decreases to a very low figure, a corresponding increase in time may not result in a satisfactory exposure. This is *reciprocity failure*. It also occurs at the other end of the scale, when intensity is very high but time very short. Reciprocity failure occurs, for example, with the long time often needed when astronomers photograph the low light intensity of distant stars or with the very short time at high intensities involved with photography by electronic flash. The point at which reciprocity failure occurs depends upon the film involved and occurs more often with color film than with black-and-white film.

In practical terms, exposure for the photographer is the particular combination of lens aperture (intensity) and shutter speed (time) selected to expose the film.

THE SHUTTER

Shutters on modern cameras are complex mechanisms, but the way in which the shutter controls the time factor of the exposure formula is a relatively simple matter. Shutters are geared so that the photographer may select either a long or a short time, or some intermediate step between the extremes. An intricate and expensive shutter may offer a choice of timed exposures ranging from 1 full second to 1/500 of a second, proceeding from one to the other in steps that halve or double the time with each step: ½ a second is obviously one-half as much time as 1 second, and 1/250 of a second just as obviously is double 1/500 of a second. The camera's shutter scale markings will be 1, 2, 4, 8, 30, 60, 125, 250, 500. The first number in this series stands for 1 full second, but all others are fractions of a second, ½, ¼, and so forth. The scale may vary from this example, depending upon the camera, but each shutter setting gives one-half the time of the preceding number and twice the time of the succeeding one.

The scale may also include *T* and *B* settings. The *T* stands for a time exposure, and when the shutter is set at this point it will stay open until the operator trips it a second time. Setting the shutter at *B* is also used for exposures longer than one second but is customarily employed only with a flexible cable shutter release. By depressing a plunger in the end of the cable, which has been attached at the other end to the shutter, the photographer holds the shutter open as long as he wants. The shutter closes when he releases the plunger. The flexible cable is necessary to avoid moving the camera while the shutter is open.

THE APERTURE

With time controlled by the shutter we have only to control intensity of the light to achieve full control of exposure. The way in which intensity control is established is mechanically simpler than the way the shutter controls time, but it is a bit more complex to explain. The size of the opening in the lens through which light flows to the film is, of course, the controlling factor in intensity. In all but the simplest lenses this opening can be varied by means of a diaphragm mounted between the elements of the lens. The opening in the diaphragm is referred to as the aperture.

Intensity of the light reaching the film varies according to the relationship between two factors: the size of the aperture and the distance between aperture and film. A small aperture and short distance can give the same intensity at the film as a large aperture coupled with a relatively long distance. For example, an aperture measuring 1 inch in diameter and 2 inches from the film gives the same light intensity at the film as an aperture 2 inches in diameter but 4 inches from the film. Intensity—the relationship or ratio between aperture and distance—can be shown by a simple fraction:

$$\text{Intensity} = \frac{\text{aperture diameter}}{\text{aperture-to-film distance}}$$

In the examples above, the fraction is 1/2 in both cases. Since this fraction or ratio is the same, the intensity is the same.

Just as a shutter speed expressed in fractions of a second is a common standard for determining the time factor in exposure calculations, so a ratio in which aperture diameter is a fraction of the aperture-to-film distance is a common standard for determining the effect of the intensity factor. And like the shutter speeds, the aperture ratio will be marked on the lens not in fractions but in what appear to be a simple series of numbers. These are *f/numbers* (sometimes called stops), the / indicating that

Most popular cameras in the 1960's: the single-lens reflex types. Recommended as a fine, precision instrument is the Honeywell Pentax.

the numbers are all fractions. The normal sequence of f/numbers is 1, 1.4, 2, 2.8, 4, 5.6, 8, 11, 16, 22, 32, 45, 64. Only a portion of this series will appear on any given lens and often the numbers on a lens will begin at 1.8, 3.5, or 4.7—at points, in other words, between the numbers in the normal series. Each lens is designed for a maximum diaphragm opening and it will be designated, then, as an f/2 lens or by whatever is the smallest number (actually the largest fraction) provided by the f/numbers on that particular lens. It will be an f/1.8 or an f/3.5 lens, for example, if the maximum opening is between normal stops.

These are called f/numbers because they are fractions of the aperture-to-film, or lens-to-film, distance and the f stands for this distance, the *focal length* of the lens. (Actually, an accurate definition of focal length is a bit more complicated than that, but we can delay an extended discussion until Chapter 7.)

Thus, f/2 indicates that the diameter of the aperture is 1/2 of the focal length; f/8, 1/8 of the focal length; f/32, 1/32 of the focal length, and so on. In any lens, the focal length remains the same, so one half of it is obviously larger than 1/8 or 1/32. To set the aperture at 2 would mean more light, greater intensity on the film than if the aperture were set at 8, and 8 would mean more light than 32.

The normal f/number series is like the shutter scale again in that each number gives one-half the intensity of the preceding number and twice the intensity of the succeeding one. The aperture in the diaphragm is a round, or nearly round, hole, and the amount of light it admits is related to its total area. Since the area of a circle is proportional to the square of the diameter, if we double the diameter we quadruple the area; to get only double the area, and thus double the intensity of the light, we need only multiply the diameter by the square root of two (1.4). An examination of the f/number series reveals that this is exactly what has been done.

The beginning photographer must remember that exposure doubles (or halves) with each step on either aperture or shutter scale. Assuming that the shutter speed remains unchanged, moving the aperture setting from f/16 or f/11 will double the exposure; moving to the next smallest f/number, 8, will again double the light, or quadruple the original exposure. Exposure will be halved if we move the aperture setting in the opposite direction, toward the larger numbers: f/22 represents one-half the exposure of f/16, and f/32 one-half of f/22, or one-fourth of f/16. Thus, f/1 will give 1,024 times as much light intensity at the film as f/32—1,024 times as much exposure if the shutter speed is unchanged. (To get a comparative figure describing the difference in light intensity transmitted by two f/numbers, square both numbers, then divide the smaller product into the larger.)

Since one step on the shutter speed scale also doubles or halves exposure by altering the time factor, we then see that changing shutter speed in one direction, for instance, doubling the time, and changing aperture in the other direction, halving the intensity, will mean no change in exposure. Thus, f/16 at 1/125 is the same exposure as f/22 at 1/60. And f/11 at 1/250 would also be the same, or f/8 at 1/500, and f/32 at 1/30.

SOLVING THE EXPOSURE PROBLEM

A good photograph does not depend solely upon proper exposure; there are other factors involved. Few pictures, however, will achieve distinction if the exposure was incorrect. Proper exposure is essential if the picture is to have fine detail in important highlight and important shadow areas. Any exposure that comes close to this objective will give printable middle tones in the negative, but only accurate exposure of the film (and correct development) will produce the delicate tone separations in highlights and shadows that are the mark of most good pictures.

The exposure problem, then, is this: to determine the proper time (shutter setting) and intensity (aperture setting) so that exposure gives a negative from which the best print shows detail in both important highlights and important shadows. If the subject is moving, for instance, a person walking or gesturing, we must select a higher shutter speed than 1/60 if we wish an unblurred image. This means we must change the aperture setting to compensate: increase intensity as we decrease time. We might, then, select 1/250 of a second shutter speed at $f/11$. On the other hand, if the subject is relatively still but we want the background to be sharp in the final print, we may need to decrease the aperture (stop down) to increase depth of field—that is, the distance between the point nearest the camera and the point farthest from the camera that will appear to be in focus in the final print. (Depth of field will be discussed more fully in Chapter 7.) We may decide upon $f/22$, and this would require a compensating increase in time, or a shutter speed of 1/60 of a second. Thus, the photographer must decide how much light must reach the film to give a properly exposed negative, and then he must decide which of the combinations of aperture and shutter speed will give the proper exposure and at the same time give the sort of image he wants.

Always a factor in exposure calculation is *film speed,* the film's inherent sensitivity to light. The higher the speed of the film, the less the exposure needed to produce a printable negative. Research has brought a doubling and tripling of film speed in recent years, and this, coupled with increased lens speeds and improved developers, has meant greater success with the probing camera lens in dimly lighted situations. In addition, experienced cameramen occasionally "push" a film considerably beyond its rated speed through particular development procedures; this practice, however, is not generally recommended for the beginner.

The film manufacturer supplies information on film speed, and with this exposure can be determined most accurately with an exposure meter (see Chapter 8), but there are more than a few times when an exposure meter is not available or cannot be used under the circumstances. Photographers must be prepared to make reasonably accurate exposure calculations without the aid of a meter.

This can be done by starting with the ASA (American Standards Association) speed of the film. If the speed number for the film is set on the shutter speed scale of the camera, then the diaphragm setting (f/number) for a normal subject in bright sunlight will be $f/16$. Let us assume the speed of the film is 125. If we set the shutter speed at 1/125 of a second (or 1/100 if 1/125 is not available), then the proper f/number (for average subject in bright sunlight) is $f/16$. With this as home base it is possible to move to other exposures for varying conditions according to the following *Daylight Exposure Table.*

The bee, busily at work on the stamen of a tulip, was photographed with a Pentax camera with 55-mm Takumar lens on a No. 3 extension tube for close-up focusing. Bee and lens were separated by about 6 inches. The camera was hand held; the film was Kodak Panatomic-X. (Floyd McCall, Denver)

23

DAYLIGHT EXPOSURE TABLE

*For average subjects, using shutter speed equal to the ASA
speed of the film.*

	f/number	EV
Bright or hazy sun on light sand or snow	22	16
Bright sunshine or hazy bright, distinct shadows, normal subject	16 *	15 *
Hazy, ill-defined shadows	11	14
Cloudy bright, no shadows	8	13
Heavy overcast	5.6	12
Open shade (subject shaded from the sun but lighted by a large area of sky directly overhead)	5.6	12

* For backlighted close-up subjects, set lens at f/8 or EV 13.

This table is only a guide; it does not guarantee perfect exposures. Variables not adequately considered in the table are time of day, geographical latitude, time of year, direction of the light, and type of subject. But at least this table puts you within range, and as you gain experience you will find it possible to produce negatives that can be made to yield satisfactory prints. If conditions leave you doubtful, then bracket; shoot first at your best exposure guess, based on the table, then shoot two more, one at the next higher f/number and one at the next lower f/number.

EXPOSURE VALUE SYSTEM

Lenses on some cameras are marked with *Exposure Value* numbers (sometimes called *Light Value* numbers) instead of or in addition to the traditional f/numbers. Exposure values also appear on some meters.

The exposure value (EV) system is a method of stating exposure with a single number given by exposure table or meter, and this number is set on a similar scale of numbers on the camera. Each number represents a specific amount of exposure (intensity by time) and when the camera is set for the matching number, aperture and shutter speed are automatically established. Any combination of aperture and shutter speed that gives the same amount of exposure will have the same exposure value. The number range can be as extensive as necessary but it usually extends from 2 to 18, depending upon the camera's lens and shutter. Just as with shutter speed and aperture scales, each EV number gives one-half the exposure given by the preceding (smaller) number and double that given by the succeeding (larger) one.

Lenses marked for use with the exposure value system will have a coupling that interlocks aperture with shutter speeds: as one is changed the other automatically changes too. For example, exposure calculation provides an EV of 15. Setting this on the camera produces an aperture setting of $f/16$ and a shutter speed of 1/125. If we want a faster shutter speed and turn the exposure dial to get 1/250 of a second, the aperture will automatically change to $f/11$. With many cameras equipped with the coupled aperture-shutter setting it is possible to override this automatic arrangement if the photographer wishes to do so.

The exposure value numbers are logarithmic and thus cover an enormous exposure range with a comparatively limited series of numbers. The series 2 to 18 is sufficient for normal use and represents an exposure range from 1 second at $f/2$ to 1/500 of a second at $f/22$, a range of 1 : 65,000. (See accompanying *Exposures and Exposure Value Settings* table.)

THE ADDITIVE SYSTEM

A new system, which may become widely used in the future, is available for determining and setting exposures without resorting to the traditional f/number and shutter speed nomenclature. For this system the logarithmic number scale is used for measuring all the values involved in the exposure formula. In the accompanying *Additive Values* table each film speed, light measurement, f/number, and shutter speed can be translated into the number that appears at the top of its column. Thus, $f/11$ has a value of 7; so do all the following: a shutter speed of 1/125, a light level of 800 footcandles, and a film speed of 400.

ADDITIVE VALUES

	0	1	2	3	4	5	6	7	8	9	10
S	3	6	12	25	50	100	200	400	800	1600	3200
L	6	12	25	50	100	200	400	800	1600	3200	6400
A	1	1.4	2	2.8	4	5.6	8	11	16	22	32
T	1	1/2	1/4	1/8	1/15	1/30	1/60	1/125	1/250	1/500	1/1000

S = ASA film speed
L = light measured in footcandles
A = aperture in f/numbers
T = time (shutter speeds) in seconds

This is called the additive system because exposure calculation is merely a matter of addition. If the film-speed value is 5 and the value of the light is found from exposure table, meter, or estimate to be 7, the total is 12. Then, any combination of shutter speed (say 1/60) and aperture (say $f/8$) whose additive value numbers total 12 will be a normal exposure.

The additive system can be used to estimate exposures if the photographer has an approximate idea of the illumination level in terms of footcandles. A footcandle represents the amount of illumination on a surface

Slow shutter-speed recorded the movement of pedestrians in a winter street scene.
(Bill Johnson, Staff Photographer, Denver *Post*)

that is everywhere one foot away from a point source of light of standard intensity. Typical footcandles include

Outdoors
Normal sunshine	6,400
Cloudy bright	1,600
Heavy overcast	800
Open shade	800
Night sports	100–200

Indoors
Home interior, day	50
Home interior, night	5–10
Offices	50–100
Schoolrooms	30–70
Sports arenas	150

The data sheet packaged with most film will show, for example, the film speed as ASA 125/5°. The number 125 is the standard film speed, and we are already familiar with it; the number 5° is the speed value in terms of the logarithmic scale and is part of the additive system.

EXPOSURE AUTOMATION

A trend that began in the late 1930's but did not gather full momentum until 1960 is the development of automatic-exposure still cameras. A multitude of designs and a failure to agree on a precise meaning of the term *automatic* have led to a good deal of confusion. It is impossible here to describe the wide variety of systems termed automatic by camera manufacturers. More than 70 different still cameras were on the market in 1964 that, their makers declared, were fully automatic.

Fully automatic generally means the camera automatically sets either the aperture or the shutter speed or both. Usually the photographer sets the film speed rating and then selects a shutter speed. He then points the camera at the subject and a built-in meter, or light-sensitive photocell,

EXPOSURES AND EXPOSURE VALUE SETTINGS

Shutter speed in seconds at Aperture:

EV	f/2	f/2.8	f/4	f/5.6	f/8	f/11	f/16	f/22
2	1							
3	1/2	1						
4	1/4	1/2	1					
5	1/8	1/4	1/2	1				
6	1/15	1/8	1/4	1/2	1			
7	1/30	1/15	1/8	1/4	1/2	1		
8	1/60	1/30	1/15	1/8	1/4	1/2	1	
9	1/125	1/60	1/30	1/15	1/8	1/4	1/2	1
10	1/250	1/125	1/60	1/30	1/15	1/8	1/4	1/2
11	1/500	1/250	1/125	1/60	1/30	1/15	1/8	1/4
12		1/500	1/250	1/125	1/60	1/30	1/15	1/8
13			1/500	1/250	1/125	1/60	1/30	1/15
14				1/500	1/250	1/125	1/60	1/30
15					1/500	1/250	1/125	1/60
16						1/500	1/250	1/125
17							1/500	1/250
18								1/500

reads the light reflected by the subject. This light energy is transformed into electrical energy in amounts corresponding to the intensity of the light. Thus, all essential elements are "programmed" or introduced into the camera's system, two by the photographer, one by the camera. The camera's mechanism automatically adjusts the aperture according to the shutter speed and film speed set by the photographer to give a supposedly correct exposure. The automatic operation happens when the photographer pushes a button or lever, usually the shutter release. And it probably is a correct exposure for many, if not most, average subjects. Of course, the camera cannot know the photographer's purpose in taking the picture, cannot know in what part of the subject the photographer's major interest lies. The result may be, in some cases, overexposed highlights or underexposed shadows. But many of the automatic cameras permit the photographer to override the automatic feature when he wishes, so in effect he has the choice of automatic or nonautomatic operation.

Some other cameras are described as semiautomatic. With these the photographer must perform a manual matching operation of some kind to set shutter speed or aperture, or both. With the most common semiautomatic system the photographer sets film speed and shutter speed, then he manually matches a needle with another pointer or mark that has been positioned automatically by the meter or photocell. When he has matched needle with pointer he has set the f/number. In some cases, turning a ring around the lens for the matching operation sets both the aperture and the shutter speed according to a predetermined program established by the film speed and the intensity of the light.

Most of the fully automatic and semiautomatic cameras are intended for the weekend snapshooter who has no desire to get involved deeply in technique, yet wants some assurance that most of his pictures will turn out. Automation, however, can provide advantages for the experienced photographer as well, if he is seeking increased freedom from the mechanics involved. Systems that permit the photographer to overrule the automation do not prevent him from applying interpretation of the subject through exposure control. But to do this, the worker with the automated camera still needs to understand exposure and its components: light, film speed, aperture, shutter speed.

QUALITIES OF A GOOD PICTURE

One assumes, then, that correct exposure, or nearly correct exposure, is required to make a good picture. What else?

Certain general qualities seem to be present in most pictures that are generally regarded as good. We must speak here in generalities, because,

Camera tools can do the job if photographers supply the creative imagination.
(Lowell Georgia, Staff Photographer, Denver *Post*)

of course, what one individual may regard as a good picture, another may reject as a failure.

Among these general qualities appears to be this one: third dimension, that is, depth. The satisfying picture usually gives an illusion of that third dimension. A second general quality of the good photograph seems to be self-containment: the picture is complete and all the parts of the picture play obvious and necessary roles in completing the message the picture has to tell; nothing is included that does not contribute; nothing is omitted that is essential. And third, the good picture, more often than not, does not try to tell everything; the photographer has, rather, left some details, some aspect of the mood, for the viewer to supply from his own experience background, just as the skillful writer leaves much to the mind of his reader.

To achieve these qualities in his photographs, the photographer must learn how things look—to his film. This means he must pay particular attention to the essential quality of things, to form, texture, detail, and mood. The values that make a picture good lie in line, form, light, and shade (add color in the case of color film) and the interrelationships between these elements of the composition. Using these pictorial elements in a manner appropriate to the subject, the photographer must select, simplify, and organize a picture that is self-contained, but leaves room for the play of the viewer's imagination, and gives an illusion of the third dimension.

With few exceptions, the best photographs are simple, straightforward expositions of a single subject; such pictures have only one story to tell and one center of interest. Too much crammed into a picture's borders results in a scattering of interest and a loss of unity. The photographer needs to think before he snaps the shutter.

SHOOTING WITH PURPOSE

A beginning photographer generally shoots haphazardly, but because he points his camera at subjects that interest him, some of the time the resulting pictures are interesting. But if he perseveres he soon must learn that shooting without thought of purpose produces a high percentage of dull and unprofitable pictures. He must aim not at the subject alone, but at expression through interpretation of the subject. His pictures must exhibit understanding through new discoveries in vision. Good photographs stem from the mind of the photographer, a mind enriched by observation, experience, and knowledge, a mind that must be cultivated and made to work if it is to produce. To talk about the practice of photography apart from what is said with the language of photography is futile.

Like a writer, a photographer must know and feel, and he can never know and feel enough.

It is generally true that the photographer draws his mental sustenance from the electricity of the scene around him. His pictures should be the result of his imagination, guided by observation, experience, and knowledge, speculating upon the significance of the scene. Understanding or comprehending becomes as important for a photographer as his equipment. Margaret Bourke-White tells a story in her autobiography illustrating this. She asked to be permitted to take pictures of Gandhi at his spinning wheel. To do that, Gandhi's secretary told her, she must first learn to spin. The photographer must first comprehend and then he can interpret and explain.

To make the interpretation or explanation meaningful, the photographer must also understand his audience. The forms and lines, shadows and textures of the print must have something more than a personal significance. What may have great personal meaning for the photographer may be meaningless for the viewers of his print. And the audience, generally, is not concerned about subtle problems in technique; only other photographers comprehend these and even they may not care.

Many subjects, universally available, lend themselves to the thinking photographer's purposes: people and their emotions, Halloween, Main Street, reflections, traffic, weather, the teen-age world, city park, a boy being a boy, light and shadow, parades. The list could be nearly endless. But whatever the subject, it is the photographer, the craftsman with imaginative vision, who makes the good picture.

Chapter 3

COMPOSITION

We live in a world in which light in an infinite variety of intensities is reflected from an infinite variety of forms. Out of the jumble of information our eyes collect from reflected light, our minds must organize unified images; these images cannot be based on visual units perceived as isolated items. Instead the images must be based on the relationships of forms, of lines, of tones, and of textures. Clarity of form and relationships in what we see is paramount if we are to function effectively and without incessantly endangering our own lives.

Survival is not at stake in the case of a photograph, but communication is. Communication is a photograph's reason for being; it must have something to report: a fact, a story, a mood, an emotion, a relationship, some insight that unveils significance in our surroundings. We want the viewer of our photographs to see and to understand, to be affected by what we saw in reality, and we want this to happen directly and without ambiguity. Each photograph must eliminate the chaos from that small part of the world upon which it is reporting. There must be no internal distraction within the report itself, no uncertainty to cloud the photograph's information or its emotional impact.

To produce an intelligible report the photographer must master the visual grammar and syntax of composition. Composition is a word used frequently in many contexts. Music is composed; so is a poem, and a novel; and a printer speaks of composing type. It always seems to mean *a putting together* of various elements so that the sum total makes a recognizable whole. Each element should contribute to the significance of the unified total. It is the relationship of each element to others that controls its contribution, and the logical development of all the interrelationships leads inevitably to the message-contributing form of the whole. In all cases the objective is communication, the transmission of a message from one person to another, and effective transmission will occur only if the code in which the message is phrased is recognizable and intelligible. From this need stem the principles of composition, whether the medium is writing, music, painting, or photography. Composition is the art of organizing an effective communication. An effective communication is one that transmits the composer's meanings with a minimum of distortion and ambiguity.

Composition in photography, like composition in writing, music, and painting, cannot be reduced to a precise set of hard-and-fast rules. This is so because composition depends upon the content of the message, and upon the purpose and viewpoint of the composer—the photographer.

Composition, quite obviously, must involve the elements being composed. The photographer begins to compose when he first perceives a visual relationship, when he realizes *this* relates to *that*. Thus, he begins to join separate items to make one, perhaps because he has noted a similarity between what once seemed to be dissimilar things, perhaps because he has discovered some coherence in apparent confusion or some new idea in the commonplace.

What elements are there that the photographer wants to put together, to arrange, to relate one to another? Elements of a picture consist of lines, points, tones, and masses that comprise the subject, its background, and its surroundings, and no two subjects can be exactly the same in these elements. Composition in music, writing, painting, or photography is not something carried about in a kit to be taken out and forced upon each new set of materials.

In all photographs the function of composition is to support and clarify content. Composition is, in fact, an inseparable part of content. This becomes especially clear when the photographic subject has been deliberately chosen for its design characteristics. The more abstract the design becomes, the more fused become content and composition, until finally the two are one. Since composition in a pure abstraction is its content, it would follow that if the composition is ineffective there can be no significant content.

But in most photographs abstraction is limited. What of those images that remain easily recognizable representations of real objects? In these cases—the vast majority in photography—content and composition can be discussed as separate parts of the picture; but even so, one still does not exist without the other. Either content or composition may be weak and spiritless or strong and vigorous, but both are present in an image of any kind, and both must be strong if the picture is to be strong. Since composition is inseparable from content and since content is as infinite in variety as subject matter, composition, too, has such infinite variety that no set of precise rules can possibly cover all situations.

Infinite, too, are the purposes and viewpoints of photographers, or the composers in any medium. If it is logic that makes possible the composing of related elements into a unified form or whole, it is purpose that determines what form an idea based on logic will assume. The photographer must have clearly in mind what message it is he wants his photograph to convey; this is his purpose. The form, or the composition, into which he shapes his idea is, to a large extent, controlled by this purpose. What must be included to convey his meaning? What is important? What is not? Elements important to his purpose must be large, or sharply outlined, or strongly lighted, or placed in eye-catching sections of the picture. Less important elements are smaller, less distinct, less well lighted, and located in less prominent positions.

As purpose varies with each photographer, so does viewpoint. Each of us sees what we want to see, or what we expect to see, since we look not with our eyes alone but with our minds as well. What we see is conditioned by past experiences and personal feelings. Consequently, no two photographers picture the same subject exactly the same way. The composition of each photograph is conditioned by what each photographer sees in the subject from his own unique point of view, a mental stance impossible for anyone else to duplicate.

Thus, it seems futile to indulge in either plain or pontifical commandments decreeing just how much dark mass will balance how much light mass, or whether five-to-eight is (or is not) a divine proportion. Composition cannot be reduced to a collection of such commandments. But neither is composition a mysterious something to be summoned only from an artistic soul, which one is born either with or without. Composition can be instinctive, but it can also be the result of planning and thought. Planning and thought, in turn, can be guided by general principles, if it is thoroughly understood that the principles have no value in and of themselves, but are only of value if they help the photographer form into an intelligible message code what it is he sees that he wants others to see.

A slavish adherence to such principles, general as they may be, can only lead to a tiresome repetition of pictorial clichés. But as guides to message coding they can help beginning photographers to greater satisfaction with their earliest efforts. Later they will find satisfaction and success coming from unconscious application of the principles filtered through their own personalities and purposes—or from conscious violation of the very same principles. Successful writers seldom give conscious attention to the rules of grammar, for long practice has built a reliable feeling for the elements of the language they are using, a feeling that makes it possible for them to violate the rules when necessary with nearly certain knowledge that their purpose will be served thereby. Such expertness generally comes only after a considerable period of experience-gathering, and the photographer may find that a few compositional precepts can speed his rise to that desired level. But it is to be hoped that every beginning photographer recognizes that lack of understanding and imagination can never be replaced by memorizing a set of precepts. No such set of rules, either general or specific, can perform by themselves.

We have already seen that the art of seeing involves not just the eyes, but the brain as well, for the brain is needed to organize what the eyes report into some sort of meaningful order. The camera has an eye—the lens —but it does not have a brain. Forms the eye and brain see clearly in the

It pays to look up when searching for pleasing compositions. Patterns make effective pictures.

three-dimensional space about us may be confusing and ambiguous when transferred, however accurately, to the two-dimensional surface of a photograph.

Order, a sequence of constituents as a device for conveying meaning, is essential for conciseness and clarity; it is the first objective in composition,

35

although order alone is not enough, since mechanical order leads to monotony. Disciplined order must be imposed on the elements of the picture by the photographer, since there is no other source from which this can come. Disciplined order comes from planning, and the more effort the photographer puts into planning his pictures the easier the planning becomes. The press photographer, of course, will not sacrifice a spot news picture of a riot while he pauses to genuflect before the altar of compositional planning, but even press photographers have time to plan the majority of their pictures. Besides, with practice, planning takes surprisingly little time.

THE SPACE-TIME SCHEME

Sometimes the photographer can physically arrange his subject into a pose that best suits his purpose. At other times he will have no such control, or he may prefer not to interfere. Nevertheless, he still has some control over two elements that greatly affect the composition of every picture. These elements are space and time. In a still photograph the first of these exists only in a limited sense and the second exists not at all. One is largely an illusion in the photograph and the other entirely so, yet both are real as elements of composition.

SPACE

In a photograph space has two important aspects. First is the flat space marked off by the picture frame itself, the format. The borders of a picture are always the first dominating and controlling elements of the composition the photographer must consider. Everything contained within the borders exists in relationship to those borders; each line is a horizontal, vertical, or diagonal line because of its relationship to the borders; each mass appears to occupy space in relationship to the borders.

The two-dimensional picture frame establishes the spatial field of the picture, and the optical elements within the picture seem to advance or recede from that frame and thus establish the second aspect of space: the illusion of a third dimension. The photograph becomes a world of its own that seems to extend beyond the flat surface of the paper on which it is printed. This third dimension is only an illusion, but a powerful one, and there are definite compositional devices that contribute to this illusion.

All devices used to create the illusion of depth or the third dimension can be lumped under one word—*perspective;* this is the term that describes the depiction of three-dimensional space on a flat plane. In photography the illusion of a third dimension is created by three principal means: *linear perspective, aerial perspective,* and *contrasts in image sharpness.* Each is capable of imparting the depth illusion alone; or they may be used in combination, and such combinations may result in the strongest illusion.

Linear perspective occurs in the actual world. A familiar example involves the converging lines of a straight stretch of highway and the diminishing size of the telephone poles running parallel with the highway. Converging lines continue to approach each other as the distance increases until finally they meet at the vanishing point on the horizon. So, if lines we know to be parallel appear to converge in a photograph, then we reason that the lines are receding into the distance, and thus we are persuaded to see depth in the picture. The same applies for diminishing size.

Aerial perspective is based on changes in tone values as distance increases. This, too, is evident in nature since haze, dust, or smoke in the atmosphere tends to make distant objects appear lighter and less distinct than close ones. Generally, the darker the object appears, the closer we assume it to be. The opposite also is true: the lighter the object appears, the farther away we assume it is. Thus, if we combine dark and light tones in our photograph, the difference in tones will tend to impart the illusion of depth. In fact, some scenes, when transferred to the flat plane of a photograph, can be given this illusion only by relying on aerial perspective, because linear perspective may not be available if there are no converging lines or series of objects of known size diminishing into the distance. When a scene is being photographed, aerial perspective actually present because of atmospheric haze or smoke will generally appear in the photographic print; in fact, it is often emphasized in the photograph. Even greater emphasis on this form of perspective can be achieved by using a blue filter over the camera lens, since this (as we shall see in the chapter on filters) exaggerates the effect of haze. In other than scenery photography, the basic effect of aerial perspective can often be created simply by arranging the lighting so that the major portion of it strikes the background, leaving the foreground relatively darker in tone in the finished print.

Perspective control through contrasts in image sharpness is also based on an effect we can actually observe when we look at real scenes and objects. The human eye can focus only on one plane at a time, and objects in front and behind the plane focused on will appear to be in various degrees of unsharpness. If you hold a card or book over one eye and look across the room with the other, you will note that you are then judging the relative distance to various objects—that is, placing them in space, by the more or less unsharp images of objects surrounding the point at which your uncovered eye is focused. The usual camera (the stereo camera is the exception) has but one eye and it can record depth in the same manner—by contrasts in sharpness. The greater this contrast between various objects, the greater will be the illusion of depth and space.

This type of perspective is frequently used in portraiture where linear or aerial perspective is undesirable. The contrast between the sharply reproduced features of the face and the unsharp background creates a feeling of space and also concentrates attention where the photographer wants it to be, on the face, the only clearly defined part of the picture. In some portraits you will note that the fuzziness of the unsharp image begins at the subject's ears. This gives a close approximation of how we see a person we are talking to when our eyes are focused on his face.

It is also possible with the camera to produce an image in which all or nearly all objects recorded by the lens will be sharp and clearly defined. In this case there is virtually no contrast in sharpness, and if an illusion of a third dimension is wanted it must be achieved by one or both of the other devices: linear or aerial perspective. The effect of linear perspective is strikingly enhanced by sharpness extending to the farthest background. An unsharp background is generally better with aerial perspective.

Two other devices, which are essentially part of these three basic means of perspective creation, may also be mentioned, since their deliberate use can often reinforce the depth illusion. These are depth or perspective through vertical location and through overlapping figures. The first is related to linear perspective. As an object moves higher on the vertical plane of the picture's surface, it will also appear to recede into the distance; normally it will also diminish in size. Depth through overlapping figures is related to all three of the basic perspective controls. Planes and masses that overlap will appear to recede behind the picture plane, and the effect is frequently reinforced by differences in tones and sharpness as well as differences in size.

One or more, in some cases all, of these devices are available to the photographer as he composes his picture in the camera viewfinder. These are not controls that operate automatically in the photographer's favor, but are rather controls he must apply with conscious effort, at least until they become as familiar to him as the rules of grammar are to the writer who

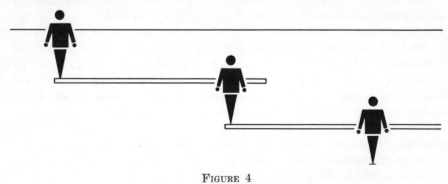

FIGURE 4
Depth by vertical location and overlapping figures.

A classic example of the S-curve in photo composition. It emphasizes the feeling of depth in addition to leading the eye of the viewer into the picture. (Norman W. Schumm, Pittsburgh)

composes a sentence without conscious concern about agreement of subject and verb.

Linear perspective can be altered by changes, sometimes very small changes, in the photographer's physical position. He can move to one side or the other, move down or up, move toward or away from the principal subject. A more distant viewpoint will reduce the effect of linear perspective—there will be less relative difference in the size of objects at longer camera-to-subject distances; while a closer viewpoint will emphasize this phenomenon of decreasing size as distance increases. Aerial perspective is controlled either by the use of filters or by adjustments in lighting. Contrasts in sharpness are controlled by focusing the lens and by setting the aperture (which controls the depth of field discussed in Chapter 7).

SPACE AND SCALE

Creating the depth illusion is generally not a difficult problem in photography; in fact, it is often quite difficult to take a picture that does not contain that illusion, at least to some degree. But another problem involving space is not always so easily solved. This is the problem of defining the scope of the space depicted within the picture's borders and the size of objects within the picture, objects that may not be readily defined in size by the viewer's past experience. This can be a problem in a large, empty hall if there are no familiar objects within the picture to scale the space enclosed by the hall. Or, to take another example, in scenery shots an impressive, massive mountain turns up in the print as a disappointing, minor hill.

The solution in both cases is to supply scale within the picture's composition, that is, a familiar element, perhaps the image of a person. Other objects can also serve: trees, automobiles, houses, animals, a chair, a fence. Images of such objects in the foreground, often to one side or the other where they serve an additional function in framing a center of interest in the background, establish a scale for the viewer's judgment of the depth, or third dimension. At other times, a familiar image of relatively familiar size placed within the depth of the picture defines the total space as large, or the mountain in the background as massive. For close-ups, scale can be supplied by smaller objects; the human hand is often an effective scale provider.

Horizons will also affect the rendition of space within a photograph. Extremely low or extremely high horizon lines create strong illusions of picture depth and space. A high horizon line puts the emphasis on depth in the land, while a low horizon will put emphasis on depth or broad expanse of the sky. Horizon lines should not, ordinarily, split the picture space into two equal parts, because the picture then tends to become static and uninteresting. Eliminating the horizon from a scenic view tends to emphasize the abstract pattern.

The choice of shooting distance is an important one in composition, not only because of the perspective involved, but because choice of shooting distance has a major effect on emphasis within the picture frame. As more is included within the frame as the shooting distance increases, emphasis generally falls to large masses rather than details. Moving closer to the subject will, of course, reverse this effect. Choice of shooting distance

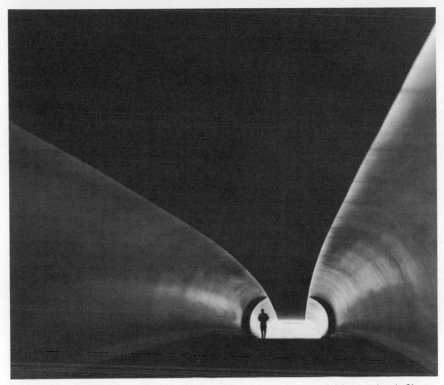

The rapid convergence of the overhead lines toward a vanishing point indicates this picture was made with a wide-angle lens. It is an effective example of linear perspective. (David Camhi, Brooklyn, N.Y.)

depends upon purpose, but the most useful admonition to the beginning photographer is against including too much, an almost universal fault in the photographs of beginners. Often the photographer's purpose gains emphasis or impact, his meaning is much more convincing and clearly stated, if he moves in close to the subject, concentrating on some particular detail—and details often provide as much information about an event or situation as an overall view.

The three basic viewpoints in terms of distance from the subject are the close-up, the medium shot, and the long shot. All are useful and all three may be called for with a single subject; only the view through the view-finder can be the final guide in any particular situation.

The photographer must constantly be searching for the best viewpoint. A step to right or left may eliminate an unpleasant fragment of background, like a tree branch seemingly growing out of Aunt Maud's ear, or a slight bending of the knees may bring perspective lines into position to put emphasis on the main point of interest.

Photographers must remember that size, either the mass of individual

These two Pentax shots demonstrate the effectiveness of lens focal length as a tool in photographic composition. The left picture was made with a 28-mm Takumar wide-angle lens while the right picture was made with an 85-mm Takumar lens. The wide-angle lens pushes the distant trees further back than they seemed to the eye, while the semi-telephoto lens pulls the background closer to the foreground.

objects or the extent of space, is not an absolute in pictures; size is always relative. Length, width, shape, and volume each gain their scale through a dynamic interrelationship with all the remaining elements of the optical environment, which includes not only the other elements within the picture but the picture margins themselves. The scale available to delineate size within the picture frame is much more limited on the flat plane of the picture than it is in the actual world surrounding us. Deliberate use must be made of perspective controls and scale relationships if the photograph's world of images is to be as attractive as the world of real objects.

TIME

There is, of course, no actual time factor in a still picture; time can only be simulated, and where the illusion of depth in a photograph may be strong and unmistakable, the illusion of time is much more subtle, in fact often escaping a casual viewer's eye if he gives the picture only a passing glance. Time in a picture is simulated by control of lines, shapes, and directions. The effort is to create some sort of visual order within the

42

pattern of the picture elements that will lead the viewer's eye on a deliberate path through the picture, thus indicating a passage of time as the eye progresses. Time may also be indicated by the blurred image, the flashing feet of a runner or the relatively sharp image of a moving figure against a blurred background. Such images indicate the movement of a subject within space, a movement that can only take place during a period of time. Time also becomes an implied element of the composition in the case of a running figure sharply delineated through a high shutter-speed. In this case time can be indicated by intelligent control of the relationship of the running figure to the rest of the picture space. If the intent is to show the figure running toward a place, then the picture space should allow extra space in front of the implied motion, space for the figure to move into. If the figure is running away from a place, then more space behind the figure will indicate this, put the emphasis on this idea, and also put emphasis on the time that has gone before the picture was taken instead of on the time that came after the shutter was snapped.

Composition or arrangement of elements within a picture can be controlled through purposeful placement of figures and objects by the photographer. Or the photographer may move about himself, rather than moving figures and objects in front of the lens. These maneuvers will be largely a matter of controlling composition through control of space. But there is a third major method of controlling the composition—through time. This is largely a matter of decision upon the fraction of a second selected for snapping the shutter, what the great French photographer, Henri Cartier-Bresson, has so fittingly called the decisive moment. His own skill at selecting the decisive moment has made this technique almost his own personal trademark. But it has not, in fact, been trademarked or patented, since, of course, it could not be; so it is a technique available to all.

When subjects are in motion, even relatively slow motion, the instant the photographer selects for taking the picture will have a major effect on the composition. Anyone who has taken more than a few snapshots has had two experiences at least one time each. First, the happy experience of discovering the image in the positive print shows perfect timing, a shutter snapped at just the right moment. The second experience, not so happy, involves the finished print that reveals bad timing, equally unsuspected. The subject had his eyes closed when the shutter snapped; or Junior, unaware that he was posing for his first picture, turned his head away just at the wrong moment. Good timing can happen by accident, but the great pictures that look as if they might have been the result of accident are more often the result of careful planning, patient waiting, or a quick sense of the decisive moment. The instant chosen to make the exposure can be all-important; a fraction of a second too early or too late and the really good picture has been missed. The photographer needs a sharp eye and quick reflexes.

CENTER OF INTEREST

Since the best composed picture is one in which elements are readily perceived as a simple, organized whole, the photographer must develop the ability of selecting viewpoints that will achieve this simplicity, subduing the distracting elements, which nearly always exist. Good photographs clarify, emphasize, and dramatize the essence of the subject so that the viewer of the photograph will gain insight into the subject.

First step for the photographer is finding the center of interest, that part of the image to which he wants the eye of the viewer to move automatically. Then he studies the image in the viewfinder for ways in which to eliminate or subdue the extraneous and irrelevant, for ways in which the remaining elements can be made to contribute emphasis to the center of interest. He attempts to simplify by moving in close, by searching for camera angles that will provide a neutral background, by setting exposure and lighting so that center of interest is highlighted and nonessential clutter hidden in shadows, by using focusing and aperture-setting to sharpen essential points and subdue the nonessential. And if maneuvering with the viewfinder before the shutter is tripped does not result in the final

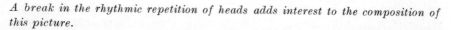

A break in the rhythmic repetition of heads adds interest to the composition of this picture.

stage of simplicity he is searching for, he plans to crop the negative when he reaches the point of making the final print.

In most photographs there should be only one major center of interest. This is, perhaps, as firm a rule as there is in photographic composition. Two others, often stated, are these: never place the center of interest in the exact center of the physical, two-dimensional space of the picture, but at the same time keep the center of interest away from the margins. The arguments usually are that central placement is apt to be dull and static, and edge placement destroys emphasis, leaving the composition uncomfortably out of balance. In many situations these arguments are valid, but for a significant number of picture subjects they are just as obviously not valid. It would appear that the secondary elements, which create the optical environment for the center of interest, have greater importance than arbitrary rules. You will find many successful and pleasing photographs in which the center of interest has been placed at or very near the picture's physical center. Less often, strong centers of interest appear near picture borders. Careful study of the total composition will reveal why the photographer selected a particular arrangement and how he managed to do it without being dull, without creating confusion rather than unity.

For positioning the center of interest, many beginners have found the *rule of the thirds* useful, although it must, like other so-called rules, be accepted with the understanding that there are many exceptions. Any photographer who always applies the rule of the thirds to his compositions will find monotony an inevitable characteristic of his work. This rule divides the picture area into thirds, vertically and horizontally. Compositional strength may come from placing the center of interest at or near one of the four points where the imaginary division lines cross, particularly the top left intersection. But, a repeated warning: arbitrary application of this system without thought for elements of the composition other than the center of interest cannot consistently produce good pictures.

PSYCHOLOGICAL FACTORS

Study of the largely psychological factors involved in the organization of lines, masses, and tones for simplicity and emphasis also can be a help. If these factors are to be of significant aid they must be applied before the film is exposed.

LINES

Two kinds of lines exist in most images: the actual and the implied. Actual lines are really seen. They are the edges of buildings, fence wires or rails, stair railings, separations between sidewalk and grass, the edges of a path or road, separations between light and shadow—anything that forms a line in the real world. Implied lines are those suggested by the shape or thrust of an object, the apparent direction of movement of a person or vehicle, and the relationships between actual lines. In our minds we often, in effect, fill in the intervals between actual lines that are moving in the same direction.

Both actual and implied lines take on compositional and emotional significance. Emotionally, a horizontal line is static, at rest, at peace; it implies calm, perhaps lassitude. A vertical line implies solemnity, dignity. The photographer's decision on format, whether the picture will be printed as a horizontal or vertical composition—that is, with the longer marginal dimension on the horizontal or vertical—often depends upon the lines of the subject. A subject with dominant horizontal lines usually calls for a horizontal format, and the vertical format better displays the subject with strong vertical lines. In either case the marginal lines emphasize the physical and psychological effects of the subject lines.

Whereas horizontal and vertical lines tend to be static, diagonal lines in the subject are the dynamic ones in composition. Diagonal lines imply

Simplicity, repetition, and a diagonal line of movement with space ahead to move into gives this picture pleasing composition. (Robert Rhode, Boulder, Colo.)

action, conflict of opposing forces, stress, and strain. Combinations of diagonal lines create a feeling of freedom, with swift movement.

But actual or implied lines are not always desirable; they may distract from the center of interest if they lead away from it. Strong lines in a building used as a background may be a disturbing rather than a contributing element. To protect himself from disappointment, the photographer must be constantly aware of lines, because, although he may fail to see them in the viewfinder, the camera lens does not, and when the image appears in the print the lines take on a prominence much more controlling than in the actual scene.

PROXIMITY

Organization of lines, masses, and tones is the vital factor in a camera-coded message, and the primary, and simplest, psychological factor in the organization of these elements is proximity. A familiar example of proximity in this sense is provided by the page of type you are now reading. Proximity of the letters builds relationships you recognize as words, which in turn form sentences. Two lines close together in a photograph in the same way become two parts of a single unit. Or any other elements close to each other on the picture surface tend to be seen together as a unit.

RHYTHM

In addition, similarity or equality among various elements tends to tie those elements into recognizable relationships: similar or equal size, shape, direction, value, texture. Often this results in a rhythm or pattern within the visual field to strengthen simplicity and emphasis. Rhythm can appear in the alternating or orderly repetition of shapes, lengths, angles, curves, directions, or intervals. In rhythm or pattern there is the risk of monotony that detracts. Often the most effective rhythm is the interrupted one, thus implying movement or change. Or two patterns may oppose each other, thus building tension and interest—if the emphasis implied by the opposition contributes to the purpose of the photographer. Compositional lines or patterns leading to such an intersection should also lead to the meaning of the picture.

STABILITY

As the elements are brought into relationships through proximity and similarity, stability becomes involved. This is, in part, a need for balance, not a precise and static form of balance that gives the imagination of the viewer no excuse for activity, but a dynamic arrangement that gives satisfaction without monotony. A perfectly symmetrical arrangement, with elements of equal size, shape, and tone at either side of the picture at equal distances from the physical center, gives balance, but ordinarily without

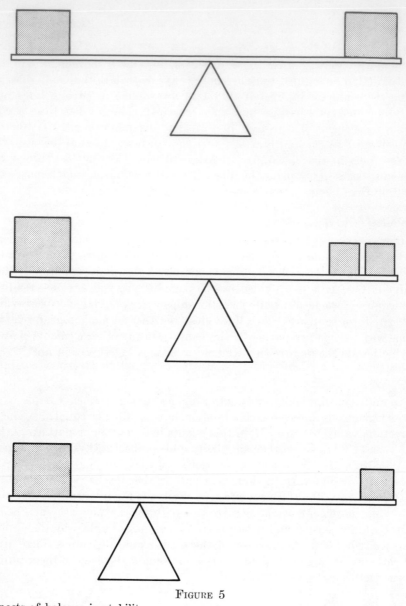

FIGURE 5

Aspects of balance in stability.

interest. There is no tension, no excitement, and no implication of movement and change, only a static, unchanging relationship. Yet complete
lack of balance, with all form and movement in one half of the picture
while the other half lacks visual interest, may be equally disturbing and
ineffective.

The mind imagines forces implied by the image masses and lines of

48

direction as imparting pressures this way or that, and these pressures seem to demand equality. The most familiar natural force is gravity. Heavy, dark masses in the photograph tend to be pulled down, with the result that a photograph containing predominantly light tones near the bottom margin and dark masses at the top is disturbing and uncomfortable to look at; just the reverse is what we normally expect, and if this abnormal arrangement is not a deliberate contribution to the photographer's purpose it becomes a distraction. Failure to pay attention to lateral balance in the picture can result in an equal distraction, but large or heavy elements near the physical center of the picture can be balanced by much smaller or lighter elements farther from the center on the opposite side. Balance, of course, is not precisely measured, but is judged by the photographer's eye.

Stability also involves the tendency for lines, both actual and implied, within the image to drive toward some sort of closed, compact shape. When we look at a picture we immediately begin a search for the simplest and most stable forms. Areas within a picture that appear to be closed and separated from their surroundings please and attract the eye because these are areas that are stable. If actual lines in the image do not form these stable areas, psychological factors come into play to fill out the broken lines, thus completing the figure. Each such stable unit either combines

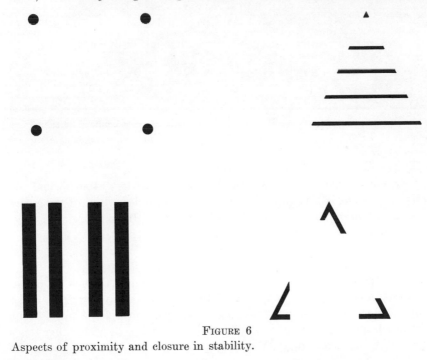

FIGURE 6

Aspects of proximity and closure in stability.

Unusual frame brings attention to the figure, adds depth, and makes this picture an eye-stopper.

with or clashes with others within the picture borders; the normal objective, of course, is a combination that makes a unified whole of the entire picture, as two or more musical notes, each by itself an individual tone, merge into a pleasing whole, serving a common purpose.

TONE

A final factor of significance in composition is tone, defined in black-and-white photography as a section of the gray scale ranging from white to black. Here again we are concerned with relationships. A single tone of gray is important only as it is related to, or contrasted with, other tones surrounding it. A middle gray may appear as either dark or light in the

Low camera angle with the wide-angle lens up very close to the foreground tulips brings you nearer to and makes the story of this picture more effective. (Duane Howell, Staff Photographer, Denver *Post*)

print, depending upon the tones next to it. If the surrounding area is predominantly black, a middle gray appears light; if the surroundings are white, or nearly so, middle gray appears dark, tending toward black. In addition, white or nearly white areas look all the whiter if surrounding tones tend toward black, and these white areas also appear larger than dark ones of equal size and shape. The lighter tones, particularly the white ones, tend to attract and hold the eye, which explains why photographers frequently strive for brightest highlights at the center of interest. Tones are also involved in the balance of the picture, since balance is not solely a matter of objects pictured, but of light and shade as well. Good photographs often contain an extended gray scale, a great number of varying gray tones between black and white, and the tones are well distributed throughout the picture. However, photography is also capable of strong graphic statements in which all or most of the dark tones are concentrated in one area of a picture, balanced—or opposed—by a second area of white.

Tones are highly important parts of a composition, and the photographer must learn to previsualize the finished print as he looks through the viewfinder, translating color, light, and shade into tones of the gray scale. He must learn to recognize large areas that will reproduce as empty spaces in the image, such as a large, empty expanse of snow or sky. These are often empty of detail and empty of interest, contributing only weakness to the composition. He must learn to recognize and correct for contrasts in tones in the image. Failure to recognize the importance of tones may mean that a line of separation between two parts of the subject has disappeared in the photographic image, letting two forms merge into a puzzling one.

POST-EXPOSURE CONTROLS

All of the foregoing compositional factors are considered, if at all possible, before the shutter is snapped. Later some controls are still available, but they are limited and can rarely produce a satisfying composition from an image that was poorly organized in the camera viewfinder. Development and printing procedures can alter tonal values, and faults in framing the subject in the viewfinder can be corrected, at least to some extent, by cropping when making an enlargement of the negative.

If unwanted elements are to be cropped out of the picture during printing, those elements must be placed at or near the margin of the viewfinder. A plan for cropping often originates before the film is exposed. Cropping, too, can change the dimensions of the visual field presented by the print and thus put greater emphasis on certain subject lines or other elements. It is wise for the beginner to look for cropping possibilities when he projects the negative image onto the enlarging easel, but experience will demonstrate that the most effective use of cropping is generally based on

The rule of the thirds illustrated. Center of interest is spaced approximately two-thirds up and two-thirds from the left. (Miss Billie Roos, Arlington, Mass.)

a plan made at the time the subject was composed in the viewfinder of the camera. There are rather severe limitations on how much a photograph can be rewritten after the photographer has left the scene where the picture was taken.

SCHOOLING THE EYE

For most persons, schooling the eye and mind to see in terms of photographic images is not a very rapid process, but there are ways in which the process can be speeded up. The capacity to see—really see—is the underlying essential, and this capacity must be learned, or perhaps more precisely, relearned, since it does seem to be a capacity most persons have as children but gradually lose as life forces upon them the necessity of seeing all objects in practical terms of functional use.

We would, first of all, urge the beginner to look about him for style and composition in nature and in all sorts of man-made objects. Look at the shape and texture of pine and aspen groves against the background of the backdrop of the Rocky Mountain peaks, or look at the play of light and shadow among the maples of the Appalachians. Look at the lines of the cloverleaf at a freeway interchange; study architecture, the old as well as the new, the complexities of Victorian structures and the starched and rhythmic simplicity of the modern city's cliff dwellings. Watch the flow of relationships among people at play, at work, and in crowds on the street. In all of these and more there are pattern and stability, and lines and tones in various stages of balance.

We would, secondly, urge all beginners to study the pictures of others, both photographers and painters. Criticize the pictures. Why do you like or dislike them? Put your answers in writing. As the persistent study of a written language gradually builds the ability to recognize the significance of relationships between letters and words, so the study of pictures gradually perfects the skill of recognizing significant and effective visual statements through the organization of pictorial elements. The skill developed in looking at the pictures of others is not at all difficult to apply to perfecting the organization of a subject seen through the viewfinder of your own camera.

We would urge a third step: analyzing the pictures of others. Much can be learned by laying a piece of thin paper over a photograph and then sketching in the main elements of the picture as they are seen dimly through the paper. This helps develop the ability to recognize the dominant elements of the composition by subduing the effect of the details. The first step here should always be to draw the margins of the picture and then to sketch the structural skeleton of the picture with as few lines as possible. Fine, artistic drawings are not the objective; rough sketches made by an unskilled hand will serve the purpose well. This step in the study process can be carried a bit further with profit by sketching paintings and photographs without laying the paper over the original picture, and finally by sketching ideas for photographs before the photograph is actually taken. These are exercises designed to strengthen mental channels used to spot the principal elements of a composition, the conspicuous and controlling lines, tones, and masses. Once a picture has been sketched or diagrammed in this way the arrangement or composition becomes clear, and if in the sketched diagram the effect is pleasing, then the composition is very likely a good one.

Looking for the reasons a picture is effective or looking for ways to convert a subject into an effective picture can be a struggle at first, but it becomes progressively easier. There may be periods of uncertainty, when the photographer is not sure just what it is he is looking for, because what he was looking for yesterday may not be what he is looking for today. But the search must never be solely for composition as an end in itself, but always for content first, and then for the composition that will provide the image form to serve the purpose. We have seen that there are no real rules of composition, and even if such rules did exist, following them would never guarantee great pictures, just as following rules of grammar will never guarantee great writing.

Since composition is organization according to subject matter and according to the photographer's purpose and viewpoint, there can be no absolute standard for any such thing as good or bad style in photography. The vital question always remains: Does it accomplish the intention? Sensitivity to these matters can hardly be acquired by memorizing rules or precepts. Distinctions are subtle and by no means universally agreed upon. Photography is a living, changing thing, and no one should try, or want to try, to bind it in a straitjacket of rules. It is employed for many different purposes, so we can do little more than echo what others have said about writing, that to do a thing in style is to do it in a way that is suitable to the occasion.

The photographer has achieved a composition with style when he has put together a few things so harmoniously that nothing can be added and nothing can be subtracted without destroying the balance of the whole. And permeating it all is the taste and comprehension of the photographer, for we cannot escape the basic factor expressed in the old saying: The style is the man.

Chapter 4
•
DEVELOPING THE NEGATIVE

After the camera work is done, moving to the final picture is generally a two-step process: (1) production of the negative from the exposed film, and (2) production of the positive, or final print, from the negative. Both operations, if performed in the usual manner, require a darkroom, although there are methods and equipment that make a darkroom unnecessary.

The darkroom and its equipment need not be elaborate, but the room must be truly dark for handling today's films, which are mostly panchromatic and thus sensitive to all colors of light. Basic equipment should include tanks for developing film, print trays, an accurate thermometer, a timer, a graduate for measuring liquids, bottles for storing solutions, a safelight, a printing frame or printing box, and, if enlargements are wanted (and they usually are) an enlarger. An enlarger timer is not essential but it is handy and desirable. Some timers will function as both an interval timer for negative development and as an enlarger lamp control for printing exposures.

The photographer must strike an exact balance between exposure and development to achieve an ideal negative, but unfortunately there are no precise and immutable guidelines to lead him to this goal. So many variables are involved, each photographer must establish his own guidelines based on general principles provided to guide his first efforts. Certain subjects and lighting conditions may demand special attention in exposure or development or both; equipment (cameras and enlargers) involved may require variations in technique; each photographer's darkroom habits exert an influence on results, and, even more important, each photographer has his own unique viewpoint. Both exposure and development, ideally, should reflect the photographer's thoughtful interpretation of the subject.

Since all photographers must solve the exposure-development problem for themselves, it follows that there cannot be any one best developer for all workers. All that can be recommended is that the beginner start with the prepared developers that come as liquids to be diluted or as mixtures of powdered chemicals packaged in cans, boxes, or packets and need only to be poured into water and dissolved according to instructions on the labels. Film comes packaged with development recommendations, and these should be followed, unless other reliable and reasonable instruction

56

is available, until enough experience has been accumulated to make experimental changes meaningful and productive. Recommendations from film manufacturer and developer supplier are based on both scientific knowledge and practical tests. These recommendations are, of course, intended for average conditions, and it makes sense to alter procedures only if experience proves the need. So that we can learn to recognize and meet this need, it is important to adhere to one film and one developer in the beginning.

DEVELOPMENT CONTROL

For any one film-developer combination the results (leaving exposure aside for the moment) depend upon three factors: temperature, time, and agitation. Rigid control of these three factors reduces film development to the same level as boiling one's breakfast egg. It is possible to guarantee a given result by developing the film for a known time at a fixed temperature with controlled agitation.

TEMPERATURE

The temperature factor is the simplest and may be considered first. The ideal temperature for most standard developers is 68 degrees F. In a few cases 70 degrees may be the recommendation. High temperatures may cause excessive softening and swelling of the emulsion gelatin and thus make it especially susceptible to damage. Lower temperatures strongly affect the activity of the developer and result in underdevelopment unless the time of development is extended to compensate. It is possible with many solutions to develop at temperatures as high as 80 degrees and as low as 60 degrees, if the time factor is altered in a reverse relationship; that is, the lower the temperature, the longer the development time; the higher the temperature, the shorter the development time. Precise factors for altering the time to compensate for abnormal temperatures cannot be provided; the best practice is to consult a time-temperature chart for the film-developer combination involved. It is inadvisable to develop at temperatures higher than 80 degrees because the possibility of damage to the emulsion layer becomes very great. It is equally unwise to develop at temperatures under 60 degrees, because most film developers do not function properly that cold.

For best results, temperature is very important, especially if developing times are short. The laboratory thermometer must be accurate. It should be checked regularly with a second standard thermometer kept just for that purpose or with a medical thermometer. Inaccuracies in darkroom thermometers are quite common.

All solutions, including the final wash water, should be kept at the same temperature as the developer if at all possible. Variations in temperature between solutions, if relatively large, may cause what is called reticulation, a cracking of the emulsion, and in the case of small-sized negatives temperature changes can cause clumping of the silver grains that form the image; these clumps show up as increased graininess in the print.

TIME

The time factor is variable, depending primarily upon the particular film-developer combination involved. Here we must again refer to recommendations supplied with the film and/or the developer. And even these are only guides; they are not absolute values. There is no such thing as a correct development time for all workers under all circumstances. Here the variables are personal perference, equipment, and agitation. We can, however, begin with the recommended times and modify them as experience dictates to meet individual requirements. A rough guide for alterations: if negatives consistently emerge too contrasty, cut development (or agitation) 20 to 30 per cent; if they are consistently too soft, boost development (or agitation) up to 50 per cent. The longer the development time,

Miss Colorado contest winner, Sally Guinn of Denver, was photographed with a Pentax camera and Kodak Panatomic-X film. The exposure index used for the film was 100 and the negatives were developed in Selectol Soft (normally a paper developer) for 3 minutes with agitation every 60 seconds. You may want to try this Eastman Kodak developer with your film to retain printable shadow and highlight detail in harshly lighted subjects. (Floyd McCall, Denver)

the more silver is formed and the blacker the resulting negative image. Contrast, or the difference between highlights and shadows, also increases with time, but only up to that point where chemical fog level begins to overtake the increase in the highlight density; then flatness or low contrast results.

AGITATION

Too often neglected by beginners, agitation is equal in importance to time and temperature. Fresh developer must be worked into the emulsion layer while the exhausted developer and by-products of the development reaction are swished out and away from the surface of the film. Agitation also keeps the solution uniform, so streaks on the negative caused by exhausted solution flowing across the emulsion do not occur. Agitation should begin the moment the film is placed in the developer and should continue for the first 10 to 15 seconds of the development period. After that agitation is usually advisable for about 5 seconds out of every 30 for the remainder of the time. (There are exceptions to this, however; see page 220.)

For uniform results agitation should be the same each time film is developed. This does not mean, however, a rhythmical and precise pattern of agitation. Such a pattern may result in development streaks, since the agitation may be more effective on some areas of the film than on others.

DEVELOPMENT PROCEDURE

To prepare for film developing, check the temperature of the developer, set the time, and place tank, tank lid, timer, and all other equipment you will need in the dark (while the film is exposed) where you can lay hands on them without a fumbling search. With all lights out, roll film must first be stripped from its paper covering; 35-mm film must be removed from its cassette by sharply rapping the projecting spool on a counter top or by prying off the opposite end with the bottle-opening end of a beer-can opener. The dry film is then wound on a clean and dry plastic or stainless steel reel. The reel is then placed in the tank and development begins.

The developer may be poured into the tank either before or after the loaded reel is slipped in. If the film is put in first, the tank lid can be put in place and the light turned on, since the lid permits pouring solutions in and out while a baffle blocks the entrance of light. However, pouring the developer in after the film is in the tank tends to create two problems: development begins on some parts of the film before it begins on other parts, so the pouring must be done steadily and rapidly; and this method increases the possibility of air bubbles sticking to the emulsion. If these bubbles are not dislodged during agitation they cause pinholes, which show up as black spots in the finished print. The pinholes occur because the air bubbles prevent the developer from reaching a tiny spot on the emulsion. Generally, slipping the loaded film reel gently into a tank already filled with developer gives better, more consistent results.

Whichever procedure is used, agitation should begin immediately and continue for 10 to 15 seconds. Gentle tapping of the tank against counter or sink helps dislodge any air bubbles. Tanks that can be inverted are best for roll films. Then, during the first period of agitation and every 30 seconds thereafter, the tank can be lifted and inverted two or three times in five seconds and then put down with a gentle tap or knock to remove the air bubbles. Whatever agitation system produces consistent results is a desirable one. If multiple reel tanks are used for only one reel, it is wise to put an empty reel (or reels) in the tank to prevent too vigorous agitation as a result of the single reel shooting the length of the tank with each inversion.

After development, the developer is poured out of the tank, rinse water poured in and out, and fixer poured in, with the light-tight lid always in place. Fixing time is generally defined as twice *clearing time*. The purpose of the fixer is to remove the unexposed and undeveloped crystals of silver halide in the emulsion. These crystals, before they are removed, give the developed film a rather milky appearance. Clearing time, then, is the time needed to remove this milky look. Twice clearing time is recommended because it is very difficult to judge the exact moment at which all the undeveloped crystals have been cleared out of the emulsion by the hypo or fixer. Film should be left in most standard fixers, with some agitation, for 5 to 10 minutes. After fixation, the lid of the tank can be removed, since all of the remaining light-sensitive halides have been dissolved by the fixer. The film is left in the tank and washed with running water; the tank should be emptied of water several times during the wash period.

Tank development with sheet films involves placing each piece of film in individual hangers, which are then lowered together into a tank of developer. Agitation should again be practiced for the first 10 to 15 seconds by lifting the hangers up and down. Let the hangers strike the edge of the tank to knock off air bubbles. Lift all hangers together, not one at a time, to avoid the corner of one hanger scratching a neighboring film.

Agitation every 30 seconds can be accomplished in various ways. If it is desirable to have the lights on, then the tank, with a light-tight lid in place, is rocked for agitation. Actually, a more efficient and reliable method involves leaving the lights off, or turning them off every 30 seconds, while the hangers are raised and tilted diagonally to allow the developer to run off one corner for a few seconds. Then the film is immersed again and relifted to allow developer to drain off the opposite corner.

Rinsing and fixing will be easiest and most efficient with sheet film if two additional tanks are available, one for the rinse and one for the fixer,

Careful exposure and development will bring out the remarkable ability of photo-graphic film to record the photographer's purpose. (Horst Ebersberg, Denver)

into which the film and hangers can be successively dipped. The lights, of course, must be out while the film is being moved from one tank to another and until it has been in the fixer for at least one or two minutes.

STOP BATH

Some readers, already familiar with film-development procedures, may have noted the preceding summary did not mention the use of a stop bath between developer and fixer. If the darkroom worker prefers a stop bath, usually a weak solution of acetic acid, to a plain water rinse, then he should continue with this practice. In most cases, a stop bath is not necessary with film and in a few cases may cause trouble, since transferring the film from the alkaline developer solution to an acid solution can cause bubbles to form in the emulsion of the film and if these burst they create pinholes.

An acid stop bath has two purposes: to stop development instantly (since most developers do not function in an acid solution), and to convert the emulsion to an acid state before it goes into the fixer, thus giving greater assurance that the fixer will be good for a relatively long period of use. Except for high-speed developers (and even here the stop bath is dangerous if it is a little too strong), the first purpose of the stop bath is not generally important with film, and a 30-second rinse in plain water leaves so little of the developer in the emulsion that it has a nearly negligible effect on the fixer. A weak acid stop bath may be advisable after a high-speed developer, since development does continue if the rinse is plain water; it is also often recommended with ultrafast films to check the possibility of fog.

FIXERS

Like developers, fixers come in convenient packages ready to be mixed with water and put to use, and they come in three principal forms. The nonhardening fixers do not contain a chemical to harden the gelatin of the emulsion; these are seldom used, because hardening is generally desired unless the print is to be toned. Acid-hardening fixers contain both an acid, to neutralize the developer and stop its action, and a hardener. Rapid fixers are usually the acid-hardening type but they reduce fixing time by about one half; they are, for this reason, popular with news photographers. Rapid fixers are not stable in the dry powder form and usually are supplied in concentrated liquid solutions.

Whatever the fixer used, the time recommended on the package label should be followed. Some of the silver image may be dissolved if negatives are left in the fixing solution for long periods. Fixing is speeded if agitation takes place during the first 30 seconds in the solution and occasionally thereafter. Thick emulsion films (the high-speed films, generally) take somewhat longer to fix than do thin emulsion films.

WASHING AND DRYING

After fixation the film must be washed to remove both the hypo and the complex silver salts that remain in the emulsion after fixing. A wash time of 30 minutes in a continuous flow of fresh water generally suffices and prevents staining and fading later on. A hypo neutralizer or clearing agent saves washing time. Thirty seconds in the neutralizer is the equivalent of 20 minutes of washing in running water. After the negatives have been in the neutralizer for a minute, washing in running water for three to five minutes gives long-lasting images.

Hypo is heavier than water and has a tendency to sink to the bottom of the tank, so it is good practice to dump the water from the wash tank (unless it has an exit for the water at the bottom) and let it refill several times during the washing period.

After washing, the film can be swabbed off in the water with a wad of cotton if you wish to remove any sand or grit from the water that may have collected on the surface of the film. The film should be dipped for 30 seconds or more in a solution of a wetting agent or detergent (such as Kodak Photo-Flo, a solution of ethylene glycol) and then allowed to drip dry. The wetting agent breaks the water into small molecules and leaves a thin, even layer of water on the film; this eliminates water spotting that might otherwise appear when the film dries. The film can be wiped slowly and gently on both sides with a damp chamois cloth or with a cellulose sponge to help prevent water-spotting, but this is a risky practice. Wiping the film can scratch or streak it if chamois or sponge is not kept scrupulously clean.

The film is hung on a line to dry, pinned up with clothespins or with film clips. The dry negatives can be filed in envelopes. Roll film is usually cut into strips for this purpose: 35-mm film into strips of six frames each and 120-film into strips of three frames each.

FILM-DEVELOPING VARIATIONS

Nonstandard, or special, techniques are available to correct known shortcomings in the negative before it is developed (underexposure, overexposure, low or high contrast, and so forth), to boost effective film speed, or to improve grain. These variations in technique can help, but usually a gain in one characteristic of the finished negative can come only at the expense of another.

Ideally, film should be developed for different lengths of time according to the subject and the photographer's purpose, but this can normally be done only with sheet films, which can be processed one at a time. Roll films on which a variety of subjects under a variety of lighting conditions have been recorded must be given a compromise development, although a single roll completely exposed under one set of conditions can receive special development to suit those conditions. Press photographers frequently develop a complete roll of 35-mm film for a few important shots, or even for a single shot, without exposing the remaining frames. When that important picture has been taken, they change rolls and waste the balance of the film; 35-mm film is cheap compared to the value of one good picture that may need special development.

FORCED DEVELOPMENT

At times photographers shoot pictures under conditions that make underexposure and/or low contrast unavoidable. Correction of both shortcomings can be secured, to some extent, by extending the development time. This is forced development, sometimes referred to as pushing the film speed. Some photographers regularly rate a particular film at about twice (or more) its ASA speed and produce negatives satisfactory for their purpose by a related decision on developer and development time. Such decisions can be based only on extensive experience.

In general, forced development is not a recommended practice. It must result in some loss of image quality. However, if the film has been underexposed, forced development may be the only way to get a printable negative. Only experience can give consistent results, but a beginning can be made by increasing development time about 50 per cent or by raising the developer temperature to 80 degrees to get approximately twice the normal film speed. Increasing development time more than 100 per cent is of almost no value, because image quality then falls off very sharply with increased fog (nonimage silver).

Agitation procedure may need to be altered for forced development. For example, in forcing Kodak Tri-X film to a speed of 1200 or higher, it is best to agitate at the beginning of the development period and then agitate again, very gently, only once about halfway through development, or agitate with a gentle turning of the tank every minute. More agitation than this can result in excessive grain.

Some developers give best results with film that, deliberately or unavoidably, has been given what would normally be considered an underexposure. Specific speed ratings or exposure indices are established for various films to be processed in these developers. The result is generally a higher effective film speed with relatively little, if any, loss in quality. But this processing is not the same as forced development, since the film has been specifically exposed for processing in a developer designed to boost film speed.

A prizewinner in the Annual Newspaper National Snapshot Awards. (Darrel M. Stuart, Logan, Utah)

TWO-BATH DEVELOPMENT

A nonstandard technique occasionally used involves development in two separate stages in two solutions. During stage one in the first solution the film emulsion is saturated with developer. Some development may or may not take place in this stage, depending upon the composition of the solution; often there is no alkali in this first solution, and therefore no development will occur. For stage two, the film is transferred to a second solution of dilute alkali or plain water, and development takes place until all the developer soaked up by the emulsion has been exhausted.

The simplest form of two-bath development is often called water bath development. In this case, stage one solution is a normal developer, while the stage two solution is plain water. The principal gain from this technique is an improvement in shadow detail of the image without building up excessive contrast or blocking the highlights with dense deposits of image silver. The film is left in the developer for about two thirds of the normal development time and then transferred to the water bath for two minutes. The film can be returned to the developer again for two minutes and then back to the water if necessary. Heavily exposed areas of the image, the highlights, soon exhaust the developer in the water bath, while lightly exposed areas, shadow regions, go on developing to build up detail. This evens out development and reduces contrast. It is important not to agitate the film in the water since this would wash the developer out of the emulsion. The water-bath technique is used principally for negatives, but it can be used for prints to soften contrast if other means, such as soft paper grades, are not available or do not accomplish the purpose. With prints the water of the second stage should be warm, but for negatives it should be the same temperature as the developer.

In the other form of two-bath development, the water bath is replaced by an alkali solution, such as a one per cent solution of borax or sodium hydroxide. The first bath is again the actual developer, that is, it contains the developing agent, but it is usually made up without the customary alkali. As a result, little, if any, development takes place in this first bath. The gelatin merely soaks up the developing agent, which is activated when the film is immersed in the alkali of the second bath. This procedure achieves the same general results as the water-bath technique.

Neither time nor temperature are critical with two-bath development, although both baths should be at the same temperature. The film emulsion layer absorbs about all the developer it can in three to four minutes in the first bath, and the developer is exhausted after three to four minutes in the second bath. At temperatures higher than 68 degrees, development in the second bath proceeds faster, but the developer is exhausted sooner, so these two factors cancel each other.

MONOBATH DEVELOPMENT

After two-bath development, processing continues as usual through rinse or stop bath and fixer. But there are other mixtures available that reduce developer and fixer to a single solution. These are called monobaths. Some developing agents function even if large amounts of hypo are present in the same solution. This means that development and fixing can take place in the same solution, simplifying and shortening processing. Development and fixation are completed in about six minutes; washing is accomplished in five, and with rapid film-drying agents, drying time can be cut to two minutes. Monobaths also are not tempermental about temperature and time. At high temperatures both development and fixation are speeded up and the two cancel each other. In addition, development proceeds to completion and then stops, regardless of the time the film is left in the solution.

Although monobath development has these advantages, it also has disadvantages. The negatives are not of the best quality, generally; they tend to be contrasty and grainy. There are no hardeners in the solution, and this increases the danger of reticulation; some monobaths cause a loss of effective film speed and a loss of tone gradation; a one-bath solution also eliminates the possibility of controlling density and contrast in development. Nevertheless, monobaths have proven valuable in emergency situations. They have been used effectively by press photographers on a number of occasions. During a goodwill tour of an American president in Asia the photographers for one news service used a monobath technique to develop film at their seats in the airplane while they were speeding from one stop to the next.

SOME PROCESSING TIPS

Developer solutions should be kept in tightly capped brown glass or plastic bottles to protect them from light and air. Developers keep longer if the storage bottle is full, since this reduces the opportunity for the developer to react with the oxygen in the air. The solution level in bottles can be raised and air eliminated by dropping glass marbles into the bottles or, if the bottles are plastic, by squeezing them to remove the air and then capping tightly. Caps or corks should be rubber or plastic, since these do not shrink or rust. All solutions should be stored at 65 to 75 degrees F. At higher temperatures the solutions deteriorate much more rapidly.

For a solution used over and over again, constant developer activity can be maintained by replenishment. Prepared replenishers are available for most standard developers. After processing each roll, an amount of replenisher indicated by instructions on the label is poured into the developer solution; it is usually about one ounce for 80 square inches of film developed. If no regular replenisher is available, self-replenishment is possible, although not as efficient. This means adding one or two ounces of fresh developer after each roll of film. Solutions designed specifically as re-plenishers are better because they contain chemicals in particular amounts to replace those depleted most during development.

Exhausted developer should never be used. Developer stored for long periods, or for relatively short periods at high temperatures, or stored in partly filled bottles for a fairly long period, are all suspect. Developers are normally as clear as plain water; after use they become cloudy and gradually begin to discolor. If the developer is badly discolored, perhaps a dirty brown, it should be discarded. Manufacturers provide data on keeping qualities and the amount of film that can be safely processed with a specific quantity of developer.

Developer that has been used even once deteriorates much faster than never-used developer. For this reason it is important not to contaminate a fresh solution with even a small amount of used developer. Small film sizes, such as 35-mm, require only 8 to 16 ounces of developer, and the best practice is to use this amount of developer only once and then discard it. This gives greater guarantee of consistent results.

Chapter 5

MAKING THE PRINT

By the time the photographer has his finished negative in hand he has already applied many skills—a selective eye, precise judgment of light and angle of view, careful handling of the film during processing. But the job is not yet done. The final step to an outstanding photograph has yet to be taken.

Making a print from the negative is basically a simple process. It involves, first of all, passing light through the negative image so that the light will form a corresponding positive image on another sensitive emulsion, which, this time, is coated on paper. Like the negative image formed in the camera on film, this positive image is invisible, or latent, until developed. So the four basic steps taken with the film must be repeated with the paper: development, fixing, washing, drying. But we can work under a dim yellowish light now, a safelight, because paper emulsions are slow relative to film emulsions and they are sensitive, usually, only to blue light.

Printmaking divides conveniently into two processes: contact printing and projection printing (enlarging). In contact printing the emulsion side of the negative is placed in tight, uniform contact with the emulsion side of the paper in either a printing frame or box; the light then passes through negative to paper. The image passed to the paper is exactly the same size as that in the negative. If camera focusing and film exposure and development were all precise, the contact print will be sharp and clear; but it will also be no bigger than the negative, much too small, in many instances, for comfortable viewing. If the negative is small, enlarging is a virtual necessity, but it is a more difficult process than contact printing. Negatives for enlarging must be of higher technical quality than those used only for making contacts. Slight unsharpness or blur in the negative image may not be noticeable in a contact print, but will be exaggerated and more than merely noticeable in a blow-up. Enlarging exaggerates, because it enlarges, all imperfections in the negative, including grain, pinholes, scratches, specks of dust or lint, or other flaws. And a heavy negative, one that has been overexposed or overdeveloped, may be adequate for a contact print but not for projection because it may be too contrasty, too grainy, or too dense to print in a reasonable exposure period.

THE ENLARGER

The enlarger is a camera in reverse. It projects the negative image onto the paper. With a camera, most pictures are taken with a relatively great distance between the lens and the subject and a short distance between the lens and the image. This results in an image much smaller than the subject. In enlarging, the conditions are reversed: the lens-to-subject (lens-to-negative) distance is relatively short while the lens-to-image distance (lens-to-enlarging paper) is great. The result: an image that is bigger than the subject (the negative). In both cases the following rule for optical magnification applies.

$$M = \frac{v}{u}$$

where M = Magnification, v = lens-image distance, and u = lens-subject distance

In enlarging u is smaller than v, so M is more than one; in the camera, ordinarily, u is larger than v, so M is less than one, actually a reduction rather than a magnification.

Enlargers in general use can be divided into two classifications: diffusion or diffusion-condenser. Even illumination of the negative is achieved with the diffusion enlarger by scrambling the rays of light in the housing around the light source and by placing an opal glass between the light source and the negative. So-called cold-light enlargers are sometimes classified separately, although they are basically diffusion enlargers; they simply employ a fluorescent grid as a light source instead of an incandescent bulb. Cold light enlargers do not work effectively with the variable-contrast papers (to be discussed later) because their light is bluish. Diffusion enlargers produce low-contrast images (which can be balanced by developing the film for high-contrast negatives) and they minimize the effect of dust and scratches on the negative. Because the light output is relatively dim, diffusion enlargers are a bit more difficult to focus than diffusion-condenser types, and the low light level also requires longer exposures.

The problem of even illumination of the negative is solved with the diffusion-condenser enlarger by directing or focusing the rays of light into a cone that has its apex at the lens. This makes maximum use of the light and gives the brightest illumination of the negative. These enlargers begin with a diffused light source, an opal bulb, but the rays of light are "condensed" or straightened out into the cone by one or two lenses placed just above the negative. There are also pure condenser enlargers that begin with a pinpoint, undiffused light source, but these create problems that

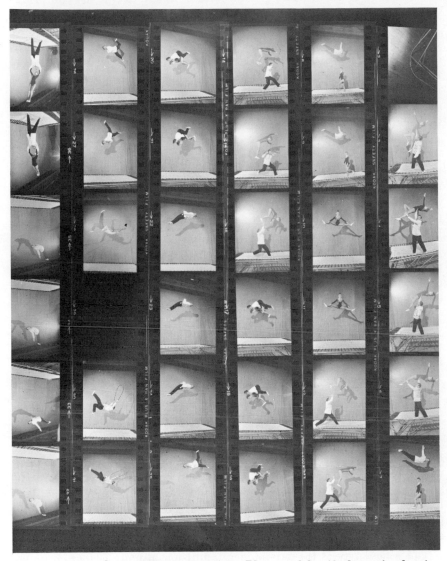

A contact print sheet of 35-mm negatives. Place an 8 by 10 sheet of enlarging paper, emulsion side up, on the enlarger easel. Place negatives emulsion side down on the paper and cover with a sheet of glass to hold negatives and paper flat and in contact. Expose with the enlarger light. Correct exposure can be determined by running test strips of a few negative frames first. The contact sheet is then available for examination with a magnifying glass to determine what negatives to enlarge and can also be used in the photographer's filing system. (David Mathias, Staff Photographer, Denver *Post*)

make them unsuitable for general work. What are really diffusion-condenser enlargers are often called condenser enlargers.

Condenser enlargers give higher contrast because some of the directed rays of light hitting the silver deposits in the negative are scattered or diffused by that silver. In the highlight areas, the dense parts of the negative, much of the light is scattered and does not reach the paper, with the result that the highlights appear whiter than they would with a diffusion enlarger. This selective scattering of light by the denser parts of the negative is known as the Callier effect, named for its discoverer, Andre Callier, a Belgian amateur physicist.

A condenser enlarger emphasizes blemishes in and on the negative for the same reason that it emphasizes contrast, since these blemishes scatter the light more than the surrounding areas; blemishes then show up on the print through increased contrast. The condenser enlarger, however, gives better resolution of detail than diffused illumination, since this resolution largely depends upon small variations in tone values within the print.

To sum up, then: the diffusion enlarger gives softer contrast and lessens the effect of blemishes, but it is less efficient and requires longer exposures or a more powerful light source. The condenser enlarger makes more efficient use of the light source, increases contrast, gives better resolution, but emphasizes grain, scratches, dust, and lint.

The most common light source in enlargers is a tungsten filament in an opal or frosted glass bulb. It is not a good idea to use an ordinary household lamp bulb in an enlarger, because the maker's name is usually printed on the end of the bulb and this can show up as a shadow image on the paper.

THE PRINTING PAPER

There are really two principal types of material used for making positive prints from a negative. The first of these is the printing-out emulsion, usually coated on a paper base. This emulsion, in which the light-sensitive chemical is silver chloride, is intended for making contact prints by daylight. The positive image gradually appears under the influence of the light, and no chemical development is necessary. Printing-out papers are seldom used today.

The second type is the development emulsion, usually coated on paper but sometimes coated on glass to make lantern plates or on a film base to make transparencies. The image does not appear on this emulsion until development. Development emulsions on the customary printing papers come in a wide variety of forms with five major characteristics:

1. *Speed.* The emulsion's sensitivity to light is its speed. Contact printing papers are coated with silver chloride emulsions, which are slow. Papers used for normal projection printing are usually chlorobromide

emulsions, a mixture of silver chloride and silver bromide. They are faster than the pure chloride papers, and the higher the proportion of bromide the higher the speed. The high-speed papers are silver bromide emulsions, especially useful for large blow-ups, such as photomurals. High-speed papers are eight to ten times as sensitive as some of the slower papers.

2. Surface texture. This characteristic is described by a variety of terms, but basically it involves the reflective quality of the surface, which can vary from a rough matte, through semi-matte, to luster, and semi- and high-gloss. To select the best paper for a particular photograph, the photographer must consider the final purpose of his picture. If purpose involves an attempt to record fine detail, or if the picture is intended for publication in a newspaper or magazine, then a glossy or semiglossy surface will probably be best, since gloss emphasizes crisp blacks, brilliant whites, and detail. For portraits, scenery, prints for exhibition, or framing, a textured surface of one sort or another may be more desirable. Personal taste is the determining factor.

3. Tint. The color of the paper on which the emulsion is coated will control its tint, varying from a white to a buff. Tints vary with manufacturers, but cream and ivory are fairly common.

4. Tone. The emulsion tone can vary from the blue-blacks or cold papers to the brownish-blacks or warm papers. The tone is largely a result of the size of the metallic silver grains left in the emulsion after processing; large grains give a blue-black tone.

5. Contrast. The contrast of a print is the impression it gives of brightness differences between various parts of the image. A print that appears to be formed of mostly middle gray tones, without any clear whites or blacks, will be low in contrast; most photographers would probably call it a flat print. On the other hand, we would call a print that seems to have a full or nearly full range of tones from black to white high in contrast, or a full-scale print. A print that emphasizes full blacks and clear white highlights may be one with excessive contrast. The contrast of a print is the result of the interaction of a number of factors: the character of the original scene photographed, the type of film used, exposure and development of the film, the type of enlarger, and, finally, the kind of printing paper used.

Such a complex characteristic of the print as contrast cannot be precisely defined or described. A certain degree of contrast has been established by a number of factors by the time the photographer prepares to make the final print; at this moment he has another factor within his control. Most printing papers are available in several contrast grades, so the photographer can select the grade that matches his negative. A desirable match depends not only upon the contrast of the negative, which can range from hard to soft, but on the preference of the photographer.

Careful printing retained the mood of the original foggy scene. This picture won $1000 in the Annual Newspaper National Snapshot Awards. (Everett C. Johnson, Arlington, Va.)

Paper contrast grades are usually classified according to the following scale:

No. 0: extra soft
No. 1: soft
No. 2: normal or medium
No. 3: hard or contrasty
No. 4: extra hard or extra contrasty
No. 5: extreme contrast

Choosing the correct contrast grade for a particular negative is one of the most difficult problems the darkroom poses. Experience is really the only method of learning to solve this problem. If a negative printed on No. 2 paper gives a print that is flat, and this is usually revealed by shadow areas that should be black but turn out to be muddy dark gray, then a higher contrast grade is needed. A few negatives may give prints on No. 2 paper that contain full blacks and whites, but little in between. This indicates a need for a softer grade of paper.

To judge a negative for contrast, examine it against a diffused light source, such as light reflected from a white painted wall, or against the ground glass of a light box. Sometimes the contrast of a negative can be judged by laying it down on a page of a book printed on white paper. The normal negative will show good tone and detail with some density in the thin (shadow) areas and the print of the book should be just readable through the most dense (highlight) areas.

Variable contrast papers are also available. To make these the manufacturer puts two emulsion layers on the paper; one is a high contrast emulsion and the other low contrast. To change image contrast the photographer exposes the paper through plastic filters held under the enlarger lens. Each filter changes the color of the light and alters the relative response of the two emulsions. Used without a filter, the variable contrast papers give approximately normal contrast, about the same as a No. 2 paper.

MAKING AN ENLARGEMENT

For high quality prints the enlarging lens (and the condenser lenses in the condenser enlargers) must be clean. Dust and lint must also be removed from the negative; use a soft brush gently; vigorous brushing may develop static electricity in the negative, and that will attract dust.

Dust is a particular problem with the increasingly popular 35-mm film. The degree of enlargement required with 35-mm negatives emphasizes the dust specks, which show up as white spots on the print. In dry air, film can easily develop a charge of static electricity, and no matter how carefully it is cleaned or brushed it attracts dust from the air faster than it can be removed. The enlarger should be cleaned frequently with a vacuum cleaner. If dust spots persist, the enlarger should be grounded with a wire from enlarger frame to a water pipe. Some photographers use a static eliminator brush; some use static eliminator cleaning fluids.

Scratches on film create a problem occasionally, again particularly with 35-mm film. These can be masked so they do not appear as thin black streaks in the print by coating the negative with a transparent grease (such as Vaseline) or oil (such as Edwal Dust and Scratch Remover). The oil is applied to both sides of the negative just before it is placed in the enlarger. After printing, the oil is wiped from the film with an absorbent tissue and returned to the negative sleeve or envelope.

Transparent negative sleeves that come bound in folders or books are best for filing 35-mm negatives. All negatives should be handled only by the edges to avoid fingerprints. Fingerprints sometimes cannot be cleaned off a negative.

When the negative is ready for placing in the enlarger, put it in the negative carrier, emulsion side down, or emulsion side toward the lens. If the negative is emulsion up, the image will be reversed in the print. The emulsion side is the side with the dull-looking surface and the side to which the negative tends to curl.

With the aperture of the lens wide open, raise or lower the enlarger to change lens-to-easel distance and thus change the size of the enlarged image. This way you can crop out parts of the image and arrange the margins of the print the way you want them. Focus accurately, still with the lens wide open. Precise focus is important. Focusing aids are available, which magnify a small section of the projected image, sometimes enough so you can focus on the grain of the silver deposit in the negative. When the negative is annoyingly dense, you can substitute a focusing negative for the one you intend to print after you have positioned the enlarger for correct composition and approximate focus. This focusing negative is made by fogging a piece of film, developing and fixing it, and then scratching a fine line in the emulsion for focusing on; an old, unwanted negative can also be used for this purpose. Or you can use a piece of torn blotting paper placed in the negative carrier so you can focus on the fibers of the paper.

Now stop the lens down to approximately the halfway point, about $f/8$. With an especially dense negative it may be necessary to leave the lens wide open, or nearly so, to keep exposure times within reason, or if the negative is quite thin you may need to stop down further than $f/8$ to avoid an unreasonably short exposure time. A middle f/stop range is recommended because it is generally the point at which the lens gives its best image resolution and because if you have made a slight error in focusing, stopping down two or three f/stops will increase depth of field and mask that error.

Switch off the enlarger light and place a test strip of the enlarging paper on the easel where it will catch a key part of the image. A test strip is a strip of paper two or three inches wide. With test strip in place on the easel, switch on the enlarger for 10 seconds. Then cover two thirds of the strip with a piece of cardboard and switch on the light for another five seconds. Move the cardboard so that only one third of the strip is covered, being careful not to move the test strip, and expose for another five seconds. Then remove the cardboard entirely and expose the entire strip for a third five seconds. Now you will have three exposures on one strip, at 15, 20, and 25 seconds. Develop this to see if one of these is the correct exposure. If not, use it as a guide to run further tests until you get the correct exposure. The test strip can also provide a guide to contrast; if the contrast appears too high or too low in the test strip you can switch to the indicated grade of paper (or filter if variable contrast paper is being used). Lengths of time other than 10- or 5-second intervals can be used; estimate the exposure from the brightness of the image projected on the easel, then bracket that estimate on the test strip. The objective is to find the correct exposure as quickly as possible with a minimum expenditure of paper. Be certain to

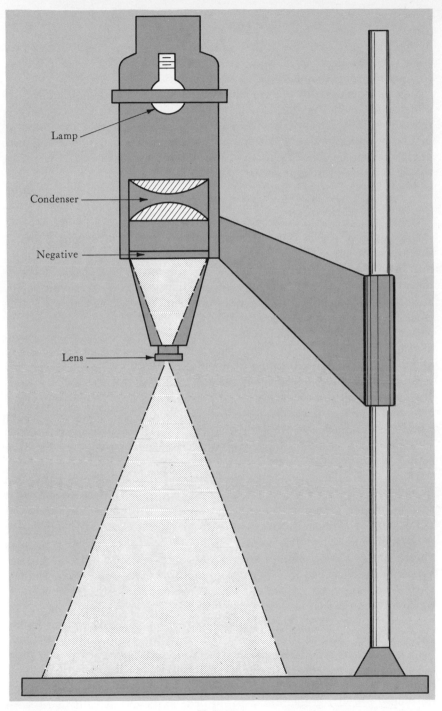

Lamp

Condenser

Negative

Lens

FIGURE 7

The enlarger.

develop the test strip the full recommended time (see instructions that come with the paper) and leave it in the hypo for a few seconds before turning the room lights on for a close inspection.

Beginners generally tend to make prints that are a little flat and a little underexposed. This may be because prints tend to lose contrast slightly as they dry and because beginners tend to be satisfied with a minimum of print development time. The best practice is to develop for the maximum, not the minimum, time. Prints will look darker under the safelights than they will under ordinary light.

PROCESSING THE PRINT

Once exposure time and contrast grade have been determined, a full-sized sheet of paper is placed on the easel and exposed. Get the full sheet into the developer quickly and all at once so that all parts begin developing at the same time. Rock the tray constantly during development for agitation or flop the print over and over. And don't forget to watch the time.

A stop bath is recommended for prints since we usually want to stop development quickly, and the stop bath will help avoid stains and development streaks and extend the life of the hypo bath that follows. Agitate the print in the stop bath for about 10 seconds and then transfer it to the hypo tray. A stop bath can be made by adding one ounce of 28 per cent acetic acid to 32 ounces of water, or an excellent choice is Kodak's Indicator Stop Bath, mixed according to directions on the bottle. This bath is recommended because it tells you when it is exhausted by changing color.

If you have sufficient room for the extra tray it is a good idea to use two hypo baths. Agitate the print in the first tray for about 30 seconds and then let it soak there for two to four minutes, with occasional additional agitation. Then transfer it to the second hypo bath and repeat for the same lengths of time. The advantages of this system are that your hypo lasts longer and you are certain of adequate fixing. Most, if not all, of the unexposed silver halides are dissolved in the first bath and left there. The second bath provides insurance that any remaining nonimage silver will be in compounds that are readily soluble in water and easily removed by washing. You can fix about two hundred 8 by 10 prints using two one-gallon baths of hypo. Mix two hypo baths to start with, then as the first nears exhaustion, pour it out and replace it with the second bath. Mix up a fresh second bath. A hypo bath nearing exhaustion becomes cloudy and foams readily. Or you can check more accurately with a strip of fogged but undeveloped film. Drop the film strip into the hypo and leave it there, with occasional agitation, for five minutes. If it has cleared to transparency in that time the hypo is still usable; if not, better discard the hypo for a fresh batch.

Do not leave prints in the hypo for a total time exceeding 10 minutes. Actually, fixing should be adequate in about half this time, if you agitate, but we usually leave the print in longer to be sure, and also to give the hardener in the bath a chance to work. But if prints are left in the fixer much longer than 10 minutes the hypo may begin to dissolve some of the image silver.

After fixing, the print should be washed for a minimum of one hour in running water—and a two-hour wash is better if you want the print to last for many years. Washing time can be reduced drastically by using a hypo neutralizer or clearing agent, such as Kodak Hypo Clearing Agent. After a two-minute soak in a solution of this agent, washing can be reduced to about 15 minutes. A clearing agent is especially recommended if the wash water is cold.

Prints can be dried, face down, on a clean white photographic blotter, in a photographic blotter roll, or on stretched cheesecloth. This is the technique for nonglossy surface prints or for producing a semigloss with a glossy surface paper. If you want high gloss from the glossy surface paper the print must be dried face down on a ferrotype plate, squeezed so all air and water are removed from under the print. (A ferrotype plate is a thin, flat sheet of steel—usually chromium-plated, sometimes black-enameled—and it is this smooth surface that imparts high gloss to prints. Glass, preferably mirror plate glass, can be used if it is uniform, free from surface defects, and has been thoroughly cleaned.) Print dryers are usually electrically heated chromium-plated drums. These drastically shorten drying time, but high temperatures can cause prints to stick to the plate. Prints can be dried by simply placing the ferrotype tin on edge or by laying it flat, print side up. The prints ordinarily pop off of their own accord when dry. Various chemical solutions are available for preparing a final rinse to promote gloss and prevent sticking and uneven drying. A 5 to 10 per cent solution of glycerin promotes even drying and prevents curl.

TIPS ON PRINTING

Exposing the negative image to the paper for approximately 20 seconds is advisable in making enlargements. This gives time for any necessary manipulations, and small errors in exposure time are not so serious. A one-second error is 20 per cent of five seconds, but only five per cent of 20 seconds. Remember that the higher you raise the enlarger head, the larger the projected image; but the total amount of light available remains the same. This means the same original quantity of light is spread out over a larger area and there is significantly less light at any given point on the

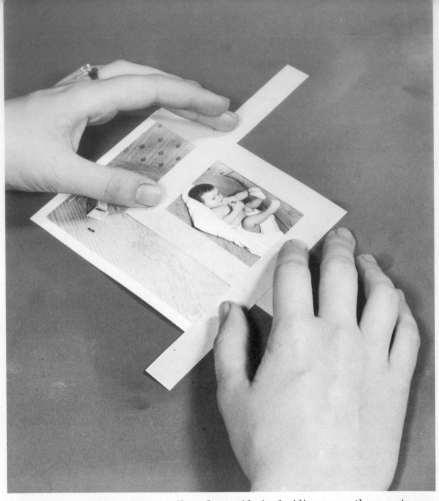

Cropping squares cut from cardboard are aids in deciding upon the way to crop a picture in reprinting.

projected image. Light intensity is inversely related to the square of the distance between the lens and the printing paper on the easel. So if the distance between lens and paper is doubled, the amount of light at any given point on the paper is cut to one fourth; in practical terms this means you must increase exposure time approximately four times, or open up the enlarger lens two stops.

The temperature of the processing solutions in print making is not so critical as it is with film processing. The developer should ordinarily be close to 70 degrees. Variations between the temperature of the developer and subsequent solutions are not important if the variations are small. The thin paper emulsion is firmly bonded to the paper base and is not likely to reticulate.

Care is essential to avoid contaminating the developer. If you use tongs to handle the print in the solutions and to move it from one tray to the next, keep one set of tongs for the developer tray only. If you handle the paper with your hands, be sure to rinse your hands after they have been in stop bath or hypo before you dip them in the developer again. And always rinse and dry your hands thoroughly before touching negatives, dry paper, enlarger, or other equipment. Some developers tend to stain fingernails; you can avoid this by always rinsing off the developer, first in hypo and then in water, before drying.

During the first few moments in the developer, nothing seems to happen to the paper. This delay is the induction period, the time the solution needs to penetrate the gelatin layer, reach the exposed silver halide crystals, and develop enough silver to be visible. The image begins to appear in 15 to 20 seconds with most papers and developers if the exposure has been a proper one. Don't be in a rush to yank the print from the developer; give enough time for full contrast to appear, including the local contrast in highlight areas that will provide the detail in those light areas.

If two or more prints wind up in the same tray at the same time be sure they get agitation; shuffle them occasionally. After the print has been in the hypo for about 30 seconds you can turn the room lights on to inspect the print; but be sure your unexposed paper is safely covered in its package or in a light-tight drawer. Study the highlights of the print. Do they have sufficient detail and texture? And what about the shadow areas and other dark portions? They should have a sort of luminous quality, even though black. Examine the contrast between highlight and shadow areas; if it is extreme and harsh you will need a low-numbered (softer) paper, or a low-numbered filter with variable contrast paper; if it is flat with blacks that are muddy you will need a harder-grade paper or a higher-numbered filter. Look, too, for blemishes such as white spots caused by dust or lint on the negative. And study local areas to see if exposure has been correct for all parts of the print; if not you will have to make some corrections by manipulating the exposure.

MANIPULATIONS

Often a highlight area in an image, such as a white shirt or even a face, comes out almost blank white in the print even though all other areas are correctly exposed for just the right amount of time and detail. Examination of the negative may show that there is detail in the highlight area as well. Paper emulsions do not have the range of exposure latitude characteristic of most black-and-white film emulsions. To retain detail in both highlights and shadows we often must resort to a bit of exposure manipulation, called burning-in and dodging.

BURNING-IN

If the first print shows exposure is correct for all areas but one or two highlight sections, the answer is the burning-in technique. Give the second

This picture was cropped to give the result shown on the opposite page.

piece of paper the same exposure as the first and then give the highlight area some additional exposure. How much can be determined by running another test strip for the highlight area alone. If the highlight area that needs burning in is the sky at the top of the picture or some other area near an edge, you can burn it in by holding a piece of cardboard or your hand under the enlarger lens so that it blocks all light from reaching the paper. Then, with the light on, slowly move the cardboard until the sky area at the top of the picture begins to appear on the paper. Keep moving the cardboard until the light reaches the inside edge of the area you want to burn in, then move back so the shadow returns to the margin. Repeat if necessary. Keep the cardboard moving constantly and give the topmost part of the sky the greatest additional exposure.

To burn-in central areas of the picture, cut a hole in a large sheet of cardboard. The size and shape of this hole can be controlled by inserting one or more fingers into the hole or by cutting smaller holes in a second and small piece of cardboard, which can be placed over the first board. After experimenting to find the exact size and shape of the hole needed as well as the position where you will need to hold the board, insert a piece

of paper in the easel and make the overall exposure. Then block out all light with the cardboard until you can move the hole into the proper position; keep the cardboard moving constantly while you let the highlight area get additional exposure. Be careful not to burn-in excessively the central part of the area while the edges get much less. Only practice can develop the necessary skill.

DODGING

Sometimes a shadow or other dark area of the print is too dark, even though highlights and middle tones are fine with a given exposure. We must make the shadow lighter by holding the light back from this area. If the too dark area is at the margin, you can shade or dodge it with your hand or a piece of cardboard. If it is toward the center of the picture, dodging can be accomplished by using a piece of cotton or cardboard on

Effectiveness of photographs can be enhanced by dramatic use of black and white tones in contrast. (J. Hugh Webb, Toledo)

the end of a length of wire at least 12 inches long. Pieces of cardboard can be cut to various sizes and shapes. One size and shape can serve many purposes because the area it shades can be varied by moving it closer or farther away from the paper and by turning it so the shape of the shadow changes. The shadow of the dodger at the end of the wire holds back light from the dark area of the print, but if you keep the dodger and wire moving slightly but constantly no shadow of the wire will show in the print. Moving the dodger up and down slightly during the exposure usually helps hide the evidence of the manipulation in the developed image.

The amount of time needed to burn-in or dodge an area varies widely, but don't be afraid to use a reasonable amount of time. It usually does little good to burn-in a highlight for five seconds when the over-all exposure of the print was 20 seconds; a good rule of thumb is: burn-in for a time equal to the original over-all exposure. Sometimes this will be too much; sometimes not enough. For dodging, try shading the dark area for about one half of the over-all exposure. You may save time and paper by running a test strip for the area to be burned-in or dodged.

Manipulation of the exposure must be planned before paper is inserted in the easel, and then must be done with care. Carelessness will result in a print that reveals your tricks; keep your dodging tool moving during the entire exposure and far enough away from the paper so that no sharp outline will show in the developed print.

84

•

Chapter 6

THE NATURE OF LIGHT

Light dominates our lives; in fact, it is impossible for us to conceive of life without light, for light is not solely the medium by which we explore our world, light is also energy vital to our survival. And light, of course, is vital to photography, for it is the physical means used to produce the image. If we are to understand the nature of photography we must understand a few fundamentals about the nature of light.

Light, we know, is something that leaves its source and eventually reaches our eyes or the lens and film of our camera. Its travels may be short and direct or long and indirect, reflected many times by objects in its path. Every object we describe as being visible is either a light source or a light reflector, and we have learned to distinguish sources from reflectors—and even more, to recognize different kinds of light sources and to identify objects by the way they reflect light.

It was inevitable then that man would want to know what it is that produces light and how light travels from place to place. How is light able to move through not only air, but through many other substances as well, through water, through glass, and even through a vacuum?

In the seventeenth century, Sir Isaac Newton concluded that light was a stream of corpuscles or some similar tiny particles fired out in all directions by a light source. It was the impact of these particles on the eye, he theorized, that created vision. Other scientists, notably a Dutch physicist named Christian Huygens, found the corpuscle theory inadequate for explaining some of the most commonly known activities of light. Huygens demonstrated that reflection and refraction of light could be explained much more simply if light were considered a wave motion. Evidence accumulated and gradually established support for the wave theory, until finally most scientists discarded Newton's corpuscle theory as untenable and accepted the wave theory. Then, in the late nineteenth century, a Scottish physicist, James Clerk Maxwell, developed the theory of the electromagnetic field and concluded that electric and magnetic energy travel in waves. Light waves, he said, are of similar nature. This proposal, that light was electromagnetic rediation of very short wavelength, was of great importance. Radiation is the emission of energy by substances or bodies of matter and its transfer through space. The sun is the most familiar source of radiant energy and sunlight its best-known form.

The electromagnetic wave theory worked perfectly in explaining a great many of the manifestations of light energy, but still did not satisfy in a number of other situations. Then, at the turn of the twentieth century, Max Planck, professor of physics at Berlin University, advanced the quantum theory. Energy, he said, is not emitted in a continuous stream, as the electromagnetic theory suggested, but in tiny spurts or packets. He gave the name of quanta to these minute energy doses; in the singular, quantum. This was the quantum theory, which became, with modification, the basis for quantum mechanics and a revolution in a major area of physics.

Four years after Planck announced his quantum theory, Albert Einstein adapted the theory to light, postulating that light, as a form of radiant energy, must also be given off in tiny packets. Einstein called these light packets photons. (A photon is, in Planck's terms, a quantum of light energy.) Einstein's theory brought us back to Newton's light corpuscles, but we were not really back where we started because we now had two theories, which were not antithetical but complementary. Light has a dual nature: it is small packets of energy called photons that travel in waves.

The aim here will be to further describe light as it manifests itself to our senses and to our intellect, so that we can explain the nature of light as it is involved in photography. But it is not possible to describe light entirely in laymen's terms; we must inevitably use some scientific terms.

LIGHT AS WAVES

The more common phenomena of light can be explained by the wave theory, the same theory that applies to all electromagnetic radiation. All of these waves of radiant energy have been organized into a broad series according to wavelength, ranging from the shortest to the longest. This is called the spectrum. The spectrum extends from the very short wavelengths of cosmic rays to the long wavelengths used in radio broadcasting. In between are the gamma rays, X rays, ultraviolet rays, visible light, infrared, and microwaves. We live in a sea of radiation, but our eyes are sensitive to only a small part of it—that part we call the visible spectrum, which we have, for purposes of this discussion, defined simply as light. Ultraviolet and infrared waves are abundantly present in the atmosphere around us, but we do not see them. All photographic films are sensitive to ultraviolet, however, and film can be made that is sensitive to infrared.

The concept of radiant energy traveling through space as packets of energy that act as though they were moving in waves is not one that is easy to picture. But we are familiar with transmission by radio waves in broadcasting, and so the basic idea does not seem completely strange. We take for granted that some sort of disturbance or condition exists that moves in waves from a central broadcasting station and this disturbance is received by and interpreted by radio sets situated many different directions and distances from the transmitting station. We may think of the sun, or any light source, as being a central station sending out waves of some sort that our eyes receive and interpret. Apparently there is no difference in kind between the two sets of waves, although there is a difference in wave dimensions. We don't know what sort of medium it is that carries these waves. What is it that moves to and fro or up and down to form the waves? Once scientists believed there was some sort of invisible, odorless substance named ether that occupied all space, even the vacuum of outer space and the space between the molecules of gas and the molecules of solids. The existence of any such hypothetical substance is now generally doubted. We do know, however, that radiant energy, including light, acts as though it travels in waves, and this is enough for our purposes.

A part of the wave theory is the hypothesis that light, as electromagnetic radiation, moves in transverse waves—that is, the wave vibration is transverse vibration. This means the vibration is at right angles to the direction in which the wave is moving. Water waves provide a familiar example of transverse vibration. If we drop a rock into a quiet pool, waves move away from the point at which the rock entered the water and in all directions. If we were to observe a single molecule of water, we would find that it moves up and down but does not move in the direction that the wave moves. Water waves, however, are not exactly the same as light waves. Waves in water only rise and fall, vibrate, in other words, in only one direction. Light vibrates up and down, but from side to side as well—in fact, vibrates in all directions perpendicular to the wave's direction of travel. (See illustration page 185.)

WAVELENGTH

Since the electromagnetic spectrum is arranged according to wavelengths, there must be a measurement of this length. This dimension of light can be visualized by again imagining the waves in a pool of water. The length of light waves and the length of water waves are both measured from a point on one crest to an identical point on the next crest, or from a point on a trough to the same point on the next trough. Wavelength is the distance between any two such identical points in a given instant of time. Near one end of the full spectrum are the gamma rays, emitted by radioactive substances, with wavelengths measuring less than one billionth of an inch. At the other end are the radio waves, undulations measuring as much as a mile in length.

The radiations we see as light fall in the very short wavelength region, measuring such tiny fractions of an inch that it is more convenient to express their length in terms of smaller units than an inch or even than a millimeter. Light wavelengths are measured either in millimicrons or Angstrom units. A micron (usually abbreviated as μ) is one thousandth of a millimeter, so a millimicron (mμ) is one millionth of a millimeter. One Angstrom unit (abbreviated as A) is still smaller, being one ten-millionth of a millimeter.

We speak of the wavelengths of light because it does not have a single wavelength. The visible region of the electromagnetic spectrum ranges from a wavelength of 400 mμ or (4000 A) to 700 mμ (7000 A). If that shortest wavelength (400 mμ) appears alone, we see violet light; a wavelength of 700 mμ we interpret as red. White light behaves as though it consisted of a mixture of all colors and thus of all wavelengths; but this presents an impossible picture for us to imagine. Fortunately we need not worry about it; we need only accept the idea that white light behaves as if all the visible wavelengths were present. When only a very narrow band of wavelengths is present we see color.

FREQUENCY

There is another unit of measurement of wave motion, called frequency. This is the number of complete waves that would pass a given point in a second of time. The longer the wavelength, of course, the fewer the number of waves that will pass a point in a second. Or, to put it another way, the longer the wavelength the less the frequency; the shorter the wavelength the greater the frequency. Frequency is inversely proportional,

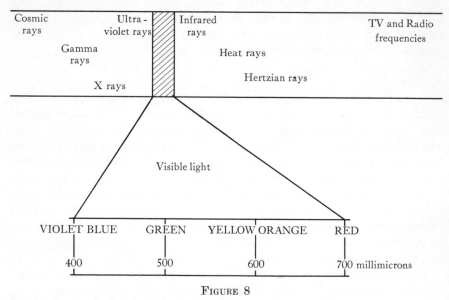

FIGURE 8

The spectrum of electromagnetic radiation.

then, to wavelength and the velocity of all light, and all electromagnetic radiation for that matter, is the product of frequency multiplied by wavelength. This formula always gives the same answer for light or other radiation traveling in space (a vacuum)—approximately 186,000 miles a second. The velocity in air is very nearly the same, but in other substances through which light can move its velocity is less because there is a change in the wavelength.

RAYS

We also speak of rays—gamma rays or light rays—as though these various forms of radiant energy proceeded along some sort of thin, straight-line beam. Actually this is another one of those concepts in physics that make no claim to be describing a phenomenon as it actually is; it is merely a tool word that helps us describe the way light behaves. No one has ever seen a single light ray and probably no one ever will, since it seems very likely that such a thing does not exist.

When light spreads out, like water waves in the pool where we dropped the rock, it travels through the air in all directions at once with the same velocity in all directions. If at any given instant we suspended the movement of the light, if that were possible, we would find the wave had reached the same distance from the source in whatever direction we took a measurement. This distance could be represented as a sphere surrounding the point light source. The sphere would be the wave front and any straight line drawn from the source to the wave front would be perpendicular to that wave front. This line would represent the direction in which the wave was traveling at that point and would be, theoretically, a light ray. This ray will continue to travel in a straight line as long as the light is traveling in a uniform medium, such as air under ordinary conditions. With the concept of light rays we can provide a coherent description of many things we must consider to understand the behavior of light.

LIGHT AS PHOTONS

It is convenient and instructive to think of light as a wave motion a good part of the time, but some of light's fascinating behavior cannot be explained by the wave theory. When we come to the way in which the radiant energy that is light is transformed into other forms of energy, we must turn to the photon theory. Photons are all about us in vast, literally unimaginable quantities as essential particles in this sea of radiation. In a single second one 50-watt light bulb will emit a quantity of photons on the order of 10^{19} and that would be 10,000,000,000,000,000,000 photons, or 10 billion billions.

As we shall see in the chapter on the chemistry of photography, the recording of the optical image created by the lens must involve a reaction between light and matter. All such reactions involve energy—gained, lost, or transferred—and in this case the energy comes from light. Or, to take another example, when light strikes some metals it causes a flow of electrical current in those metals, which consists of the movement of electrons. The electrons are set in motion by the impact of the light. This phenomenon is the basis of the photoelectric cell. When light strikes the metal of such a cell, each photon, as it strikes, transfers its energy to an electron, and this energy boost allows the electron to escape from its atom. The movement of these freed electrons is the electrical current. The stronger the light, the greater the number of photons and the greater the number of free electrons; therefore, the stronger the current. Thus, a photoelectric cell can give an accurate measurement of the light's intensity.

This example of light and an electrical current can be reversed, too. Look for a moment at the case of the incandescent bulb in a reading lamp. What makes the wire filament within this bulb give off light? In this case the electrical current heats the wire and the heat is a sort of excited movement of the wire's molecules, atoms, and electrons. The excited electrons circling the nucleus of each wire atom jump outward from one orbit to another, getting farther and farther away from the nucleus. But these same electrons can reverse the process, jumping back to orbits closer to the atomic nucleus. As they do this they release the energy previously absorbed on the outward journey and this energy is again in the form of quanta, but now we call them photons instead, because this is the energy we identify as light. So electrons jumping back and forth alternately absorb and emit energy, and when they are emitting energy they are sending out light. This light takes the form of photons, but light's photons are not all identical. Photons are of various energy magnitudes depending upon the structure of the atom emitting them. We are all familiar with the idea that atoms vary in mass; an atom of iron is not identical with an atom of oxygen. So quanta or photons vary in magnitude according to the frequency of the radiation; a photon of blue light is not identical to a photon of red light. The higher the frequency of the radiation (or the shorter the wavelength) the larger the magnitude of the quantum. Actually this gets into an area where only mathematics can describe the situation, a realm beyond the scope of this book.

These photons sent out by the reading lamp can, in turn, be used to excite the electrons of the metal in a photoelectric cell, and thus the energy is converted back into an electrical current. Or the photons can be used as energy to create a chemical change in the emulsion of film. And this change is the basis for the photographic image.

LAWS OF GEOMETRICAL OPTICS

Optics is a branch of science concerned with the behavior of light. Up to this point we have been primarily concerned with physical optics: the composition and character of light. Now we need to turn to the geometry of the paths light rays follow—geometrical optics.

RECTILINEAR PROPAGATION

One of the most fundamental principles or laws of geometrical optics states that our imaginary light rays travel in straight lines as long as they are moving through a homogeneous medium, such as air. This is not such a difficult notion to grasp, since we are all familiar with the straight beam of a flashlight and the straightness of shadows, which would not exist if light bent itself around corners. Another version of this law is that light always takes the path that requires the least amount of time, and as everyone knows, the shortest distance between two points is a straight line. This explains many things about light. Light emitted from a point source or light reflected from a single point on an object travels in all unobstructed directions in straight lines, so a surface sensitive to light, such as the surface of film, reproduces a pattern corresponding to the original subject.

REFLECTION

Among the most familiar of light phenomena is reflection. Any object that is nonluminous, that does not of itself emit light, can be seen only by reflected light that has originated at a luminous source. This applies not only to subjects with highly polished surfaces, such as mirrors, but to all nonluminous objects. All such objects reflect some light and absorb some. Glass mirrors, polished metals, a white snowbank, or a white shirt reflect most of the light, absorb very little. Black objects absorb most of the light, reflect very little. A red object absorbs all or most of the visible spectrum's radiations except those of the longest—the red—wavelengths. Objects of other colors appear colored for the same reason: they absorb some wavelengths and reflect others.

Light reflected from a highly polished surface obeys a simple but important law. The reflected ray of light bounces off at an angle from the surface equal to the angle made by the way it struck the surface—the incident ray. Stated simply: the angle of reflection equals the angle of incidence. If the angles were not equal the light would be traveling by a longer than necessary route from luminous source to object and thence to your eye. And this could not be true, because light always takes the shortest route, and simple geometry shows that the shortest route occurs when the angles are equal. In addition, the reflected ray always lies in the same

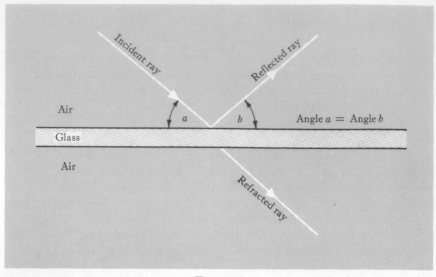

FIGURE 9
Reflection and refraction of light.

plane as the incident ray: a horizontal incident ray results in a horizontal
reflected ray. This sort of reflection from a polished surface is called
specular reflection.

But the surfaces of many objects we see by reflected light are not highly
polished; they are rough, providing many different inclines from which
the light bounces. The result is *diffuse* reflection, rays of light scattered
in many directions. Actually, the angle of reflection still equals the angle
of incidence, but the rough surface provides so many different angles at
which a unidirectional light beam strikes that the reflected light is widely
scattered. Many surfaces, of course, lie between the polished and the rough,
with the result that light reflected from them is both specular and diffuse.

REFRACTION

When light strikes the surface of opaque objects, some is absorbed, some
is reflected. But what happens when light strikes a transparent object,
such as glass? A little light is absorbed, a somewhat larger amount is reflected, but some travels on through the transparent medium to emerge
on the other side. These penetrating rays, however, have quite probably
undergone a change. We say the light has been refracted. Refraction occurs
because the velocity of light varies inversely with the density of the medium it is passing through. The denser the medium, the slower light's
speed. Its speed is greatest in a vacuum, only slightly less in air, but significantly less in glass or water. Light's speed is reduced about one third

Reflected images often add to the photograph. (Bill Johnson, Staff Photographer, Denver *Post*)

in glass, although this varies with different kinds of glass, and about one fourth in water. The speed of light in a vacuum (186,000 miles a second) divided by the speed of light in a transparent substance such as glass (in some glass about 124,000 miles a second) gives the *refractive index* of the substance. Using the two figures given above, the refractive index of the glass would be 1.5. The refractive index of water is about 1.3. The refractive index is never less than 1 and rarely exceeds 2. The higher the index number, the greater the bending power of the substance, that is the denser it is, and the slower light will travel in it.

When a light beam traveling through air strikes the surface of a sheet of glass it is always slowed down, and its direction may or may not be changed, depending on the angle at which it struck the surface dividing air and glass. If it hits perpendicularly to the surface, it slows down in the denser medium of the glass but does not change direction. But if the beam strikes at an oblique angle, part of the beam hits the glass first and slows down, while the other side of the beam is still traveling at air speed. Inevitably the beam is slewed around or bent and continues through the glass in a new direction. As the beam emerges at an oblique angle from the opposite surface of the glass it bends again, in the reverse of the first change but for the same reason: one part of the beam emerges first and resumes air speed, while another part is still dawdling along, at about 124,000 miles a second, in the glass. The refracted beam, after it has emerged from a piece of glass with parallel sides, is offset but parallel to the original beam. The degree of refraction depends upon two factors: the angle at which the light strikes the glass and the difference in the speed of light in the two mediums. The greater the angle, the greater the change in direction, and the greater the difference in speed, the greater the change.

Is refraction an exception, then, to the law of rectilinear propagation? Not really. You will recall that light travels by the quickest route, ordinarily a straight line, but when light moves from one transparent medium into another, as from air into glass, a straight line is often not the shortest time route.

DISPERSION

If we send a beam of light through a transparent medium that does not have parallel sides, a somewhat different situation prevails. This difference can be observed by using a prism, a triangular piece of glass. The light, if it strikes the first surface at some angle other than the perpendicular, is refracted as before and travels on, at somewhat reduced speed, through the prism. When the light reaches the opposite surface, which is inclined at an angle to the first, it is refracted again, but this time not in the opposite direction to the first change, but in the same direction. The two refractions do not cancel each other and return the light beam to an offset

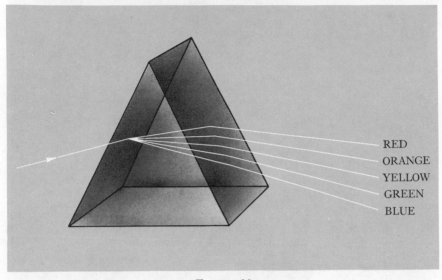

RED
ORANGE
YELLOW
GREEN
BLUE

FIGURE 10
Prismatic refraction and dispersion.

but parallel path; their effect is cumulative, so that the change in direction is accentuated.

But the prism causes something else to happen, too. A transparent material, such as glass, has a different refractive index for each wavelength of light. The index increases as wavelength decreases. Thus, a glass prism has a higher refractive index for blue light than for red. This means that blue light is bent more going through a prism than red, and the other colors (wavelengths) fall in between. So when we send a beam of white light, containing all the visible wavelengths, through a prism, it emerges not as a single beam of white light, but as the separate colors of the visible spectrum. This phenomenon is called dispersion.

CRITICAL ANGLE

When a ray of light travels from a denser medium to a thinner medium, for example from glass to air, it is, of course, refracted. If the ray strikes the surface between the two mediums at just the right angle, it is bent just enough so it skims along the boundary between the glass and air. The incident angle at which this occurs is called the critical angle. If the angle is greater than this, the light ray will be totally reflected, that is, refracted so much that it will turn back into the glass and never emerge at all, at least not at that particular surface. The ray will, very likely, emerge at some other surface of the piece of glass. This principle is used in construction of reflecting prisms in binoculars and in the viewfinders of some

Subjects such as this challenge the photographer's ability to see, to compose, to expose, to print.

cameras. Actually, the construction of these prisms is more complex than this explanation indicates, because the light may be bounced about a number of times, so that the image will emerge unreversed and right side up.

DIFFRACTION

Light can be deflected from its straight-line course by still another circumstance. When light rays touch the sharp edge of any opaque mate-

96

rial, they are bent slightly, and some of the light creeps into the region of the shadow. This is called diffraction.

Light moving through a small opening, a circle or a slit, in an opaque sheet of cardboard will form a round spot or bar of light on another piece of cardboard held behind the first, an image of the opening. But if we decrease the size of the opening, the edges of the image begin to blur and the size of the image gets larger until finally a point is reached where the image is badly distorted. This is the effect of diffraction. Normally, we notice diffraction of light very little, because openings in barriers are

Light caught by lens and film can record atmosphere and mood. (Yseult Mounsey, Montreal)

many, many times larger than the wavelength of light, and diffraction, or the spreading of light, is only pronounced if the width of the opening comes somewhere close to being equal to the wavelength. The wavelength of the longest visible radiation is less than 1/25,000 of an inch.

Diffraction causes dispersion of white light just as refraction does, because the longer the wavelength the greater the diffraction; so red rays are deflected the most. In fact, diffraction is used to split light into its colors. Lines are scratched with a diamond on a piece of glass, as many as 30,000 lines to an inch, to form a grating, and when light is passed through the slits between the lines it is diffracted and split into its various colors. The diffraction grating is a much more efficient device for splitting light into all its constituent wavelengths than a glass prism. Such a grating reveals that there are literally thousands of colors in sunlight, each with its own wavelength and each slightly different in hue from its closest neighbors in the spectrum.

Photographers should take note that the smaller the aperture used to admit light to film, the greater the diffraction effect. Actually, even the smallest aperture setting on almost all cameras is still so much greater in diameter than the wavelengths of light that the diffraction is minor. Nevertheless, it is well to remember that stopping the diaphragm down as far as it will go cannot increase the sharpness of an image that is already sharply focused; it will, in fact, decrease that sharpness because of diffraction, although perhaps not enough to be particularly noticeable. A point can be reached with a pinhole camera where reduction in the size of the hole results in an image so blurred by diffraction as to be useless.

POLARIZATION

A final phenomenon we should note involves a change in the vibration of light waves. Ordinary light waves vibrate in all directions that are at right angles to the direction of travel. If all of this vibration is eliminated except vibration in one direction or in one plane, that light ray will still be there, only weaker. Such a light ray is said to be polarized.

Certain crystals will polarize light because they are transparent to electromagnetic radiation only if the waves are vibrating in one specific plane. We might think of an ordinary light ray as a wooden, circular rod, the circular shape indicating the multidirectional vibration. The polarizing crystal is a sort of double-bladed saw. As the light strikes the crystal it is sliced (actually absorbed) down both sides. The only part that gets through is a thin slice through the center, so it comes out of our crystal saw no longer a rod but as a flat board. The board will be standing on edge, lying flat, or in any other position in between, depending upon the orientation of the crystal that did the sawing. This is a description of plane-polarized light. Light can also be circularly polarized; in this case the plane of polarization is not flat, but twisted like a spiral staircase.

The naked eye is unable to tell any difference between ordinary light and polarized light. The reflected light from most surfaces is polarized to some degree, and this is the reason why so-called polaroid glasses keep the glare of a bright day from blinding us. A polarizing filter over the camera lens can also eliminate unwanted reflections. (See Chapter 10 on filters.) Polarized light is important in many scientific fields, since it can be used to photograph subjects that are not visible under ordinary light.

Chapter 7

THE LENS

Because light travels in straight lines, we can form an image without a lens—in the pinhole camera. If we could permit just one ray of light from each point on a subject to squeeze through the pinhole, since each ray travels in a straight line, each would illuminate a separate point on a screen (or film) and thus create an image. There are, however, two major difficulties with this idea. First, a single ray of light from each point does not create a very bright image, and second, such a tiny pinhole, if it could be achieved, would create so much diffraction or spreading and interference of the light rays that the image would be useless. We can increase the size of the pinhole to admit more light from each point on the subject and thus increase the brightness of the image. Increasing the size of the pinhole also reduces the effect of diffraction. The bigger pinhole admits more light rays from each point on the subject, but these rays do not travel on the same path. Instead, they spread out and illuminate, not a point on the image, but a circular spot; this spot gets bigger as the pinhole gets bigger, and the bigger the spot, the less sharp the image. The ideal size of the pinhole becomes a compromise between sharpness of the image and light-gathering ability, but the best possible compromise means exposures of at least many seconds and probably several minutes.

We must turn to reflection and refraction of light to collect great bundles of light rays from a single point and redirect them all to meet again at another point. This gives us both advantages we are seeking: a brighter image and a sharper one.

Mirrors, of course, reflect light, and a symmetrically curved mirror will gather a bundle of rays from a given point and bounce them back so that they all meet at another predetermined point. The reflection principle is used in astronomy, as for example in the 200-inch mirror telescope at Mount Palomar, California, but mirror optics are generally impractical for most photography. The mirror bounces the light back in the same general direction from which it came, and some recording apparatus must be placed in the path of incoming rays to catch the reflected image. With the large mirror optics used in astronomy this is practical; with the small cameras used in ordinary photography it is generally impractical.

We then turn to the prism and refraction. A simple glass lens, circular in form and with its two surfaces curved, acts like a great many prisms arranged in a circle with their bases toward the center. All rays of light passing through the lens are bent except those that pass directly through the center; the rays striking the lens at points farthest from the center are bent the most.

The foregoing describes the fashion in which a simple lens, like a reading glass, works, but actually such a lens does not function perfectly. The rays of light entering the lens from a single point source are not brought back to a precise point because of a number of optical defects called aberrations. Because the lens surfaces are spherical, rays entering the outer and thinner portions of the lens do not come to a focus at the same point as rays striking the center and thicker part of the lens; and since glass disperses light into its component wavelengths, a lens produces a spectrum instead of a point image. There are other aberrations as well, but we need not get involved in a detailed discussion of these, because the manufacturers of photographic lenses have reduced all of them to the point where they rarely cause us any trouble. Aberrations are reduced or corrected by combining a variety of simple lenses into one complex lens and by using various kinds of glass.

SIMPLE LENS TYPES

Simple lenses are classified according to the way in which they bend the rays of light entering them. Some refract light so that the rays leaving the lens are bent inward and toward one another and so eventually meet. These

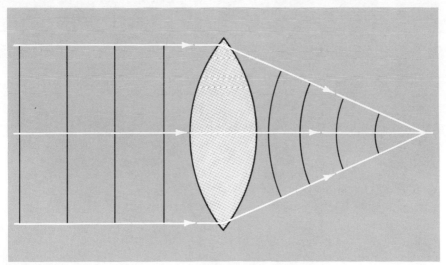

FIGURE 11

Converging or positive lens.

At top is the actual photograph of the image formed of an illuminated arrow through a pinhole. To admit sufficient light, the pinhole was made larger than normal; consequently the image is considerably diffused. At bottom the opening in the front of the box has been enlarged and a lens inserted; the image is brighter and sharper.

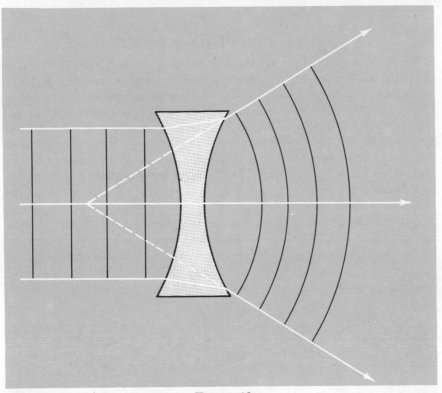

FIGURE 12

Diverging or negative lens.

are converging or positive lenses, since they converge a beam of parallel rays of light to a point behind the lens. Such lenses are thicker at the center than at the edges. The only other general type of simple lens, bends the rays outward and away from one another. These are diverging or negative lenses, and rays of light coming from them seem to have come from a point in front of the lens. Such lenses are thicker at the edges than at the center.

A positive lens has at least one convex surface, that is, a surface that curves outward. The opposite surface may also be convex, or it may be flat or concave (curving inward). A negative lens always has at least one concave surface, while the other surface is either concave, flat, or convex. The degree of curvature and the relationship between the two sides have a great deal to do with how the lens bends the light. A lens may be convex on one side and concave on the other and be either a positive or a negative lens, depending on whether rays of light are converging or diverging as they leave the lens.

THE COMPOUND LENS

The lens manufacturer selects a number of these simple lenses (or *elements,* as they are called), combining 4, 6, or even as many as 12 or more into a compound lens, which reduces the aberrations to practical limits. The aberration in a negative lens is usually opposite the corresponding aberration in a positive lens in direction; so correction is accomplished by balancing these opposing influences on the light. It is impractical to eliminate all the aberrations; the lens designer simply attempts to reduce them all as far as he can without producing a lens prohibitive in cost. This task becomes progressively more difficult as the aperture (or speed) of the lens is increased.

In the arrangement of the compound lens, some of the elements are cemented together with transparent cement; others are mounted separately and accurately spaced in a cell consisting of threaded metal rings.

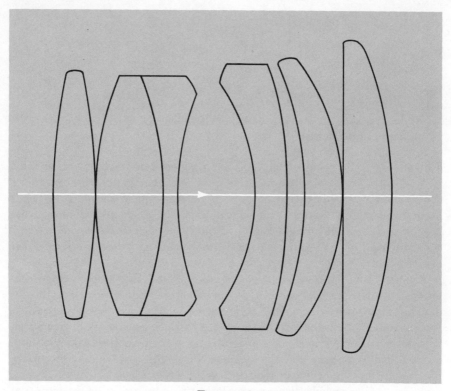

FIGURE 13

Diagram of modern, high speed, six-element lens, the 55-mm Super Takumar.

Manufacturing a lens depends, first of all, upon the solution of complex mathematical problems concerning the many variables involved. Electronic computers have greatly speeded up this part of lens design, one reason high quality and high speed lenses have been more widely available at cheaper prices in recent years. However, lens design and manufacture is still a laborious and time-consuming process; few manufactured products require any higher degree of precision in design and production than a photographic lens.

Another factor that has made high speed and relatively sharp lenses available is the development of new kinds of glass. Lenses can be made of any number of substances, but they are usually made of glass—but not just ordinary glass. Glass for lenses, or optical glass, must be designed for control of the refraction of light and must have a high degree of homogeneity or uniformity in both chemical composition and physical state. Ordinary glass consists of silica and sand mixed with several alkaline bases such as lime, potash, or soda. But optical glass can include any one or more of at least 30 different chemical elements.

Optical glass is composed essentially of a very pure variety of sand, specially selected for freedom from iron. Mixed with this sand is any one or more of a wide variety of metallic oxides, selected to give the glass particular properties. Since World War II some optical glasses have been made using oxides of lanthanum, cerium, thorium, and lithium, as well as other elements, some of which are called rare earth elements, so the new glasses have been called rare earth glasses.

By selecting from among the approximately 100 different kinds of optical glass available, the lens designer can develop a combination of lens elements to meet specific requirements, keeping in mind the shape of the elements as well as their physical composition. Different types of glass refract the light to different degrees, and some of the newer materials offer a high refractive index, compared to ordinary glass, with low dispersing power. In some cases each of the elements within a compound lens is made of a different kind of optical glass.

Adding elements reduces aberrations but also increases the reflection of light back and forth between the surfaces of the lens elements. This internal reflection is known as *flare* and is particularly noticeable for any object that is very much brighter than its surroundings, such as the sun or a lamp. Flare increases with the number of uncemented (glass-air) surfaces. It can be eliminated by cementing two elements together, but this means the concave curve of one element must exactly match the convex curve of the next, and it severely limits the freedom of the lens designer. The answer to this problem was the development of lens coating. The surfaces of the lens elements are coated with an extremely thin layer of a metallic fluoride, often magnesium fluoride. Eliminating the reflection

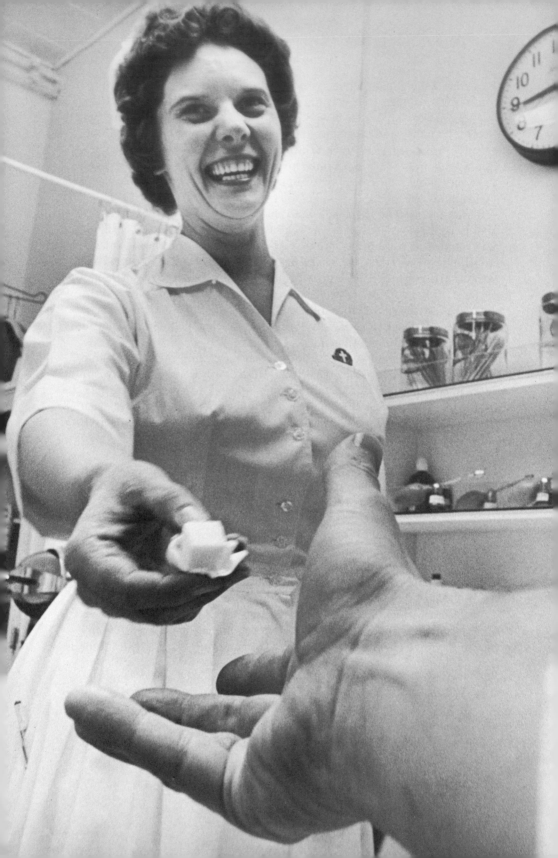

depends upon a phenomenon of physical optics known as *interference;* the refractive index of the coating layer is such that light reflected from its upper (air-fluoride) surface equals that reflected from its lower (fluoride-glass) surface and the layer is just thick enough for the light reflected from the upper surface to be out of phase by half a wavelength with the light reflected from the lower surface. The result is interference and no light at all. Coating offers other advantages besides reducing flare light. Practically no light is lost by reflection in a coated lens, and the energy so saved increases the transmitted or image-forming light. A glass surface coated with a correct layer of fluoride transmits up to 99 per cent of the incident light. Thus a compound lens with eight glass-air surfaces, all coated, transmits more than 90 per cent of the light, while a similar but noncoated lens may transmit only 70 per cent. Lens designers are then free to use more air space separations between lens elements and thus achieve an improved total lens design.

In summary: the photographic lens is a composite or combination of various simple positive and negative lenses, differing in optical properties and curvature, so the best possible compromise is achieved between one aberration and another within a previously established cost limit.

FOCAL LENGTH

Two of the characteristics of the photographic lens are fundamental. One of these is relative aperture—the diameter of the lens opening relative to the distance between lens and film. Relative aperture has already been discussed in Chapter 2 in connection with exposure. Here we must turn to the second characteristic, focal length, which was only mentioned in passing in that earlier discussion. Focal length is important because it determines the size of the image projected on the film for any subject at a given distance from the camera.

First we must establish a definition for focal length. When light rays come from a point on a subject at infinity, those rays may be considered parallel when they reach the lens. The lens bends these rays so that they converge to form an image of the point from which they originated. The distance from this image point to the optical center of the lens is the focal length. In simpler terms, the definition of focal length is often given as the distance between lens and film when the lens is focused at infinity. But in actual fact focal length is not measured from either the rear surface of the lens or from the physical center of the lens. It is measured from what

Getting Salk vaccine in a sugar cube. The proper lens, properly used, can tell the story. (David Mathias, Staff Photographer, Denver *Post*)

is called the rear nodal point. This is the point from which emerging light rays seem to come as they converge toward focus. It is a point usually within the lens and often close to the physical center. But with some lenses, as we shall see in the discussion of the telephoto and retrofocus lenses, this rear nodal point may be either in front or behind the actual lens. However, the photographer seldom needs to measure the focal length of a lens, since this characteristic is almost always marked on the front of the lens mount, in millimeters, centimeters, or inches.

It seems fairly safe to assume that most pictures are taken with the lens focused at some point short of infinity. For subjects closer to the camera, the lens must be moved away from the film plane; the closer the subject the greater the distance between lens and film if the image is kept in focus. Lens-to-film distance varies but slightly for subjects 50 to 100 feet away, but varies rather radically for subjects close to the lens. Great accuracy is needed in focusing for subjects at close range. With a lens of long focal length there are greater shifts in lens-to-film distance than with a lens of short focal length.

But the fact that lens-to-film distance changes as lens-to-subject distance changes does not alter focal length. It remains the same for any given lens because it is based on entering light rays that are parallel, and these occur only when the subject is at infinity, or so distant that for practical purposes the rays may be regarded as entering the lens on parallel paths.

Although a given lens does not alter its focal length, with the exception of the so-called zoom lenses, a single camera can be used with a variety of lenses, each with a different focal length. Photographic lenses are frequently identified in relative terms as normal, short, or long in focal length. But these designations are not absolute. A lens may be short focal length for a large negative but the same lens would be long focal length for a small negative.

A lens is generally regarded as normal if its focal length is approximately equal to the diagonal of the negative. Judging by the focal length of the lenses that are standard equipment on 35-mm cameras marketed today, a normal or standard lens for the 35-mm negative, with a diagonal of a little less than 45 mm, may be any focal length from 40 mm to 58 mm. Both 45 mm and 50 mm lengths are common on rangefinder models of the 35-mm camera, while 50 mm, 55 mm, and 58 mm are common on single lens reflex 35's. So what is normal with these cameras is hardly susceptible to precise definition; and the same is, to somewhat lesser extent, true of all other types of cameras.

A normal focal length lens produces a perspective in the uncropped print that appears approximately normal when we view the print from normal viewing distance. Or from another approach, a normal lens can be defined as a practical one for the lens designer who is striving for a good quality optical objective that can satisfy a large proportion of the camera's users without involving abnormal cost. Designers, for example, found it easier to meet the requirements of through-the-lens focusing with the single lens reflex camera if they used a focal length somewhat longer than the diagonal of the film.

The best we can do is simply accept what has come to be regarded as normal in lens focal length: something approximately equal to the diagonal of the negative to be covered by the image the lens projects. A lens, then, with a focal length significantly greater than the negative diagonal is a long focal length lens; one with a focal length noticeably shorter than the negative diagonal is a short focal length lens.

The longer the focal length, the greater the size of the image on the film when the subject remains at a given distance. In fact, image size and focal length are directly proportional; doubling the focal length results in doubling the size of the image.

ANGLE OF VIEW

Since image size increases with focal length, it logically follows that the longer the focal length of the lens, the less of the subject the lens will get

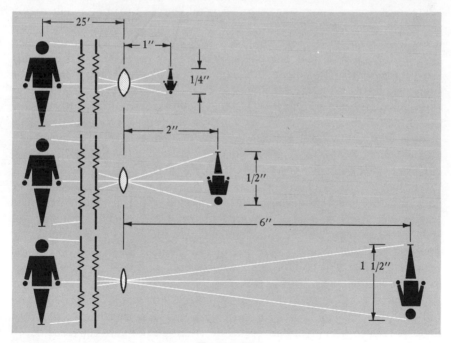

FIGURE 14
Image size and focal length are directly proportional.

on the negative. Or, to state it another way, the greater the lens focal length, the less the lens angle of view.

For example, if we want to increase the size of the image of an aspen tree surrounded by pine trees without moving the camera closer to the subject, we change to a lens with a longer focal length. But since the size of the negative remains the same, this means the aspen will occupy a larger part of the negative and of necessity a proportionate amount of the surrounding pines will be eliminated from the negative image.

With a single camera, then, but with three or more lenses for that camera, the photographer has considerable flexibility in photographic point of view. The short focal length or *wide-angle lens* encompasses more of the scene at any given distance. Thus the wide angle lens can be used relatively close to a central subject without eliminating from the negative the surrounding environment. Such a lens also exaggerates the spatial separation between objects within its angle of view. The long focal length lens, on the other hand, in effect reaches out to bring objects closer, so the photographer can take the picture from a relatively distant position but keep the image large on the negative. Thus, we see why newspaper and magazine photographers, and many other professional photographers, prefer a camera with interchangeable lenses. The photojournalist with, for example, a single 35-mm camera and several lenses can function effectively in close quarters with a wide-angle lens. On the other hand, the same camera with a long lens serves him well at sports events. Although he may have to remain in a specific assigned position, he can still pull in large-sized images with 100-mm to 1000-mm lenses. The long lens permits the photographer to shoot at considerable distance from the subject without sacrificing the tight cropping in the viewfinder that eliminates unnecessary detail, provides close-up views without the camera being close.

Interchangeable lenses are most commonly used with the 35-mm camera. In 1940 only a half-dozen 35-mm cameras featured interchangeable lenses, ranging in focal length from 38 mm to 500 mm. Twenty-five years later more than 50 such cameras offered interchangeable lenses, ranging from 18 mm to 2000 mm. Abnormal focal lengths are especially suited to these small cameras. With a large camera that uses film measuring four by five inches, the normal lens is approximately six inches in focal length. To double that focal length would require a 12-inch lens. With the 35-mm camera (normal lens 45 mm to 55 mm), a four-inch lens doubles the normal. The image magnification factor is the same in both cases (twice normal), but it is achieved with the 35-mm camera at much less expense and bulk. And the image magnification comes with less sacrifice in depth of field. A 12-inch lens must be stopped down to $f/24$ to give the same depth of field as a four-inch lens set at $f/18$.

Wide-angle lenses are generally considered to begin, for the 35-mm

Wide-angle lens let the photographer stand close to the foreground subject and background is still within the picture frame and within the depth of field. The perspective has exaggerated the distance between foreground and background. (Lowell Georgia, Staff Photographer, Denver *Post*)

Wide-angle (28-mm) lens on the Pentax camera used close to the nearest subject; all subjects closely related in the composition, yet the children were standing arm's length apart. (Floyd McCall, Denver)

camera, with the 35-mm lens. However, many photojournalists make the 35-mm their standard lens, keeping it on the camera most of the time; they seldom use a lens of normal focal length (45 mm to 55 mm). They do frequently use 28-mm and 21-mm lenses. The most widely used of the long lenses for the 35-mm camera are the 85-mm and the 105-mm. Following these in popularity are the 135-mm, the 200-mm, and the 400-mm, used mostly to get close-up views of sports action, views that can be duplicated only by the spectator with binoculars; but the binocular view is a fleeting one; the photograph is there for leisurely study.

Angle of view expands as focal length decreases: the 21-mm lens on the 35-mm camera will give an angle of view of approximately 90 degrees, double the angle of view of the 50-mm lens. With this increasing field coverage comes increased problems. A picture magazine editor once said that when he evaluates the work of a new photographer he pays particular attention to pictures made with the wide-angle lens. This is the area, he said, where the men are separated from the boys.

The wide-angle lens has been rated as the most difficult to master because it stretches out to include more of the area and more of the objects that surround the principal subject. Care must be taken to move in close enough to the subject to avoid losing it in the midst of a variety of distracting and unwanted images of other objects. If the negative must later be cropped during printmaking to eliminate unwanted parts of the image, the value of the wide-angle lens has been nullified. In addition, the wide angle of view increases the need for squaring the camera with horizontal and vertical subject lines.

A 35-mm single lens reflex camera, such as the Honeywell Pentax, is the best tool for learning to use lenses of varying focal lengths, and especially for the wide-angle lens, because you can actually see what the lens is putting in your picture frame. With a camera like the Pentax you can study the picture in the finder, watch what is happening in the corners, observe the lines in your subject, particularly those straight lines near the edge of the frame, and observe the relative sizes of images within the picture's depth. With the Pentax the authors have found they can study the subject through the taking lens, moving closer, then still closer, moving to one side or the other, moving up or down. Often the right view suddenly appears in the viewfinder, a startlingly new view of the subject that will add both impact and meaning to the picture. Searching for this viewpoint is half the fun of wide-angle photography.

PERSPECTIVE

Many photographers, when they first begin experimenting with interchangeable lenses, are puzzled by the apparent perspective distortions of the short and long focal length lenses. Short lenses exaggerate the distance between near and far objects within the field of view, and near objects seem excessively large. A friend's face is imaged with a distressingly large nose. Long lenses, on the other hand, compress distance; two objects along the same line of sight but separated by several feet appear in the photograph to be crowded upon a single square foot of ground.

The clue for understanding this is a simple one. Focal length determines image size, but it has no effect on actual perspective, which is the comparative size of objects at different distances from the lens. Perspective is controlled solely by the distance between camera and subject.

Let's ask John and Tom to pose for us. Both are six feet tall. We place John 10 feet from the camera and Tom at 20 feet. If the image of John, nearest the camera, measures two inches, the image of Tom, twice as far from the camera, will measure only one inch: doubling the distance reduces image size by one half. Now we will ask John to move out to a point 30 feet from the camera. This time Tom is closest at 20 feet, but his image remains one inch tall. John is only 50 per cent farther away than Tom, so his image will be reduced not by one half, but only by one fourth. His image will be three quarters of an inch. Yet the two men were the same distance apart in both poses—10 feet.

Pictures taken with short, normal, and long lenses without changing camera position exhibit precisely the same perspective. The short lens appears to distort perspective because it is ordinarily used with the camera close to the nearest object we want on the negative. Image sizes of more distant objects decrease rapidly because that short distance between camera and nearest object is quickly doubled or tripled by the distances to objects farther away. The long lens is used when the nearest object to be pictured is many feet from the camera; image sizes of more distant objects decrease at a slower rate. The perspective provided by a lens with other than the normal focal length is never actually distorted, but it appears strange because the viewpoint is strange. With the short focal length lens we see the subject from an abnormally close viewpoint. With the long lens we see the subject from what appears to have been a close viewpoint, but the perspective remains that of a distant view. The view and perspective of a long lens can be duplicated by enlarging a small section of a negative made with a normal or short lens.

The long lens can be used effectively to pull subjects widely separated in the actual scene into closer relationship in the photographic image. Suppose we want to take a picture of a farm scene. We find picturesque shocks of grains in the foreground and the farmhouse in the background. We are using a 35-mm camera with a 50-mm lens. But when we stand at 10 feet from the grain shocks the image of the house is too small. The answer? Let's make two changes. We will move back with our camera to 20 feet from the grain shocks and change to a 100-mm lens. The image size of the grain shocks remains the same; doubling the focal length of the lens has been exactly balanced by doubling camera-to-subject distance. But what of the farmhouse? Its image is nearly doubled in size because distance from camera to house has been increased only a fraction while lens focal length was doubled. If we can change both lens focal length and camera position we have vastly increased control over picture composition.

TELEPHOTO AND RETROFOCUS LENSES

Photographers frequently refer to any lens with a longer than normal focal length, one that gives larger images at a given camera-to-subject distance, as a telephoto lens. No great harm results from this nomenclature habit, although it is often incorrect. In the true telephoto lens the physical placement of the lens is closer to the film plane than the focal length indicates. For example, one Takumar 200-mm lens is only 138½ mm long, or just 3½ mm longer than the common 135-mm lens, which is not a telephoto.

For 35-mm cameras, focal length is usually achieved for all long lenses up to 135 mm by increasing the physical distance between film and lens. Beyond that, focal length is achieved with special optical construction using two groups of lenses. The front group is a converging or positive lens system, while the rear group is a diverging or negative unit. Each of these groups will include more than one element for correction of aberrations. Light rays are converged by the front unit but the rear unit partially cancels this convergence. As a result the cone of light reaching the film appears to converge from a point somewhere out in front of the complete lens. In other words, the rear nodal point of the lens is not inside the lens at all, but somewhere out in front of it. (See Figure 15.)

The retrofocus lens is, in effect, just the reverse of the telephoto; it is farther away from the film plane than the focal length would indicate. This is achieved with an optical construction that is the reverse of the telephoto lens: the diverging or negative group of lens elements is the front unit, while the converging or positive group is the rear unit. The optical center of the lens is somewhere in space behind the rear group. (See Figure 16.)

The retrofocus design has been of value with the single lens reflex camera because it gives additional space between lens and film without increasing focal length. This permits the mirror to operate unimpeded by the lens.

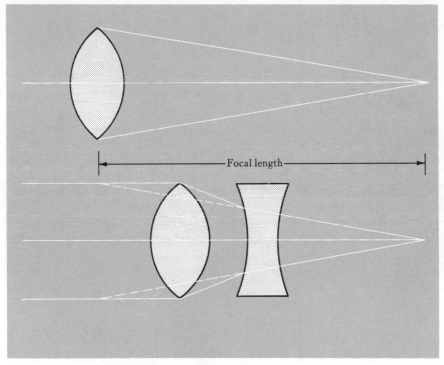

Focal length

FIGURE 15

Long lens and telephoto lens of the same focal length. The bottom lens is a telephoto lens and so is actually shorter in physical length than its focal length, because of the negative element.

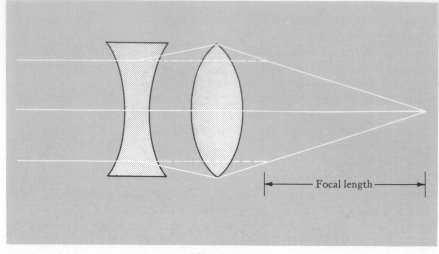

FIGURE 16
A schematic diagram of the retrofocus lens.

ZOOM LENSES

Zoom (variable focal length) lenses have been relatively common for movie and television cameras, making it possible for the cinematographer to shift quickly from a distant and wide-angle view of the subject to a close-up shot without moving the camera or removing one lens and inserting another. It was all done with a single lens. Application of the zoom principle to still cameras had no significant development until about 1958. Since that time there has been a fairly rapid proliferation of zoom lenses for 35-mm still cameras of the single lens reflex type.

A zoom lens provides a continuously variable focal length over a limited range; that is, it provides an infinite number of focal lengths between two extremes. The extremes may range from a moderately short focal length to a moderately long one, or from an approximately normal to a medium long one. Or both extremes may lie within the long focal length region. An example is the Super Takumar Zoom for the Pentax, a fully automatic $f/4.5$ lens with a zoom range from 70 to 150 mm.

A zoom lens also keeps the f/number constant no matter what the focal length setting and maintains reasonably sharp focus throughout the zoom range. Accurate focus is generally maintained best if the lens is first focused while it is set at its longest focal length. Even so, there will be some loss in image sharpness with zoom lenses and each photographer must judge for himself whether this is crucial in his work. The problem of

A telephoto (400-mm) lens allowed the photographer to use a distant perspective that compressed nearly a dozen blocks into what looks like one. (George Crouter, Staff Photographer, Denver Post*)*

maintaining focus poses the major difficulty in designing zoom lenses. Focal length can be changed quite simply by changing the distance between components or groups of simple lenses within the total complex lens. But such a change shifts the image plane, the plane at which the film must be positioned if the image is to be in focus. So the zoom lens design usually provides a way to shift two groups of lens elements simultaneously: one group shifts to change the focal length and the second group shifts to keep the image in focus.

With zoom lenses it is generally advisable to stop down, and this usually dictates the use of films with at least moderately high speeds so that you can stop down and yet retain a fast shutter speed. The high shutter speed is important to avoid the blurred images that may result from camera shake. Zoom and telephoto lenses are best employed on tripods to keep the camera steady. When they must be used with the camera held in the hands, steady hands and fast shutter speed become vitally important.

AUXILIARY LENSES

Attachments are available that increase or decrease the focal length of the fixed lens in some cameras. Auxiliary telephoto attachments feature the normal telescopic construction with the front converging or positive group of lens elements and the rear diverging or negative group. The reverse is true of the wide-angle auxiliary, which has a diverging or negative group in front and a converging or positive group in the rear. These auxiliary lenses are simply placed in front of the camera's normal lens. Such attachments are useful within a limited range of focal length shifts. However, it should be noted that there are other limitations in many of these auxiliary lenses. Vignetting (image fading at the negative corners) can occur with some of the telephoto attachments, and the wide-angle auxiliaries sometimes give out-of-focus images at the negative edges. With auxiliary attachments in place, exposures must often be made with apertures no greater than 5.6, and edge-to-edge sharpness for big enlargements requires settings of $f/11$ or $f/16$.

Many of the auxiliary lenses are relatively low in price, but unfortunately image quality usually corresponds. Noteworthy exceptions, in both price and image quality, are the wide-angle and tele Rollei Mutars, designed for use, of course, with the Rolleiflex, a twin-lens reflex camera, and a popular one with professional photographers. The authors have found that the Rollei Mutars give exceptionally high-quality images. The Mutars are complex optical objectives made up of several components to match the regular Rollei lenses. They effectively increase or shorten the focal length of the camera lens with virtually no loss in speed. Without physically altering the regular lens or interfering with the camera mechanism,

FIGURE 17

Rollei camera with Mutar auxilliary lens attached.

the telephoto Mutar provides a magnification of 1.5 times (boosting the regular 75-mm lens to 113-mm), while the wide-angle Mutar extends the normal 56-degree angle of view to a wide 72 degrees. In both cases the photographer has an absolute check on the picture in the finder screen.

In a few cameras the front component of the lens can be removed and replaced with either a special telephoto or wide-angle component, designed specifically for the camera. The rear component of the normal lens remains permanently attached to the camera. Results with these cameras can be excellent in image quality, but, again, the range of possible shifts in focal length is limited.

Depth of field is controlled by aperture. Both photos were taken with a 55-mm lens on a Pentax camera. The aperture was f/1.8 for the photo at the left, and f/11 for the photo at the right. Position of the camera did not change. (Floyd McCall, Denver)

DEPTH OF FIELD

Anyone who has examined photographs at all critically will have noticed that often images of objects that were both near and far from the camera appear to be in focus in many pictures. But the briefest study of optics shows that a lens can be focused on only one plane at a time. How is it possible for objects both closer and farther away than that plane to be in apparent focus in the picture? The answer lies in the optical phenomenon traditionally given the label *depth of field*.

Depth of field is, in fact, a result of the limitations of the human eye and not the result of any optical magic produced by the photographic lens. A lens images a point as a circle (called in photographic literature the *circle of confusion*). But the unaided eye cannot resolve extremely fine detail, so all circles smaller than 1/100 of an inch in diameter look like points. The image may actually be out of focus, but if the circles of confusion are so small that the eye cannot detect them, it makes no odds; the image appears sharp.

When we focus on a point 10 feet from the camera, only that point and

120

all other points at precisely the same distance will be of maximum possible sharpness in the image. Points on other objects closer and farther away from the camera will be reproduced as circles in the image, with the circles getting larger and larger for objects farther and farther away from the plane on which the lens is focused. Finally, the circles of confusion get large enough for the eye to detect them—actually, the eye sees a blurred

Wide-angle lens and low angle of view got this high impact result. (George Crouter, Staff Photographer, Denver *Post*)

This photograph was taken with the 28-mm lens on the Pentax camera. The following shots were taken with the various Takumar lenses shown in this picture, camera-to-subject distance being increased with each lens change to keep the girl approximately the same size in the viewfinder. Her position was not changed. (Floyd McCall, Denver)

Taken with the 35-mm lens.

. . . the 55-mm lens.

. . . the 85-mm lens.

. . . the 105-mm lens.

. . . *the 135-mm lens.*

. . . *the 200-mm lens.*

. . . *the 300-mm lens.*

. . . *the 500-mm lens.*

image. The distance between the nearest object and the farthest object that appear to be in focus is the depth of field.

A rule of thumb has practical value. The depth of field will normally be divided so that approximately one third will be in front of the point focused upon and about two thirds behind it. This one third/two thirds rule is, however, only an approximation. As the lens is focused closer to the camera, the depth of field is more evenly divided, until the point where the camera is focused at a distance equal to twice the lens focal length, giving an image the same size as the actual object. At this point depth of field is extremely shallow, but equally divided on either side of the point of focus. Many cameras include scales that give approximate depth of field, but if depth of field is critical it must be determined by consulting a table or by mathematical formula.

Obviously, depth of field depends, for one thing, upon our own critical standard: how much blur are we prepared to accept? The more critical we are the less the depth of field will be.

Enlarging, of course, also affects depth of field, because enlarging the image also enlarges the circles of confusion or inherent, always present, blur in any image. If the negative image is to be enlarged, normal practice with most professional photographers and universal with 35-mm negatives, the circles of confusion in the negative must be about 1/500 of an inch in diameter or less, so that when they are enlarged they will not exceed 1/100 of an inch in the print.

The size of the circles of confusion (the sharpness or critical rendition of object points) in the negative image is controlled by the angle between light rays approaching the film—that is, the angle between rays originating at a given subject point. The smaller this angle, the smaller the circles of confusion—or the sharper the image.

The angle of the light rays is controlled by two factors: the size of the lens aperture used for making the exposure and the distance between lens and object. As the diameter of the lens aperture is reduced, the angle between the converging light rays is reduced, thus increasing depth of field. Likewise, as distance between lens and subject increases, the angle between the light rays is reduced, and depth of field again increases—until the far limit of depth of field reaches infinity, beyond which, of course, it cannot go.

Lens focal length is sometimes listed as another factor controlling depth of field. But actually this is simply another way of saying that lens aperture controls depth of field. It is true that a lens with a focal length of two inches, set at $f/4$, gives greater depth of field than a lens with a focal length of four inches, also set at $f/4$. But the difference in the depths of field is accounted for by the actual, physically measurable diameter of the opening in the lens diaphragm. In the example of the two-inch lens, that

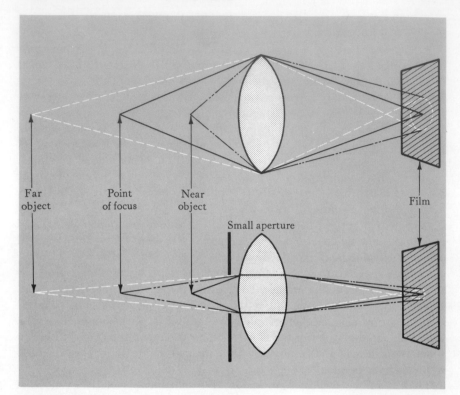

Far
object

Point
of focus

Near
object

Film

Small aperture

FIGURE 18

Aperture and depth of field. As aperture is decreased in size the cones of light are narrowed and circles of confusion at the film become smaller, resulting in greater depth of field.

opening measures one half an inch (one quarter of two); with the four-inch lens the opening is twice that diameter, one full inch (one quarter of four). *F*/4 on the short focal length lens gives the smallest base for the cone of light converging toward the lens, and thus the smallest angle between the converging rays. However, we must remember that the image size with the four-inch lens is twice as large as the image projected by the two-inch lens. If we move closer to the subject with the short focal length lens, so that we have images of equal size, then depth of field at any given *f*/stop will be the same with the two lenses. The short focal length lens offers an advantage in increased depth of field at any given *f*/stop *if* we are willing to accept the decreased image size. But if image size is the same, depth of field will be the same.

To summarize: the two important factors controlling depth of field are aperture diameter and distance focused upon, and the most important of these from a practical viewpoint is aperture diameter. If great depth of field is desired, stop down to the smallest aperture (largest *f*/number) possible consistent with correct exposure (adjusting shutter speed, of course, to compensate for the smaller lens opening). If shallow depth of field is desired, use the largest aperture (smallest *f*/number) feasible.

For most photographers, determining depth of field precisely, down to the final inch or even foot, is seldom, if ever, necessary. But for the record, depth of field can be determined in the following way:

The simplest and easiest method is first to find the *hyperfocal distance:* the distance from camera to the nearest point in acceptable focus when the lens is focused at infinity. If we can accept as within acceptable focus all circles of confusion that measure no more than 1/1000 of the focal length of the lens, hyperfocal distance can be determined simply by multiplying the diameter of the lens opening in inches by 1,000. The answer, of course, will be in inches. (Multiply by 1,500 or 2,000 for more critical definition.)

For example, to determine the hyperfocal distance for a two-inch lens with aperture set at *f*/4, first find the diameter of the aperture by dividing the *f*/number into focal length, since *f*/numbers are fractions of focal length.

2 (focal length) ÷ 4 (*f*/number) = ½ (aperture diameter)
½ × 1000 = 500 inches
Hyperfocal distance = about 42 feet

Usually focal length is marked on the front of the lens in millimeters. One millimeter = 0.03937 inch—or one inch = 25.4 millimeters (for most calculations 25 will do). A simple method of converting millimeters to inches is to multiply the millimeters by four and mark off two decimal places.

With hyperfocal distance known, the limits of depth of field can be found from the following:

$$\text{Near limit of depth of field} = \frac{H \times D}{H + D}$$

$$\text{Far limit of depth of field} = \frac{H \times D}{H - D}$$

H = hyperfocal distance
D = distance focused upon

Of occasional value is the knowledge that maximum depth of field will occur for any given *f*/number when the lens is focused at hyperfocal distance. Depth of field then extends from one half the distance focused upon to infinity.

COLOR CORRECTION

The term color correction has often been used in connection with photographic lenses, and too often the assumption has been that a color corrected lens is one intended for taking good color pictures. This is a misinterpretation of the term. Color correction is a correction for chromatic aberration, the tendency for the different colors (or wavelengths) in white light to be refracted different amounts and thus brought to a focus at different points. (See page 95) A color corrected photographic lens brings all rays, regardless of wavelength, to focus at very nearly the same point, so near there is no ordinarily detectable difference. Thus, color correction is just as important for panchromatic black and white film as it is for color film.

A lens corrected for two colors is known as an achromat, and if such a lens is properly designed and manufactured it focuses all colors or wavelengths so closely together it will meet customary photographic demands. A lens corrected for three colors is called an apochromat, but these are quite expensive and slow in speed (offer a relatively small maximum aperture). No lens is fully corrected for all wavelengths present in white light, and even if one could be made it would hardly be a practical improvement, since today's lenses project as finely detailed an image as today's films can record.

CLEANING THE LENSES

Photographic lenses should be treated with respect and care. Optical glass is softer than ordinary glass and thus more easily scratched or otherwise damaged.

Lenses should be kept clean but not with the same casualness as most persons use in cleaning their eyeglasses. Dust on the surface of the lens should be blown off or brushed off with a soft camel's hair brush. Fingerprints or other smears should be removed by breathing on the lens and then gently wiping the surface with lens cleaning tissue.

So-called lens cleaning fluids are not recommended except for occasional use. Frequent use of such fluids may result in etching the metal content of the optical glass by the solvents in the fluid, or the fluid may seep between glass elements of the lens and dissolve the cement holding them together. Do not use the specially treated cleaning cloths or cleaning papers designed for use with eyeglasses. If any solvent (plain water or pure grain alcohol will do) is used to remove stubborn smears on the glass, use only a very little by moistening a wad of lens tissue and immediately dry the lens with another clean tissue. Lenses should never be taken apart for cleaning except by a trained technician.

Chapter 8
•
LIGHT AS A LANGUAGE

The tonal nuances upon which the photographic image depends are created and conditioned by subtle variations in the emulsion's response to light. Form, texture, volume, space, mood—all depend upon contrast in tone values, and these are all elements that contribute meaning to a photograph. To contribute and control this meaning, the photographer must control light.

Yousuf Karsh, internationally famous for his revealing photographic portraits, phrased it superlatively well. He said simply: "Light is my language." So it is for all photographers; and like writers, some photographers use their language well, with distinguishing style; others use it poorly, with a style distinguished only by its triteness. Control of light must begin for the photographer with an understanding of the basic response of his material to light.

The photographer must learn to relate light intensities reflected from various parts of the subject to the gray scale tones that will be produced by silver deposits on his finished print. In between the subject and the print, of course, lies the negative; so it is of the negative he must think first.

Variations in light intensities that strike the film during exposure create the all-important tone-modulating power of the negative. The light that records the positive image is modulated by the deposit of silver in the negative. The greater the silver deposit in a given section of the negative, the less the light passed by that section to the printing paper; and, of course, the reverse is also true. The less light the negative passes, the lighter the tone in the print; the more the light, the darker the print tone. And the variations in the negative silver deposit can give a wide scale of tones between the two extremes. Make a drawing with black ink on a white sheet of paper; the result has contrast, or a brightness range, from the black of the ink to the white of the paper. But it has only those two tones, black and white. The photograph includes intermediate tones of gray, in some cases a great many intermediate tones, in other cases only a few, but without some of these intermediate tones the photograph can give no impression of roundness and depth.

The relative range of tones from black to white is recorded on the film in silver deposits, or densities, and is the negative's version of the range of light intensities reflected by objects in the scene being photographed. Two

129

variables are involved in light reflected by the photographic subject: the ability of each surface to reflect light and the amount of light striking each surface. A whitewashed wall in direct sunlight reflects perhaps 500 times as much light as a black velvet cloth in the shadow of the wall. Somewhat less, but still extreme, is the difference in light reflected from the white shirt of a man standing in the sunlight and the light reflected from the shaded trunk of a tree nearby.

This difference in the intensity of the light reflected by the brightest and the darkest part of the scene has been called by various names. In the scientific literature it is usually referred to as the luminance scale; in other publications it has been called the brightness scale. For purposes of simplification in this basic discussion we will call it the contrast range, or simply the contrast of the subject, because it is this range of light intensities reflected from the subject that will be translated by exposure and development of the film into the contrast range of the negative and the print. Contrast is the difference in visual brilliance between one part of the subject or image and another, and as such it is the result of what the eye and brain of an individual observer perceive. We can measure the luminance scale (contrast range in the subject) with a light meter, or we can measure the density scale (contrast range in the images on film or paper) with a densitometer, but in neither case can we assume that we have a measurement that corresponds exactly to what the brain perceives. Psychological factors, impossible to measure, are involved. However, we can, by controlling exposure and development of the film, translate subject contrast as we see it into what will be a generally pleasing image contrast. This image contrast may closely approximate subject contrast, or it may be radically different. Whatever the image contrast, it should be controlled by the photographer, not by accident, to give a result at least approximating what the photographer saw (not merely with his eyes, but with his mind and emotions as well) in the subject. This is, of course, the problem of tone reproduction, and tones determine the entire nature of the final picture. Unfortunately, the theory of tone reproduction is extremely complex, and we can consider only its basic outlines in this introductory survey.

LIGHT AND SHADE

Fundamental to understanding tone reproduction is an understanding of light and shade in photographic subjects. This knowledge must be accumulated through experience and we shall attempt to present here only the most elementary of guides.

Shadows outdoors on a sunny day are darkest when the sky is deep blue and cloudless. In such a situation 90 per cent of the light at the earth's surface at midday comes directly from the sun; only 10 per cent comes as reflected light from the sky. This means shadows are only one tenth as bright as their surroundings. But a cloudless day is unusual. On an average day about 20 per cent of the light comes reflected from the sky and clouds, and the range between highlights and shadows is less extreme. When the sun is low in morning or late afternoon, the shadows are also brighter, because a still larger percentage of the total light on the scene comes from the sky.

Sunlight alone is harsh; shadows are an intense black; subject contrast is extremely high and nearly impossible to encompass on negative and print. This situation comes close to existing at high mountain altitudes on a clear day.

Skylight alone, the situation that generally prevails on an overcast day, can be depressing on a landscape scene, since shadows shrink and become vague if they exist at all. Skylight alone, however, as a soft, diffused light, can be flattering for outdoor portraits. But complete lack of shadow means a lack of modeling; objects have no volume, no third dimension.

A situation approximating sunlight alone can occur indoors under strong direct lighting and the result is the same: extreme contrast from dark detail-less shadows to brilliant highlights, another situation difficult to control in image tones. This often occurs in sports arenas where a high percentage of the light is direct and harsh. In many other indoor situations the lighting is more nearly natural, assuming that *natural* here means something approximating sunlight plus skylight on an average day. Indoors direct light from a lamp is the sunlight and indirect light bouncing from light-colored ceiling and walls performs the function of the skylight. If the percentage of indirect light is low the contrast range is likely to be too extreme for ordinary exposure and normal development of the film to bring out detail in both shadows and highlights.

The highlight-to-shadow contrast in the average photographic subject is approximately 160 to 1; that is, the highlights are approximately 160 times as bright as the deepest shadows. For unusually contrasty subjects in brilliant sunlight or under a high percentage of direct lighting indoors this ratio may be much higher, perhaps 1,000 to 1, and for a gray seascape on a dull, overcast day it will be much lower, perhaps 10 to 1.

The average photographic film can produce a contrast range of about 200 to 1 so it can handle the average subject without difficulty. In addition, the contrast range of the negative image is normally less than that of the subject because of *flare light*, light scattered and reflected within the lens and camera. Although the antireflection coating on all glass-air surfaces of most modern photographic lenses reduces flare light, it does not eliminate it. When this flare light strikes the film it has a much greater effect on shadow areas than on the highlights. One unit of flare light added

Dramatic highlights and black shadows add impact. Also important were timing, to catch the gesture, and the choice of camera viewpoint. (David Mathias, Staff Photographer, Denver *Post*)

to 100 units of image-forming light in the highlights is only a one per cent increase; but one unit added to one unit of image-forming light in the shadow areas is a 100 per cent increase. The result is a compression of contrast—highlights and shadows are brought closer together in relative silver deposit densities. Although flare also occurs in the enlarger, where it may further reduce the contrast range of the image, normally the effect of flare is much less in the enlarger than it is in the camera.

Printing papers can handle a much shorter contrast range than the film. Glossy surface papers reproduce contrasts on a scale of approximately 70 to 1, although the average for glossy prints is closer to 50 to 1. Semimatte papers average about 36 to 1, and matte papers, about 20 to 1. This compression of subject contrast to the limits of the positive image is of practical importance to the photographer. It means he must, in some cases, accept compression of the tonal scale, but he can usually control where that compression will take place.

The contrast of the negative is related to, but not always an accurate reproduction of, the contrast in the scene. The range of densities or contrast of a negative is the result of a combination of factors, including the brightness range of the subject, the exposure given the film, the inherent contrast of the film emulsion (it varies with different films), and the development of the negative.

Highlights, such as a white shirt in the original scene, cannot be reproduced with pleasing detail in the print if exposure has been so great as to block up that area of the negative image. Light will be blocked from moving through that negative area if the silver deposit (density) is too heavy. On the other hand, there will be no print detail in shadowed areas of the subject if exposure has been too little, because the silver deposit in shadow areas of the negative image is then so slight it has no effective light-modulating power, and the almost uninterrupted flood of light results in a thoroughly blackened area on the print.

The photographer's problem, then, is to make sure he gives enough exposure to create detail-recording silver deposits in important shadow areas without blotting out detail in the highlights with an excessive amount of silver there.

With most black-and-white photographic films a rather wide range of exposures gives negatives that, in turn, give satisfactory prints. This range of possible, if not all ideal, exposures is known as the latitude of the film. Photographers, particularly news photographers working under less than ideal conditions, may have to rely on this latitude on occasion, but all photographers should have a thorough understanding of the two rules on which the art of correct exposure is solidly based :

  1. Find the least possible exposure that will permit reproduction of the desired amount of detail in dark areas of the print and at the same time produce a range of print tones matching the photographer's preconception of the picture he wants to produce.
  2. Find the right combination of *f*/number and shutter speed to satisfy requirement Number 1 and at the same time produce the photographer's desired result in blurred or frozen motion and in shallow or great depth of field.

Application of these rules, which take into account the brightness range of the subject, must be related, in addition, to the characteristics of the film emulsion and to the planned development procedure. This makes it evident that exposure is not a fixed and immutable figure even for a given subject, a light condition, and film speed.

FILM SENSITOMETRY

Trial and error, if carried through enough trials and enough corrected errors, can lead to a decision on the exact combination of film, exposure, and development needed to produce a satisfying photograph of a particular subject. But there is a realm of photographic science that can help shorten this process, a realm known as sensitometry. Photographic sensitometry is concerned with the measurement of the response of photographic emulsions to exposure and development; its aim is to eliminate, or at least greatly reduce, the trial-and-error work in establishing what results can be expected from a standardized method of treating the film emulsion. Exact sensitometric methods are only available in a properly and elaborately equipped laboratory, but even so a knowledge of sensitometry can be of immense aid.

Sensitometry is based on investigations near the end of the nineteenth century by two Englishmen, Ferdinand Hurter, a chemist, and Vero C. Driffield, an engineer, who were also both amateur photographers. Modification and expansion of their work have established present-day standards that are almost indispensable to all photographers.

Sensitometry deals with the relationship between exposure and the densities of the silver deposit in the developed film emulsion. To establish

Backlighting is a dramatic form of lighting. The sun, actually in this picture, caused the shadows to reproduce blacker and the highlights on the crests of the small waves to be whiter, making the waves appear angry and violent. (Lowell Georgia, Staff Photographer, Denver *Post*)

reliable data for any given film emulsion, precise control must be maintained over both exposure and processing. Testing of an emulsion is started by subjecting it to a series of standard exposures in which each exposure step exceeds the preceding step by a constant factor, such as two or the square root of two (1.41). An instrument capable of giving such a series of accurate and reproducible exposures is known as a sensitometer. After exposure the test material is developed under tightly controlled, standard conditions. The result is a gray scale progressing in precise steps from white to black because each step or increment in exposure established a corresponding increment in silver deposit density in the negative. Finally, the test negative is examined in a densitometer, an instrument that measures the light-stopping power of each of the density steps.

DENSITY

The contrasts between various silver deposits in the photographic image establish the nature and quality of that image. The blackening created by the silver deposits is referred to as the density of the image. There are two general aspects of density: the over-all blackness of the negative image, what we might call the average density, and the density range or scale, the difference between the highest and the lowest densities, often referred to as the contrast of the negative. But to understand the meaning of density precisely enough to understand sensitometry, we must begin with two other terms: transmission and opacity.

Transmission is the light-passing characteristic of the negative.

Opacity, the light-stopping characteristic of the negative, is the transmission value inverted—or the reciprocal of transmission.

To illustrate: if the incident light, the light falling on the negative, is given an arbitrary value of 100 and we then measure the amount of this light that gets through the negative and find it to have a value of 50, we would then say the negative is transmitting 50 per cent of the light, or its transmission is 50/100 or one half. Invert the transmission value to get opacity: 100/50 = 2. Or, in effect, opacity is incident light divided by transmitted light.

Opacity describes the extent of blackness created by the silver deposit in any selected part of the image, but it is not a useful concept in sensitometry, because it varies in an arithmetical fashion and thus provides a long and clumsy series of numbers to deal with. In addition, opacity is not directly related to the way we see the differences in tones within the image; we see those differences as a logarithmic scale, not an arithmetical one.

Perhaps an abbreviated review of logarithms will make this clearer. On the next page we have printed on the top line an arithmetic series of numbers. On the second line, a geometric series of numbers.

0	*1*	*2*	*3*	*4*	*5*
1	10	100	1,000	10,000	100,000

Now any number in the arithmetic (top) series is the logarithm of the number paired with it in the geometric series on the bottom. These are logarithms to the base 10, because 10 is the number in the geometric series paired with unity in the arithmetic series, and are known as common logarithms. The common logarithm of 1,000 is 3.

In looking at a negative, we see a step in the density scale from 1 to 10 as the same as a step from 100 to 1,000. With logarithms we can give equal space on the graph to each such step and keep the graph within a reasonable space.

Density, then, is defined as the logarithm of opacity. If the opacity is 2 (one half of the light transmitted, one half of it stopped), the density is the logarithm of 2, or .3.

Some typical transmission, opacity, and density values are as follows:

Transmission	*Opacity*	*Density*
1	1	0
½	2	0.3
¼	4	0.6
1/10	10	1
1/16	16	1.2
1/100	100	2
1/200	200	2.3
1/1000	1,000	3

Densities larger than three are rare, since to exceed that density more than 99.9 per cent of the light would have to be absorbed.

THE CHARACTERISTIC CURVE

For a sensitometric test, the density measurements of the silver deposits in the film exposed in a sensitometer are usually made with a recording densitometer. This device not only reads the densities but automatically plots them on graph paper, and from this graph we get the characteristic curve of the emulsion tested. The curve, sometimes called the H & D curve because Hurter and Driffield first used this system, provides a complete description of the response of the film to exposure and development.

The curve describes in graphic form the relationship between density and exposure. Because density is a logarithmic expression, exposure is transposed into logarithmic terms, and for purposes of the characteristic curve becomes known as log exposure, or log e. The plotted curve shows the density of each step of the series of varying exposures made in the

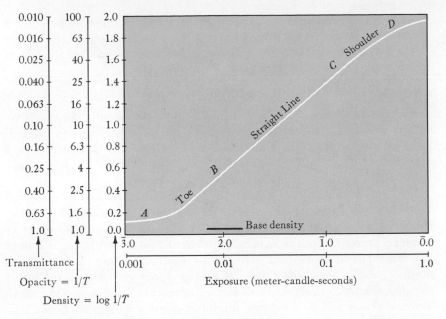

Transmittance

Opacity $= 1/T$

Density $= \log 1/T$

FIGURE 19

The characteristic curve.

sensitometer, and each density step is shown as a function of the exposure that produced it. According to theory, equal increases in log exposure should give equal increases in density. If this were true the graph would not form a curve, but a straight line. Density, in fact, is not exactly proportional to log exposure. The curve has the shape of a stretched-out, italic capital S. The bottom curve of the S (sections A to B in Figure 19) is called the toe of the curve. The toe begins above the baseline, because a certain minimum density is contributed by the film base and gelatin. The first few exposures are so small no silver develops in the negative and there is no density beyond base density; then, at the threshold of the emulsion, some slight silver deposit begins to build density and the curve turns upward. As exposure increases, the steepness of the curve increases, until finally we reach the straight-line section of the curve (B to C in Figure 19). Here equal increases in log e bring equal increases in density. The straight-line section occupies the major portion of the curve's length, but the line finally curves into the top of the S (C to D); this is the shoulder. Here again equal increases in exposure do not result in equal increases in density. Finally a point is reached when an increase in exposure makes no change in density, and the line of the curve is horizontal. If exposures are increased to much greater figures—enormous overexposures—the curve

137

actually begins to bend downward again; increases in exposure here bring decreases in density. This effect has been given the term *solarization*.

The characteristic curve is a summary of three important properties of the emulsion: speed, exposure range, and contrast.

SPEED

It would be extremely difficult, if not impossible, to get predictable results in photography if we had no idea of the light sensitivity of the emulsions we use; determining exposures would present the frustrations of a nightmare. One of the most important functions of sensitometry is to provide us with guides to emulsion sensitivity or speed.

The greater an emulsion's ability to record with silver deposit densities at low levels of exposure, the greater its speed. But for practical purposes this must be assessed as the emulsion's ability to separate two or more low-level exposures into recognizably different density levels, for it is only the difference in tones that give a photograph meaning. Low-level exposures, usually the shadow areas of a subject, are recorded on the toe of the characteristic curve. As these exposures reach a point where the curve begins a perceptible vertical rise, minimum density differences begin. The speed of the film lies somewhere along this section of the curve. Modern speed rating systems are based on the gradient (that is, the rate of ascent, the steepness) of the curve at the point where these first usable differences in density appear. The smaller the exposure at this point, the greater the speed of the film.

The method involves drawing the characteristic curve and selecting the exposure at which the slope or gradient on the toe is 30 per cent of the average gradient. The average gradient is based on that section of the curve extending from the point at which minimum differences in density occur and a point above that representing a 1.5 increase in log e.

If 30 per cent of the average gradient gives a point on the curve that represents an exposure of .01 meter-candle-second, then the speed of the film is taken as 1/.01 or 100. This speed figure is an expression of the minimum necessary exposure with this film, and using this figure as the basis for figuring exposures will inevitably mean some of the densities—in particular the shadow areas—will fall on the toe of the curve. But investigations and tests of recent years have shown this to be desirable. The tones are somewhat compressed in this region, but this compression is counteracted by the characteristics of printing papers and enlargers.

Because it was feared photographers would get a high proportion of underexposures using such a speed rating, the speed figure was converted into an *exposure index* by dividing it by a safety factor, usually 2.5. In our example above, with the film speed of 100, the exposure index would have been 100/2.5 or 40. But as photographers became more skillful and exposure meters became common items of equipment, this safety factor was more a handicap than a help. Today's film speeds are generally very close to being the same as the speed determined in sensitometric tests. Present safety factors are on the order of 1.2. Photographers frequently establish their own personal exposure index for a particular film, based on their standard method of exposing and developing that film. This index may be either higher or lower than the film's speed. The term speed should properly be reserved for the sensitivity figure established by sensitometric testing; any other figure used in figuring exposures should be called an exposure index.

EXPOSURE RANGE

The exposure range, or latitude, of the film appears on the characteristic curve as that section between the toe and the shoulder, or approximately the straight-line portion of the curve. The straight-line section is that area where equal increments of exposure produce equal increments of density. Here the tone relationships in the negative most accurately reflect the contrast relationships in the subject. However, we have already seen that some of the toe region is advantageous. So we had best modify our definition of exposure range to the range of exposure values through which density increases at a useful rate. This would carry our exposure range down to the point where the slope of the curve begins to flatten out and up to a point where the slope again turns toward the horizontal. We can use the shoulder of the curve, but we shall find as a matter of practical results that the toe section is much more useful. The least exposure that will give useful separation of tones (detail) in the shadows will place those shadows on the toe of the curve but keep the highlight areas, for most subjects, well below the shoulder. This means highlight areas in the negative will have useful tone separations—they won't be blocked up—and they will serve to modulate the light that strikes the printing paper, giving us detail and sparkle in the print highlights.

CONTRAST

With a negative, the term contrast means the range of brightness values that have been recorded on the film in silver deposits or densities. In a contrasty negative there is a noticeably wide separation between the extremes, that is between the almost clear, minimum density regions and the dense, highlight areas. There may or may not be a great number of individual density steps between the two extremes.

Contrast on the characteristic curve is shown by the slope of the curve, the angle the line of the curve makes with the horizontal. The steeper this line, the higher the contrast. In other terms, contrast is the relationship between the rate of change in density and the rate of change in exposure.

Automobile lights on a mountain road were recorded with a telephoto lens on a 35-mm camera. (Bill Johnson, Staff Photographer, Denver *Post*)

If density increases rapidly with each exposure change, contrast is high. If density moves up 10 units while exposure, the horizontal factor, is moving across only 8 units, we have a steep grade or slope—high contrast. It could be expressed as a ratio determined by dividing 8 into 10, which would give 1.25. This is, in fact, a measurement of contrast and it is called *gamma*. In mathematical terms gamma is the tangent of the angle formed if the slope of the straight line portion of the curve is extended to meet

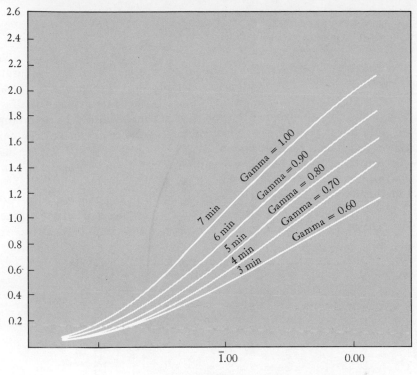

2.6
2.4
2.2
2.0
1.8
1.6
1.4
1.2
1.0
0.8
0.6
0.4
0.2

Gamma = 1.00
Gamma = 0.90
Gamma = 0.80
Gamma = 0.70
Gamma = 0.60

7 min
6 min
5 min
4 min
3 min

1̄.00   0.00

Log Exposure

FIGURE 20
Gamma increases with development time.

the baseline. If the straight-line section of the characteristic curve rises only 8 units while moving (via exposure) 10 units horizontally, gamma would be 0.8.

Exposure range and, to a large extent although not entirely, speed are properties of the emulsion alone. A given emulsion also has a certain inherent contrast, but the contrast in the negative also depends upon development. Development factors that affect contrast (or gamma) are the choice of developer, time, temperature, and agitation during development.

If we increase time, temperature, or agitation, we steepen the straight-line section of the curve—we increase gamma. Certain emulsions can be developed to a much higher gamma than others, and certain developers, notably those with a large proportion of alkali or a strong alkali, produce a higher gamma than others. No matter what film-developer combination is used, however, and no matter how much we may increase time, temperature and agitation, there is a limit to how far we can push contrast. This limit will vary with film and developer, but it is known by the general term of gamma infinity.

141

The practicing photographer, of course, will not have the elaborate equipment necessary for sensitometric testing, but he can use the ideas of sensitometry to control his results. Knowing the interaction of the factors involved, he can confidently expect consistent results if he maintains reasonably strict control over those factors. Equally important, he can confidently predict results when and if he alters those standards; one factor can be changed, usually development time, while others are kept standard, and the results are predictable.

Familiarity with gamma as it is translated into the range of densities in a negative makes it possible to control contrast by consulting a time-gamma curve for the film-developer combination to be employed. A typical

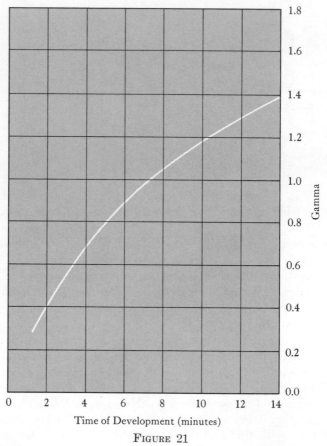

FIGURE 21

Typical time-gamma curve.

time-gamma curve is given in Figure 21. A gamma of 0.8 is probably an average figure for most negatives. A gamma that exceeds one is relatively high.

Beginning photographers are often surprised to see the apparent thinness (general lack of overall density) in the negatives produced by many professionals. This is usually because they have been conditioned by seeing what were really overexposed negatives, that is, negatives that were given significantly more exposure than was really necessary. The professional photographer takes full advantage of the speed of his film, letting shadows fall on the toe of the curve, because he knows that the result will be an easier negative to print for sparkling highlights and it will have less grain and sharper image lines.

The emulsion of a photographic paper responds to light in essentially the same way as the film emulsion does, so characteristic curves can also be drawn for papers. The highlight densities of the negative (ideally kept below the shoulder of the curve) are reproduced on the toe portion of the paper's curve. This means that if the highlights in the negative fall on the shoulder where contrast is compressed, they will be compressed even more on the toe of the paper's curve. The result is cumulative loss of contrast and detail in the highlights, both vitally important for a full-scale, sparkling print. Shadow areas of the negative, on the other hand, although somewhat compressed on the toe of the film's characteristic curve, are helped by the paper because in normal circumstances they fall on the straight-line portion of the paper's characteristic curve, where the contrast is highest.

EXPOSURE METERS

Methods of determining film exposure vary widely from the guess-and-hope system of the weekend snapshooter to the precise and painstaking Zone System of an Ansel Adams. Aids range from exposure charts sometimes printed in camera instruction books or enclosed with data sheets packaged with film to the photoelectric exposure meters. Anyone who takes his photography seriously will sooner or later come to the exposure meter.

Meters measure the light reflected from or incident upon a subject. The photoelectric cell, usually made of selenium, releases an electrical current when struck by light; the stronger the light, the larger the current. A galvanometer measures this current, its pointer indicating an exposure recommendation that the meter's scale translates into shutter speeds and lens apertures, based on the speed of the film being used. The photographer must make the final decision on the particular combination of shutter speed and aperture.

As increasing film speeds made photography possible in situations where the light level was exceptionally low, photographers found their standard selenium photocells too insensitive. Booster (larger) cells were made available, but the real answer came with the development of the cadmium sulfide cell. While selenium cell meters depend upon the tiny current generated when light strikes the cell, CdS meters monitor the current from a battery —the more light, the more current the CdS cell passes. Readings in extremely low light situations are thus possible. And the CdS meters are small, since the cell itself is usually smaller than a dime and the mercury batteries used with them are the size of a button. The battery needs to be replaced only once a year. Built-in meters on recent models of 35-mm cameras are usually of the cadmium sulfide type.

There are two general types of meters: the reflected light meter and the incident light meter. The first measures light reflected from the subject; the second, light falling on the subject.

The incident light meter reads the light falling on the subject and takes no account of the reflection capabilities of the subject; it assumes the subject is a middle gray. Actually, the incident meter is calibrated for an average subject, and for this type of meter, average means a subject that reflects 18 per cent of the incident light. The light-sensitive cell of the incident meter is usually covered by a dome-shaped diffuser, so that it reads all the light from every source on one side of the subject. For accurate measurements it should be used near the subject, not at the camera position, unless lighting on both subject and camera position is obviously the same. Often the lighting at the two positions is not equal, and if the subject position is inaccessible, the incident meter cannot provide an accurate guide to exposure.

Conventional procedure with a reflected light meter simply involves standing at camera position, meter in hand, with meter aimed at the scene to be photographed. Outdoors the meter is generally tilted slightly downward to offset the inflated reading a bright sky background will give. The meter strikes an average from all the light intensities reflected from the scene. It does not matter to the meter whether the subject is a bright snow scene, a gray alley on a dull day, or the dark shadows of a forest. The meter strikes an average; it scans the scene, whatever it may be, and reports only one suggestion, an exposure that would give a middle gray print tone for the average brightness value of the subject. This average, of course, depends upon how much of the scene the meter reads—that is, on its *acceptance angle*. If it reads a wide angle, then it will perhaps include in its average of brightness values a relatively large expanse of sky, or other regions that may not be included in the photograph.

Taking close-up readings is a more accurate method and avoids the chance that reflection from a sky area or from some other exceptionally bright (or dark) area within the meter's acceptance angle may upset the

Sun, fog, a solitary fisherman, and an alert photographer—the result was a $1000 prizewinner in the Annual National Newspaper Snapshot Awards. (Richard M. Tarkington, Lawrenceburg, Tenn.)

average. But with the close-up method the photographer must do the averaging, and this usually means taking a reading of two or more areas of the subject, ranging from important shadows to highlights. If moving in close with the meter is not possible, the substitution method may work. The meter reading can be taken from the photographer's own hand, with the hand held so the light falls on it in the same way as it falls on the intended subject. For close-up readings the meter should be held as close as possible without casting a shadow on the area being scanned.

The exposure meter, whatever its type, cannot know the photographer's purpose. It cannot know, for example, that the photographer's main interest lies in recording detail in a relatively small and dark area and that he has ignored a large and bright background. The photographer must think about what the meter has reported. Each photographer must calibrate his meter to his own use, according to his equipment, his developer, and the type of negative he prefers.

Spot meters make possible accurate readings of small areas of a distant subject that cannot be conveniently approached for close-up measurements. These meters read only a small section of the subject, even when used at a considerable distance, because of their narrow acceptance angles. An example of this type of meter is the excellent Honeywell Pentax 1°/21° Meter. The viewing screen for selecting and locating the subject covers an angle of 21 degrees. In the center of this screen is a circle defining the one-degree angle of acceptance of the cadmium sulfide light-sensitive element. The specific area to be read for exposure is centered in this circle. The 1°/21° meter, like other long-distance, spot-reading meters, is rela-

FIGURE 22

Honeywell Pentax 1°/21° Meter.

tively expensive, but it is ideally suited for use with the so-called Zone
System of photography.

THE ZONE SYSTEM

A reflected light meter held up to any surface will give a reading to
render that surface in the photographic print as a middle gray tone. This
is your clue to a technique for determining exposures that will be something more than approximately correct for you and your equipment.

A superb teacher and photographer, Ansel Adams, years ago developed
a Zone System of exposure determination that has much to offer all photographers. Complete control through the Zone System requires extensive
knowledge and experience but a little more than a nodding acquaintance
with the system can improve those final prints.

By dividing the brightness range of the subject into ten separate zones,
the photographer can use the exposure meter and the darkroom to control
tonal values. He can darken or lighten tones, as he prefers, to emphasize
his interpretation of the subject.

The ten zones are

Zone 0: maximum black; film base density only; total black in the print.
Zone I: still black; no texture.
Zone II: dark gray; some suggestions of texture; the darkest part of the
print in which a hint of detail will appear.
Zone III: dark gray with noticeable detail and texture.
Zone IV: medium dark gray; the average open shadow with full detail and
texture.
Zone V: middle gray; the value of a neutral gray test card.
Zone VI: medium light gray; average skin tone values that are not in
shadow.
Zone VII: light gray.
Zone VIII: texture and some detail.
Zone IX: pure, glaring white; no texture, equal to the white of the paper
stock.

We can relate these zones to relative exposure factors in terms of increased or decreased exposure from the middle value, Zone V.

Zones:	0	I	II	III	IV	V	VI	VII	VIII	IX
Relative										
Exposure:	1/32	1/16	1/8	¼	½	1	2	8	4	16
Relative										
f/stops:	64	45	32	22	16	11	8	5.6	4	2.8

A Zone VI density in the negative image has had twice as much exposure
as a Zone V density; a Zone IV density only half as much as Zone V. Also,

Only backlight will capture the somber beauty of the sand dunes.

one step on the zone scale is equal to one step on the f/number scale (and, of course, on the shutter speed scale as well).

A close-up meter reading indicates an exposure to render the area as Zone V in the image; one stop more exposure puts it in Zone VI; two stops more, Zone VII; three stops more, Zone VIII; four stops more, Zone IX. In the other direction: one stop less exposure than the meter indicates renders the subject area as Zone IV; two stops less, Zone III; three stops less, Zone II; four stops less, Zone I; five stops less, Zone 0 or no effective exposure at all.

Suppose we take a reflected light meter reading of a subject's face and it gives us an exposure of 1/125 of a second at f/16. But we remember that the meter reports on any brightness value it faces so it will be rendered in the print as a middle gray, and middle gray is Zone V. But skin tones are best reported as Zone VI, normally. So we increase exposure to 1/125 at f/11 (or 1/50 at f/16). Thus, we see we can place any brightness value of the subject in any zone. Suppose we read, close up, the exposure for a brightly lighted snowbank. Metered exposure is 1/250 at f/32 —middle gray, Zone V. But we want to render the snow in the print as white with texture and some detail: Zone VIII. So we increase exposure three stops: 1/125 at f/16. An example with a shadow area: meter reading

1/125 at $f/8$ for middle gray, Zone V. We want the shadow area on Zone III. Correct exposure: 1/125 at $f/16$.

All of the above assumes an established normal development, which must be based on film and developer being used to establish that one-stop, one-zone relationship. For full control of the Zone System the photographer must also establish standards for abnormal development that can move a brightness value in the subject either up or down on the print zone scale. This is possible because variations in developing time change the densities of the low values (Zones 0 to III) very little, the middle values (IV to VI) somewhat, and the high values (VII to IX) radically. An increased development time boosts a Zone VI to VII or even VIII. A decrease in development time drops a Zone IX subject brightness down to a Zone VIII or VII in the print. Exposure controls the placement of the low values; exposure plus development controls the placement of the high values. This is the same as the old photographic adage: "Expose for the shadows; develop for the highlights."

An example of the application of this technique: A meter reading of a shadow area indicates an exposure of 1/125 at $f/8$. We close down two stops to place the shadow in Zone III (1/125 at $f/16$). But a reading of the skin tones in direct light indicates an exposure of 1/125 at $f/11$ (Zone V). We would like the skin tones rendered as Zone VI. If we increase exposure to 1/125 at $f/8$ to accomplish this, our shadow area would then fall in Zone V. So we expose the shadow where we want it, Zone III (1/125 at $f/16$), but increase development time to boost density of the skin tone image to Zone VI. Or we can print on a higher contrast paper.

With a high-contrast subject, keeping both shadow and highlight detail within the range of the printing paper's limited scale may pose a problem. Again the indicated solution is to expose for the darkest important shadow area to place it on the appropriate zone, then reduce development time to keep important highlight areas from slipping above VIII. Only testing with a particular film and developer combination can produce the precise development time needed. Or the two-bath development technique explained in Chapter 3 may be used.

Determination of normal and abnormal development times must be done by testing with a particular film and developer. Testing may begin at the recommended developing time, then variations can be tried on the order of 50, 70, 125, and 150 per cent of the recommended time.

The Zone System can produce either literal interpretation of subject brightness values or tonal distortion to emphasize the photographer's personal view of the subject. Shadows can be produced as any shade of gray or black and highlights as light gray or white.

Chapter 9

LIGHTING WITH FLOOD AND FLASH

Outdoors the photographer must take the lighting as he finds it. He can exercise some control by maneuvering his camera position, by using reflecting surfaces, or by adding light from a flash. But the main source of light is beyond his direct control. When he moves indoors the situation changes radically; here the light is often that supplied by and completely controlled by the photographer.

Indoor lighting control demands familiarity with only a few simple lighting tools: the spotlight, which gives a hard and relatively narrow beam; the floodlight, which gives a broad, soft, and general beam; flash, of various kinds and dimensions, and reflectors, white or aluminized boards specifically designed for photographic use, or white paper, cardboard, cloth, a light-colored wall or ceiling, or board covered with aluminum foil.

The effect of any direct light source (not including reflectors) is controlled by

1. Varying the angle at which the rays of light strike the subject by raising or lowering the light source.
2. Varying the position of the light source, so it shines from in front of the subject, from behind, or from any point in between.
3. Varying the distance between the light source and the subject.

These are the most common controls; others may be available in studios with extensive lighting equipment. These additional controls may include varying the power of one or more lamps, filtering the light with diffusion screens or color filters, or modulating the light with various shields or shades.

Any single light source can provide any one of the following six basic forms of illumination on the subject.

1. Front lighting is flat and relatively shadowless; that is, the shadows are not visible, or at least only partially visible, from the camera position. A subject with roundness or volume will appear to be flattened out by front lighting; it no longer seems to occupy space of its own but seems merely to be a rather flat shape plastered to the background.

2. Side lighting tends to make features stand out by casting shadows visible from the camera position. The subject seems to gain volume or roundness under side lighting, takes on more of an identity separate from the background.

3. Top lighting tends to give the same result as side lighting, emphasizing projecting features and depressions, but it is an unusual, and thus unnatural, form of lighting.

4. Lighting from below, seldom encountered under normal circumstances and also unnatural in a photograph, casts shadows upward and projecting features are brightly lighted on the underside, while the upper surfaces are in shadow. It sometimes can be used for dramatic effect in photography, perhaps to add to the hobgoblin effect of a Halloween picture.

5. Back lighting casts shadows toward the observer, or the camera, and provides a rim of light about the subject.

6. Diffuse lighting is indirect or reflected light. The lamp is aimed, not at the subject, but usually at the ceiling, sometimes at a wall or at the intersection of wall and ceiling. This gives a soft diffused light, often a more natural-looking light than direct lighting methods.

THE FIVE FUNCTIONS OF LIGHTS

Lighting effects are produced primarily by the placement of the lights. There is virtually no limit to the number of lights that can be used, and if three or a half-dozen lights are employed, then the arrangements possible are infinite. However, learning to control the lighting arrangement is not so difficult as it may seem, because there are really only five functions that any one light source can fulfill.

1. The key light.   In this case the lamp is being used as the principal source of illumination; it dominates all others that may be employed. It casts the most important shadows; it is this light that holds the picture together. If the key light does not dominate, there are likely to be conflicting shadows, resulting in a confusing and incoherent picture.

2. The fill light.   This lamp is placed to open up or fill in the shadows cast by the key light. The intention is not to eliminate these shadows but merely to throw enough light into them so that detail in the shadows can be readily recorded on the film. Although the shadows cast by the key light appear to the photographer's eye to have detail, in fact they very likely will be black and without detail as far as the film is concerned. But the fill light must cast no shadows of its own. The fill light will do its job properly if it is positioned at or near the camera and on the opposite side of the camera from the key light.

3. The accent light.   This lamp is placed to provide distinctive highlights, such as a rim or halo about the subject's head, or to put highlights on the hair, cheek or forehead. This lamp adds extra sparkle and brilliance to the finished print. A frequently used accent light is one placed behind the subject and aimed at the camera; a bare bulb (one without reflector) placed behind the subject often serves this purpose and at the same time illuminates the background; a reflector, perhaps a mirror, can also be used for accent if placed on the side of the subject opposite the key light.

4. *The background light.* This lamp creates tonal contrast between background and subject and is aimed at the background, usually from a position behind or to one side of the subject.

5. *The bounce light.* In this case the lamp is used as an indirect source of illumination, with its rays bounced off any convenient reflecting surface. This means ceiling or walls of a room or a reflector board, if the photographer has such among his equipment. Effective bounce light demands a light-colored surface; dark walls and ceilings absorb too much of the light. The light, of course, is colored by the hue of the reflecting surface, a factor of importance in color photography.

With the five functions of light sources known, it becomes possible to work out lighting arrangements to meet all situations. The authors do not advocate slavish adherence to a standardized arrangement of lights, but a knowledge of the standard can provide a point of departure for individual expression in the language of lighting.

Lights are generally arranged to produce either modeling or texture. Modeling light, intended for people, solid objects or three-dimensional subjects, is designed to convey depth and roundness. This is accomplished by lighting one side of the subject, leaving the other side in shadow with a gradual transition from light to shadow. This creates places of differing tone values in which the nearer parts of the subject contrast with those farther away.

Light that appears to be most natural generally shines downward on the subject. This indicates that the first step in designing a basic lighting setup should be placement of the key light on a plane higher than the subject. We have already seen that side lighting provides modeling by casting shadows visible from the camera position, so a key light position to one side of the subject is also indicated.

We place the first light, what we plan to be our key light, at about a 45-degree angle to the front and about three or four feet above the subject. Exact positioning should be determined by the appearance of the subject under the light and not by any rule of thumb. The angle at which the light rays descend on the subject depends to some extent upon how far the light is away from the subject. Approximately two thirds of the subject is in the direct rays of the key light, the rest in shadow. We must lighten the shadow area so that the film can record some detail there. To do this we add the fill light, placed near the camera but on the opposite side of the camera from the key light. The fill light must be of less intensity than the key light, be farther away than the key light, or be covered by a dif-

Flash made it possible to catch this revealing moment and win a $1000 prize in the Annual Newspaper National Snapshot Awards. (Charles M. Mason, Lockland, Ohio)

fusion screen (one layer of white handkerchief will do in an emergency) to avoid eliminating the key light's shadows.

Next we plan, if necessary, for lighting the background. There are no rigid rules for this. The background may be lighter or darker in tone than the subject. The purpose is to achieve a separation between subject and background in the print.

These three lights may be enough, or we can add to the illusion of volume or roundness in the subject by back lighting. In this case the direct rays of the light placed behind the subject and aimed toward the camera must be blocked from reaching the lens. The backlight gives a more pronounced feeling that the subject is occupying space of its own, separate from the background.

Or another sort of accent light may be used: a spotlight aimed down at the subject from the side opposite the key light, to add the sparkle of highlights.

All sorts of variations are possible from this standard lighting arrangement, including such extremes as profile lighting (a strong light placed to illuminate just one half of the subject's face, leaving the other side in a shadow that can be filled in or left dark). Or silhouette lighting, generally best achieved with a strong backlight diffused through a screen such as an uncreased white sheet.

If an important aspect of the subject involves texture, then strong side

More than one flash lamp was used to give lighting in depth. (Duane Howell, Staff Photographer, Denver *Post*)

lighting is required. Light must strike the surface at such an acute angle, literally skimming the surface, that even tiny projections will be brilliantly lighted on one side and cast strong shadows on the other. How strong the light and how acute the angle will depend upon the desired effect with each textured surface.

FLOOD LAMPS

The best way to learn to control light is to begin with flood lamps, which are nothing more than ordinary incandescent lamps putting out a more than ordinary amount of light because they burn under an electrical overload. Since their filaments burn at an unusually high rate, flood lamps have only a fraction of the life of ordinary lamps.

The most common types of flood lamps for still photography are the 250-watt or No. 1 lamp, the 500-watt or No. 2 lamp (both for use in reflectors), and the reflector floods, which have their own built-in reflectors, available in broad-beam and medium-beam floods and spots. Wattage is generally 500 for the broad beams and spots, 375 for medium beams. Flood lamps also come in two color temperature ratings, 3400° K for Type A color films and 3200° K for Type B color film. The 3200° K lamps last

154

much longer but give a bit less light. Either can be used with black-and-white film. (Color temperature is explained in the discussion of flash bulbs.)

No more than three 500-watt lamps should be used on the usual electrical circuit. The number of lights that can safely be used on a single circuit can be determined by multiplying the voltage by the amperage of the fuse. For example, 110 volts times 15 amps, the usual fuse on a home circuit, equals 1,650 watts.

Exposure with floodlights should be determined with exposure meter readings. If a meter is not available, refer to the guide number chart printed on the carton in which the floodlights were packed.

FLASH: BULB AND ELECTRONIC

Flash, the most practical of artificial light sources for photography today, has made picture-taking possible and relatively simple in almost any situation. But it was not always thus. As recently as the early 1930's flash photography was regarded, quite justifiably, as a risky undertaking, for it meant taking pictures with magnesium powder bonfires. A press photographer sprinkled one to three teaspoons of this explosive powder into a long, narrow pan. Then, with considerable perturbation, he held this pan overhead with one hand while he steadied his camera, usually a large and heavy Graphic or Graflex, with the other. He pressed a release on the flash-pan handle to fire a powder cap, igniting the magnesium, and to compress, simultaneously, the air in a rubber tube leading to the camera's shutter. The air pressure tripped the shutter as the powder exploded. If he worked quickly, the photographer could reload both flash-pan and camera in time to get off a second shot before the smoke from the first drifted down to obscure the subject—assuming the subject was intrepid enough to stay around for a second performance. Often, for these indoor pioneer flash pictures, the photographer took with him as principal assistant a fireman who stood by with extinguisher in hand, which was needed often enough to make this a wise precaution.

Today firemen can attend to more conventional duties while photographers carry with them safe and easily portable supplies of light, instantly employed and precisely controlled. The photographer has his choice of two forms of packaged flash: the conventional and expendable flash bulbs or the reusable but initially more expensive electronic flash.

FLASH BULBS

The conventional flash bulbs, some relatively large but many no larger than a fair-sized peanut, contain a wire filament covered with an explosive primer paste. The rest of the interior of the bulb is loosely filled with aluminum or zirconium wire or foil, surrounded by an atmosphere of oxygen at reduced pressure. An electrical current moving through the filament heats up and ignites the explosive primer, which in turn ignites the metal wire or foil, and it is the rapid, controlled burning of this metal bonfire that gives the picture-taking light, a short but intense flash. Bulbs are also made that do not contain the metal, but only an extra amount of the primer paste; with these it is the burning of the paste that provides the light.

The outer glass surface of all flash bulbs is coated with a layer of lacquer, sometimes a pale blue and sometimes clear, to prevent a shattering explosion of the glass. The bulbs with the blue coating are intended for use with color film. The blue coating raises the *color temperature* of the light to match daylight color film.

The color of a light source varies with its temperature. An incandescent lamp is luminous because it is hot, and the hotter it is, the whiter is the light. An iron poker placed in a fire first of all becomes dull red in color; then, as it gets hotter, it becomes a brighter red, then yellow, and finally, as it approaches the melting point, white. To say that something is white-hot is to indicate a higher temperature than red-hot. When a perfect black-body radiator, one that does not reflect any light falling on it, is white-hot, it is emitting appreciable amounts of all the visible radiations of the spectrum. Color temperature, then, is a measure of the whiteness of the light from a luminous source, but this is temperature based on the absolute scale, a scale that begins at –273° C (absolute zero). Temperature on this scale is expressed in degrees Kelvin (K), after the British physicist, Lord Kelvin. Thus 0° C is 273° K and 100° C is 373° K.

Color films are balanced for a particular quality or color of light, so the color temperature of light sources used with these films becomes of great importance. To the eye, sunlight and light from electric lamps seem the same, white, but their color quality is actually quite different. The color temperature of daylight is approximately 6500° K, depending upon the proportion of direct sunlight and reflected skylight; light reflected from the blue north sky can be 10,000° to 18,000° K. The color temperature of an incandescent electric bulb will be about 2800° K.

The color temperature of most clear flash bulbs is approximately 3800° K. This relatively low color temperature means the light is rich in yellow and red rays. The blue-coated bulbs have an approximate color temperature of 6000° K. The blue coating filters out some of the red and yellow rays, leaving an energy distribution with a higher proportion of blue rays; thus the light is whiter. These blue-coated bulbs, then, are designed for use with color films balanced for the average color temperature of daylight.

Flash bulbs are also rated according to their light output, measured in

Flash and good timing on the shutter finger caught the right moment.

lumen seconds. A lumen is a unit of light or luminous power, and the quantity of light in lumen seconds is the power of the source multiplied by the duration in seconds. A standard 100-watt light bulb produces approximately 2,000 lumens in one second. Flash bulbs produce 4,000 to 100,000 lumen seconds in a time period that lasts, usually, less than 1/25 of a second. Small (AG-1 and M2) flash bulbs produce approximately 7,000 lumen seconds (4,000 to 6,000 if blue-coated). No. 5 and 25 bulbs produce about 20,000 lumen seconds (9,000 if blue-coated), and larger bulbs produce from 33,000 to 100,000 lumen seconds.

Flash bulbs, like any bonfire, gradually build to a peak light output and then fall off to zero again. Since they vary in the time required to build to peak, bulbs can be classified on this basis as well. There are fast peak, medium peak, and slow peak bulbs—F, M, and S for short. F bulbs (those containing no metal wire or foil) peak in about 5 milliseconds. (A millisecond is 1/1000 of a second.) M bulbs peak in 15 to 20 milliseconds, and S bulbs in about 30 milliseconds. An additional classification is the FP (or flat peak) bulb, designed for use with the focal-plane shutter; it reaches peak output in approximately 20 milliseconds and holds that peak for 20 to 50 milliseconds, to give the focal-plane shutter time to move across the film.

ELECTRONIC FLASH

In 1851 a British pioneer in photography, William Henry Fox-Talbot, received a patent for the use of a high-speed electrical spark as a photographic light source. He had demonstrated his device by taking a picture of a London newspaper. Not a particularly remarkable achievement, even in those pioneer days of photography, except that the page from the newspaper was whirling rapidly at the time the picture was taken. The picture showed the printing unblurred; it was sharp and clear. This was in the day when exposures were made by removing a cap from the front of the lens and then replacing it after an estimated or counted exposure period. Fox-Talbot had made his picture of the spinning newspaper by using an electric spark as his light source. The duration of the light from the spark was so brief that the movement of the image on the film was insignificant. This was the first electronic flash.

Taking pictures by the light of a spark did not become an everyday occurrence in the nineteenth century, since it was a cumbersome method. It involved an electrical generator cranked by hand to build up a large charge of static electricity stored in a series of Leyden jars. Two wires connected to the Leyden jars led to an open-air spark gap. When the electrical circuit was closed, the electricity jumped the gap and the resulting spark, like a flash of lightning, lasted for only a tiny fraction of a second.

In the twentieth century, in the 1930's a Massachusetts Institute of Technology professor, Dr. Harold E. Edgerton, perfected some significant improvements on the Leyden jar-spark technique. In place of the muscle-tiring hand-cranked generator he used alternating current. The Leyden jars were replaced by modern electrical capacitors (devices that hold or store an electrical charge, also called condensers). The open-air spark gap was replaced by a glass tube filled with one of the rare inert gases, usually xenon.

The typical electronic flash unit, patterned after the system developed by Dr. Edgerton, includes five fundamental parts:

1) A power supply that provides the electrical energy for

2) one or more electrical storage capacitors, which hoard this energy until

3) a triggering circuit, activated by the camera shutter, spills all the stored power through

4) a gas-filled flashtube, which converts the electrical energy into light, which

5) a reflector directs toward the subject.

The stored charge flashing through the gas-filled tube gives a powerful blast of light for a small fraction of a second. The duration of the light pulse is usually taken as the time required for the light to rise from one third of peak value to peak and then to fall again to one third of peak. Most portable electronic flash units, the most popular for today's photography, give a flash duration somewhere between 1/500 and 1/2000 of a second. This is the same as a shutter speed in the same range, as long as the existing light at the photographed scene is not intense enough at the film plane to create an image-forming reaction with the silver halides in the emulsion. This, in fact, is one of the major advantages of electronic flash: it allows the photographer to take pictures of high-speed action, sports events, without worrying about high shutter speeds. He must only make sure that he has used a shutter speed fast enough to prevent any ghost image from being formed by the existing light. This usually means a shutter speed of the order of 1/200 of a second.

Electronic flash has other advantages. Each flash tube will last for 10,000 or more flashes; there is no need to replace a bulb after each picture. Batteries used with the unit need to be replaced or recharged occasionally, of course. A small C cell unit like Futuramic gives from 60 to 200 flashes before the batteries are exhausted. A medium-power wet cell or nickel cadmium unit delivers 80 or more flashes before needing recharging. High-voltage dry cell units usually deliver 500 to 1,000 flashes before exhaustion. Units that use alternating current—that is, units that can be plugged into a wall socket—last indefinitely, and some units can be used with either batteries or A.C. source. Some, too, can be plugged into an A.C. source periodically for recharging the batteries and thus will last for extensive periods.

Operating cost for each electronic flash picture is only about 1/10 of a cent, although, of course, initial investment cost is relatively high.

Electronic flash is ideal for use as a shadow fill light for outdoor shots, and the color quality of the light, ranging in the most popular units from 5800° K to 6500° K, is very close to that of daylight, an important factor in color photography.

Electronic flash is also easy on the eyes of the photographic subject, since the very brief duration of the flash does not have the same blinding effect as the conventional flash bulb; this makes it especially desirable for sports photography—in fact, many athletic groups prohibit all but electronic flash.

After each firing the electronic flash unit needs a brief period to recharge the capacitors. This is usually referred to as the recycling time and it can vary with the most popular units from 4 to 12 seconds. Most units are equipped with indicator lamps, which flash on when the charge has reached about 80 per cent of full capacity.

SYNCHRONIZATION

Since bulb and electronic flash supply an intense but brief illumination, some method must be provided to ensure that the shutter of the camera is open while the flash is at its peak. This is called synchronization. Synchronization depends, first of all, upon the type of shutter involved: front (at the lens) leaf shutter, or back (focal-plane) shutter.

A front shutter takes somewhere between two and four milliseconds to open and about the same time to close. For a shutter speed of 1/100 of a

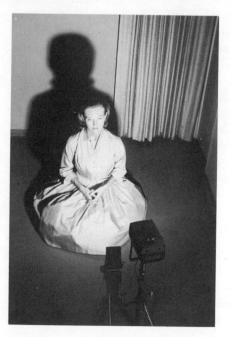

This series of pictures, made by the authors on Panatomic-X film exposed at an index of 100 and developed in Selectol Soft, illustrates lighting with multiple flash units. The lights used were No. 52 Honeywell Modeling slave units. Photos of the studio were taken with a Pentax fitted with the 28-mm lens and connected to a Strobonar 65D electronic flash. This flash was bounced from the ceiling to trip the slave lights in the studio. Each portrait was taken with the Rolleiflex camera shown in the studio pictures. This first photo shows the least desirable lighting: one flash attached to or close to the camera. Results are flat and lack modeling.

When only one flash is used, best results are obtained by holding the flash unit at arm's length to the side and above or straight above the camera, depending on the attitude of the subject. This avoids the flat look, puts in some shadows, and adds a bit of modeling.

Bounce flash—here bounced off a wall, although usually it is bounced off the ceiling. Exposure must be increased two to four stops, depending on distance from light to reflecting surface to subject and on ability of the surface to reflect light. Bounce gives softer lighting, with shadows and modeling.

Two lights—for additional modeling and accents. The subject has here been caught at the intersection of the line of sight from the camera and the line between the key light and the accent or back light. This technique gives us an accent rim light but leaves harsh shadows.

Three lights—adding a third light, a shadow fill light, to the left and slightly behind the camera. This is a typical setup for triangular lighting. Note we still have the highlights from the accent light but shadows thrown by the key light are now soft and natural.

Four lights—a decision must be made by the photographer. If he has four lights available, he must decide whether to use the fourth on the background or as another accent or back rim light. Here we have used the fourth light on the background to lighten its tone and subdue shadows.

Five lights—the background light used again in this setup. But a fifth light has been added as an accent light to rim the right side of the model's head. There are many variations of these lighting setups, of course. Frequently the accent lights are spot lights.

second the blades are fully open for a total time of about eight milliseconds. This means the shutter starts to close in 12 milliseconds (or less) and will be fully closed in 16 milliseconds. But the common M bulbs need 15 milliseconds or more to reach peak light output. This discrepancy between shutter and flash peak is even more pronounced at higher shutter speeds.

If we could be content to take all flash pictures at slow shutter speeds, say at 1/30 of a second, we could start flash bulb and shutter at the same time. At 1/30 of a second the shutter is open for nearly 40 milliseconds; in that time the bulb has reached peak and started to fade. But we usually prefer higher shutter-speeds, so we must give the bonfire in the bulb a head start if peak light output is to match the fully open shutter. This is the purpose of the synchronization settings on the camera.

The camera with a leaf shutter often gives a choice of synchronization settings. A setting marked X is intended primarily for electronic flash, which peaks in less than one millisecond. In this case the starting of the flash may be delayed, instead of the opening of the shutter. In fact, in cameras set for electronic or X synchronization, it is customary to have the electrical contact for firing the flash made only when the shutter blades reach the fully open position.

Some leaf shutters have an F setting for the fast peak bulbs; the opening of the shutter is delayed only two or three milliseconds after the flash bulb is ignited. And F peak bulbs can be used on the X setting at shutter speeds of 1/100 of a second or slower.

The M setting on the shutter is designed for the medium-peak bulbs. The electrical contact to fire the bulb is made first and after a predetermined delay, established through a gear-train or springs or through an electrical solenoid magnet, the shutter opens. On some cameras this delay period is variable to allow for synchronization at various shutter speeds.

With the focal-plane shutter, synchronization has different dimensions. This shutter has a slit that travels across the film. The slit, for example, may be set to expose each point on the film for 1/200 of a second, but it may take 1/50 of a second to travel completely across the film. The focal-plane shutter used in small cameras is usually the self-capping type; it automatically caps or closes the slit after an exposure so that there will be no exposure when the shutter is recocked, pulling the curtain back across the film. The shutter consists of two separate curtains, actually, and gives a range of high speeds and a range of low speeds. When the shutter is fired at a high speed, the first curtain starts to rush across the film gate. A short interval later the second curtain follows so that an open slit crosses the film. At slow shutter speeds, however, the first curtain flips across the film gate to uncover the entire negative area before the second shutter even starts. After a time interval established by the shutter setting, the second curtain makes its trip to close the shutter and end the exposure.

This means, then, all flash bulbs, and electronic flash as well, work with the focal-plane shutter at slow shutter speeds (1/50 of a second or slower). With higher shutter speeds, however, the normal flash bulbs give uneven illumination on the film, and electronic flash, with perhaps a flash duration of only 1/1000 of a second, exposes only that small part of the negative that happened to be uncovered during that 1/1000 of a second.

This is the reason for the FP bulbs, which give a relatively even illumination for the entire period of the focal-plane shutter's travel across the film. However, we should note again that other flash bulbs and electronic flash can be used with the focal-plane shutter at the slow range of shutter speeds. Also, the midget bulbs, such as the AG-1 and the M3, work at some of the higher focal-plane shutter speeds because they give a relatively flat peak.

EXPOSURE WITH FLASH

Distance between flash and subject is the critical factor in flash exposure. The amount of light falling on the subject is inversely proportional to the square of the distance. A flash bulb six feet from the subject puts twice as much light on the subject as the same bulb at eight and one half feet, or four times as much light as the same bulb at 12 feet. To simplify exposure determination, manufacturers of films and flash equipment publish *guide numbers,* which have been calculated by a formula developed by the American Standards Association. This formula takes into account the lamp's effective light output at a particular shutter speed, the speed of the film, and the reflector factor. The reflector factor depends upon the shape and surface (polished or satin finish) of the reflector and the size of the flash bulb.

The appropriate guide number is determined by consulting a chart furnished with flash bulbs, with film, or with the flash equipment. The photographer must know the speed of his film and usually must decide upon a shutter speed. With these two elements known he can find the appropriate guide number from the chart. Dividing distance in feet from flash lamp to subject into the guide number then gives him the f/number.

It is important to remember, however, that guide numbers are strictly that—merely guides. Variations in equipment, development, photographers, and subjects cannot be allowed for in the general formula. The numbers are intended for average indoor subjects, in an average size room, with light-colored walls and ceiling. If the room is small with surfaces that will reflect a lot of the light, one or perhaps even two stops less exposure should be used than the guide number indicates. If the room is large, such as an auditorium, you can expect little help on exposure from light reflected by walls and ceiling. Correct exposure is probably at least one stop

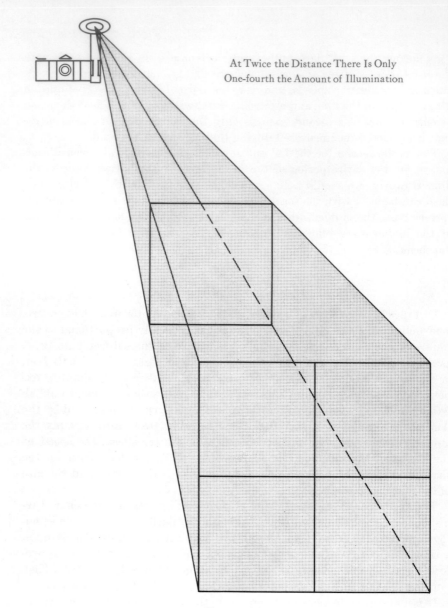

At Twice the Distance There Is Only
One-fourth the Amount of Illumination

FIGURE 23

The inverse square law.

more than that indicated by the guide number. Open up at least one stop, too, when shooting with flash outdoors at night.

To allow for the variations in your own equipment, it is wise to make a series of test exposures with a particular flash bulb or electronic flash unit at the shutter speed you will use most often. The subject should be 10 feet from the flash lamp, and the distance must be measured carefully. Then make a series of exposures of the same subject at half-stop or full-stop intervals. Half-stop intervals are recommended for color film, full-stop intervals for black-and-white film. Process normally and select the negative or transparency that represents the best exposure. Your own personal guide number for that film and shutter speed is then the product of the lamp-to-subject distance times the f/number used for this best exposure. A card marked with the f/number used can be included in each shot for easy identification. The time and film expended on such a test will return dividends in later correctly exposed flash pictures.

Consistent underexposure with flash may be the result of any one of a number of factors, or of a combination of these factors. With conventional flash bulbs the most common cause of failure is weak batteries. Or synchronization may be faulty because of equipment or photographer failure. Often the photographer fails to recognize the synchronization demands of the particular bulb he is using. The first check involves making certain bulb and camera synchronization setting are compatible. Flash failure may also result from poor contacts in the circuit. The bulb base and connections between camera and flashgun must all make close contact. Circuit breaks can also result if the cord between camera and gun is frayed and cracked.

The light output of electronic flash units and thus exposure calculation with them depends upon several factors. A common unit of measurement for electronic flash is the watt-second, a measure of the energy stored in the capacitors. Ratings vary from 35 watt-seconds to 200 watt-seconds for the popular portable units and from 200 to 60,000 watt-seconds for large, studio lights. But the watt-seconds rating does not give an accurate measurement of effective light output. Light output varies not only with the watt-seconds of energy applied to the flash tube, but also with the efficiency of the tube, with the efficiency of the reflector, with the distribution of the light from the reflector, and with the number of flash heads fired from a single power source. To provide a guide number for an electronic flash unit, the manufacturer usually provides a measurement of the useful light output in effective candlepower seconds (ECPS). Then,

$$\text{Guide Number} = \sqrt{0.063 \times \text{ECPS} \times \text{film speed}}$$

But, again, the photographer must regard any guide number only as a starting point until he has completed a series of tests.

Guide numbers for electronic flash remain constant for shutter speeds ranging from open flash to 1/25 of a second through 1/500 of a second, because the duration of the flash is less than the shutter speed.

APPROXIMATE GUIDE NUMBERS
For Portable Electronic Flash Units *

Output of Unit in Effective Candlepower Seconds

Film Speed	350	500	700	1,000	1,400	2,000	2,800	4,000
25	24	30	35	40	45	55	65	80
40	30	35	40	50	60	70	85	100
125	50	60	75	90	100	120	150	180
160	60	70	85	100	120	140	170	200
200	75	90	100	120	150	180	210	250
400	95	110	130	160	190	220	270	320

* This table is intended as a starting point for determining correct guide numbers with specific equipment.

FLASH TECHNIQUE

The general principles outlined at the beginning of this chapter apply to lighting with flash. Subjects may be illuminated with a single flash lamp or with several, and the effect of each depends upon its placement in relation to the subject. Practice and experimentation with floods will provide invaluable background for anticipating results with flash, although flash lighting is more intense and builds greater contrasts in the image.

SINGLE BULB TECHNIQUE

Single flash at the camera, *on-camera* flash, is the simplest method of making flash pictures. But this tends to produce flat lighting with no modeling effect; the roundness or volume of the subject is de-emphasized. There are no shadows to create depth and texture. The only shadows visible in such a picture are usually on a wall or other background, and often this results in tone mergers that make it impossible to tell where the image of the subject ends and the shadow begins. If the picture must be taken with on-camera flash, the subject should be more than three feet and less than six feet from the background, whenever possible. This will give enough room for the shadow to fall away to the rear, where it is hidden from the lens, but the background will not be so grossly underexposed as to place the subject in black and cavelike surroundings in the final print.

Significant improvement in picture quality in flash pictures comes from a simple rule: use *off-camera* flash whenever possible. If the equipment in use permits, the flashgun is removed from the bracket holding it to the camera. The lamp is then held at the end of its cord, or as high as the photographer can reach above the camera, and pointed down at the subject. Camera must be held in one hand and flashgun in the other. This position for the flash, high and off a foot or two to one side or the other of

One flash bulb was used off to the camera's right, and high. No light at the camera.
(Robert Rhode, Boulder, Colo.)

the lens, will eliminate the flat, washed-out lighting of on-camera flash. Shadows appear on the subject's face to add roundness or the third dimension. Black shadows on the background drop much lower and are usually well hidden. The subject stands out from the background, occupying space of its own, instead of appearing to be a flat cutout plastered on that background.

On a longer extension cord a single lamp off camera can provide believable simulation of natural lighting. A bulb placed so that it is hidden from direct camera view in fireplace or near a campfire produces a realistic imitation of firelight; or a flash bulb fired from a position near a normal indoor lighting fixture, perhaps hidden in a lampshade, simulates the light from that fixture. Remember: placement of the light is all-important in achieving desired effects, and exposure must be based on lamp-to-subject distance, not on camera-to-subject distance.

In placing any flash lamp, watch for mirrors, windows, enameled walls, eyeglasses, or other shiny surfaces that may bounce the light into the camera lens. This is specular reflection and can be avoided simply by remembering that angle of reflection will equal angle of incidence.

Soft, diffused lighting for pictures that look very much as though they were taken with natural indoor lighting can be achieved with either *bounce* flash or *bare-bulb* flash. With bounce flash the light is aimed at a reflecting surface, usually the ceiling or a nearby wall. The resulting diffused light creates natural-looking highlights and open shadows with printable detail. Bare-bulb flash gives much the same effect if the bulb is placed high and away from the camera. This technique simply involves firing the bulb without a reflector.

Exposure must be recalculated with either bounce or bare-bulb technique because in both cases the light is not concentrated on the subject. This means much of the light is lost, so exposure must be increased. How much to increase exposure depends upon the size of the room and the color of the walls and ceiling. For bounce, exposure can be estimated on the distance from flash to reflecting surface to subject. Divide this total distance into the guide number for a basic f/number, then open up one more stop to compensate for the light absorbed and scattered by the ceiling or other reflecting surface. In general, a bounce shot requires two full stops more exposure than direct flash. If the ceiling is high, 12 feet or more, or dark in color, the lens should be opened one additional stop. High, dark ceilings, however, do not generally provide enough reflection for effective bounce flash. For bare-bulb flash the same rule of thumb applies: open up at least two stops more than the indicated exposure for lighting with a reflector— more if the room is large, perhaps less if the room is small with many bright, reflecting surfaces.

In some cases, for bounce flash, you may be able to measure the proportion of the light the reflecting surface will absorb. Take an exposure meter reading with the meter pointed toward the room light and then a second reading with the meter pointed toward the reflecting surface. If the meter drops a stop or a stop and a half, that is the amount to open up.

Whenever the flash bulb is placed close (less than six feet) to a person who will not be shielded by the reflector or some other protector, always place a clear plastic shield over the flash bulb. There is always the one chance in a thousand that the bulb will explode.

Because the light falls off at twice the rate of the increase in distance, it is difficult to light a subject of depth, such as a row of persons or a crowd, with a single flash. Subjects close to the light receive a disproportionately high share of the illumination. If exposure is based on the distance to the closest person, the image of the farthest will be underexposed; if exposure is based on the distance to the farthest person, the image of the closest will be grossly overexposed, and probably unprintable. Recommended procedure in such a situation involves removing the flashgun from the camera, holding it high and aimed at the farthest subject. Calculate exposure for the distant subject. Let spill light from the edge of the reflector illuminate the close subject. It may also be possible to bounce the flash off the ceiling to cover a large area evenly.

MULTIPLE FLASH TECHNIQUE

Better pictures can usually be made with more than one flash lamp, either bulb or electronic. Multiple flash permits application of the basic principles outlined earlier in this chapter; modeling can be improved, contrast reduced, texture emphasized, pleasing highlights created with accent lights.

The basic setup includes two lamps: one high and to one side of the subject and the other on the opposite side of and near the camera. The first is the key light on which exposure is based, and the second is a shadow-fill light. The key light must put more illumination on the subject than the fill light. The balance of the light intensity from the two lamps can be controlled in several ways: by using different sized bulbs, by diffusing the light from the fill lamp, or by putting the key light closer to the subject.

Generally it is easier to use the same size of bulb in both lamps; then if the two lamps are the same distance from the subject, one layer of clean, white handkerchief over the fill light will cut its intensity about one-half, giving a lighting ratio between key and fill lights of approximately 2 to 1. You can check this with the handkerchief or other white cloth you intend to use as a diffusing screen. Simply take a meter reading of an outdoor scene through a clear glass window, with the meter held close to the inside surface of the window. Then read the same through the handkerchief flattened against the glass. Compare; if the first reading is $f/11$ and the second (through the handkerchief) is $f/8$, the handkerchief will cut the light from the flash by one half.

Light ratio is also easily controlled with the same size of lamp by simply placing the key light closer to the subject than the fill light. Remembering the rule that the light intensity is inversely proportional to the square of the distance, then, if the key light is at six feet and the fill light at 12 feet, the lighting ratio is 4:1; key light at six feet and fill light at 10 feet, lighting ratio is 3:1; key light at six feet and fill light at eight and one-half feet, lighting ratio is 2:1.

A small amount of fill light can be obtained if the photographer holds the flashgun out in front at arm's length and aimed back at his own white shirt front; this will give about one eighth the light he would get aiming the flash directly at the subject.

More flash units can be added to the basic setup to give background

Four Strobonar electronic flash units were used to light the picture shown at the top. All four lights are visible in the bottom picture, taken to show the lighting setup. The Pentax camera that took the top picture is also shown in the bottom picture. It is on a tripod near the bottom left, just underneath the paper flower decoration near the center of the window. (Floyd McCall, Denver)

lighting or highlight accents or to balance the illumination on close and distant areas of a subject in depth. The variations are infinite and can only be hinted at in a brief outline of techniques.

Multiple flash requires lamps on extension cords plugged into the flash-gun at the camera or *slave* units. Extensions put an extra load on the bat-teries, which must be fresh or synchronization failures are likely. Slaves are self-contained flash units not connected to the camera's flashgun by wires. An electric eye built into the slave unit reads the flash at the camera and trips the slave flash. This takes place very quickly, but some delay is involved with conventional flash bulbs. It is best to use shutter speeds on the order of 1/30 of a second, to be sure the shutter will still be open to catch the peak of all slave unit bulbs. With electronic flash at camera and in slave units, leaf shutter speeds of 1/200 of a second or faster are en-tirely feasible because electronic flash peaks in less than one millisecond.

Exposure calculation with multiple flash is usually no different than with a single flash lamp aimed at the subject. Exposure is still based on the distance (in feet), between the key light and the subject divided into the guide number. And the guide number is selected just as though only one flash bulb were being used. This is so because in normal multiple flash setups each lamp is lighting a different part of the subject, and one—the key light—dominates to give coherence to the image. However, if you aim two or more bulbs at the same part of the subject to get more light, the following applies:

For two bulbs, multiply the single flash guide number by 1.4.
For three bulbs, multiply by 1.7.
For four bulbs, multiply by 2.

Multiple-flash technique has sometimes been simulated, depending upon the subject, with a single flash unit. This is the *open-flash technique.* In-doors or out, wherever the existing illumination is quite low and the sub-ject immobile, the shutter can simply be opened and the scene painted with light by repeated flashes from a single flash unit. The existing light must be low, so that the film will not be overexposed during the long period the shutter is open. With the camera on a tripod or other firm support to keep it immobile, the photographer can move about, flashgun in hand, firing as many times as he wishes. This same technique can be used to burn-in the image of weak light sources, candles, Christmas lights, Fourth of July sparklers, with a time exposure and then the scene is flashed with one bulb to expose other nonluminous details. The flashgun that has no switch to do this job can be flashed when it is not connected to the camera by short-ing out the unit with a paper clip.

Open flash is often used for subjects with considerable depth, and this requires a small diaphragm opening, ($f/22$ or $f/32$) for extensive depth of field in the image. Exposure can be established with the open flash guide number for the film-flashbulb combination. This is usually the same as the

Shadowlike images of the photographer illustrate the technique used in lighting a subject of considerable depth with multiple flash, leaving the camera lens open while an electronic Strobonar is fired from different positions. Figures of men provide scale, defining the space. (David Mathias, Staff Photographer, Denver Post)

guide number for shutter speeds up to 1/30 of a second. Dividing the f/number selected into this guide number gives the distance in feet the flash should be held from the subject each time it is fired.

In dark areas it is possible for the photographer, if he is wearing dark clothes, to move about freely, even passing in front of the camera lens while it is open, without his image registering on the film. If an assistant is available he can place a cap over the lens between flashes to eliminate the chance of unwanted light recording on the film.

SUN AND FLASH

Flash illumination is used effectively to open up shadows cast by brilliant sunlight outdoors or to balance indoor lighting with the light on an outdoor scene that will be included in the picture through a window.

Using flash outdoors is usually intended to fill in the shadows enough to record detail without eliminating those shadows. This is an especially useful technique with color film, for which blue bulbs or electronic flash must be used so that the color temperature of the flash matches that of the sunlight.

Exposure is based on the sunlight. The distance the flash must be from the subject is calculated from the guide number and the f/number selected for the sunlight exposure. For example, if the exposure selected for the sunlight is f/16 at 1/125, look for the proper guide number for the film-flashbulb combination at that shutter speed. Assuming the guide number is 160, then dividing f/16 into 160 gives us 10 feet. That is the distance at which flash would approximately balance sunlight, in other words, eliminate the sunlight's shadows. To keep the shadows, the flash must be moved to approximately 14 feet; sunlight to flash ratio is then approximately 2:1. Moving the flash back to 20 feet from the subject gives a ratio of 4:1, sunlight four times as strong as flash.

If it is inconvenient—and it often is—to move the flash, then the reflector and bulb can be covered with a clean, white handkerchief. This will cut the light from the flash by one half. Or the flash can be fired without reflector, reducing the light by one half again, or bounced off a convenient reflecting surface.

You can juggle the flash-sunlight relationship by changing the shutter speed, since flash exposure, especially with electronic flash, is controlled primarily by lens opening. Changing the exposure from f/11 at 1/125 to f/16 at 1/60 will give the same exposure as far as sunlight is concerned but will reduce the exposure from the flash.

The exact ratio between sunlight and flash is largely a matter of personal preference. For color pictures the desirable ratio is often 2:1 or 3:1. Color intended for magazine or newspaper reproduction generally needs a greater amount of fill light than color transparencies shot for projection on a screen.

The same general technique applies in lighting an outdoor subject in the shade with a background in sunshine, or in lighting an indoor scene to balance it with the sunlight on a scene visible from the camera position through a window. Exposure calculation begins with determination of the exposure for the sunlight; then the f/number so obtained divided into the proper guide number gives a distance from flash to subject. Adjustments must again be made to get the proper ratio between sunlight and flash, and this depends on the photographer's purpose, the personal interpretation he wishes to give the combined indoor-outdoor scene. Flash fill can also be used to open up shadows on an indoor subject positioned next to a window.

•

Chapter 10

FILTERS FOR BLACK-
AND-WHITE PHOTOGRAPHY

Important tools in photography are filters, since they significantly increase the photographer's ability to control the image. In black-and-white photography, filters can bring the image into closer conformity with the subject as the eye saw it. Or, just the opposite, light reaching the film can be so altered as to distort reality to serve the photographer's creative purpose. Filters can make the image of white clouds stand out in dramatic relief against a dark sky, can penetrate haze as though it were not there, or put atmospheric haze into an image when little existed in the actual scene. Filters can put contrast into the black-and-white reproduction of two different colors of equal brightness, or can make two different colors merge as a single brightness value in the print.

Filter-makers will, quite willingly, supply photographers with a hundred or more different filters; they will even make filters to special order. But the great majority of filters are intended for scientific or experimental photography. The average photographer can get along quite comfortably with three or four filters for black-and-white work, and he will rarely need more than eight. Most photographers find use for filters of only three (at the most four) different colors, but they may use filters of two different intensities within one or more of these basic colors. The three most common filter colors are yellow, red, and green. The fourth, occasionally used, is blue. The blue filter has no wide application in black-and-white photography; it can be used to increase the effect of atmospheric haze in scenic shots and sometimes is useful in copying work. Yellow filters are among the most useful because they darken the rendition of blue, a wavelength of light to which all film emulsions are overly sensitive, and thus make other colors, particularly yellow, green, and red, appear lighter by comparison in the black-and-white print.

BASIC PRINCIPLES

Filtering, of course, involves the removal of undesired matter from a substance passed through the filtering device. In physics it involves the elimination or reduction of electromagnetic radiation of certain wavelengths without greatly altering others. A light filter, then, is like a sieve that allows some wavelengths (colors) to sift through but stops some or all of other wavelengths.

Very few subjects for photography are black and white; most reflect selected portions of the visible spectrum, which the eye interprets as colors. An apple looks red because it absorbs a large proportion of the short wavelengths—the violet, blue, and green—but reflects most of the long wavelengths—the red. The leaves of the apple tree, however, absorb much of the red as well as the blue, and reflect mostly the green rays. With a photograph we attempt to translate these or other colors that the eye sees into black and white or the intermediate tones of gray. This translation of the brightness values of colors to the brightness values of the gray scale is quite often somewhat less than perfect, because even panchromatic film, although sensitive to all the visible spectrum, differs from the eye in its degree of sensitivity to the various wavelengths.

Special dyes added to the film emulsion have extended the sensitivity of the silver halides to the longer wavelengths, even into that region of the spectrum to which the human eye is insensitive, the infrared band. But two major discrepancies between sensitivity of eye and film remain. All film, including panchromatic and even infrared-sensitive film, is especially sensitive to ultraviolet, which the eye does not see at all, and to violet and blue, which the eye sees not as bright colors but as relatively dark ones. In addition, the eye sees green as bright while pan film sees green as relatively dark. Put another way, it amounts to this: peak sensitivity regions of eye and film do not match; the film's peak sensitivity falls in the blue region of the spectrum, while the eye's peak sensitivity falls in the green region.

We can correct for this by altering the proportions of the various wavelengths (colors) that reach the film, thus darkening some areas in the final print and by comparison apparently brightening others. This is the basic principle behind the use of colored filters in black-and-white photography. Although colored filters are generally identified by the filter's own color, which is the color it transmits, it is often more instructive to think of filters in terms of the colors they absorb. The colors absorbed are the ones darkened in the print, and it is this darkening that explains the filter's effect. No filter actually brightens any color, since it obviously cannot amplify the light reflected from the subject. It is only because a filter alters tone relationships in the black-and-white print, darkening some tones so that others appear lighter by comparison, that we can speak of a filter brightening any color.

The functioning of a filter with black-and-white film can be observed by looking at a scene that includes a number of colors, preferably including blues, reds, and greens, through a photographic filter or, if the filter is not available, through a sheet of colored cellophane. A green filter or green colored cellophane will darken blue, purple, orange, and red; greens, and yellows to some extent, will appear to be brightened by contrast.

If a filter absorbs all wavelengths equally it will be gray in color. If it absorbs some wavelengths but not others it will be colored. It will be the color of the wavelengths transmitted, or complementary (opposite) in color to the wavelengths absorbed. If the filter looks green, it will transmit green light and absorb red and blue. But it may not absorb all the light reflected from red and blue objects. It may let some of these rays pass, depending largely upon the density of the filter's color; the denser or heavier its own color, the more of the other colors it will absorb. In addition, most objects do not reflect pure color of a single wavelength. More often an object that looks blue is reflecting some green rays and possibly even some red. The green rays get through the green filter, of course, and reach the film, thus recording some exposure, and the object is generally a tone of dark gray in the print, not black.

FILTER ABSORPTION CHART

Color of Filter:	*Colors it will absorb:*
Blue	Red, some yellow, and some green
Yellow	Violet, most of the blue
Green	Red, some blue
Red	Violet, blue, most of the green

Filters can be used in two ways in photography, to modify the light falling on the subject (a filter over the light source) or to modify the light passing through the lens before it reaches the film (a filter in front of the lens). Those filters designed to be used in front of the lens are the most important in black-and-white photography and the ones we are primarily concerned with in this chapter.

FILTER FUNCTIONS

In black-and-white photography there are two purposes for which filters are used most frequently, and a number of other secondary purposes, purposes for which filters are used only occasionally or rarely. The two principal purposes are correction and contrast. Secondary uses of filters

Correction filter separated clouds and sky in the image. Also note the actual and implied lines in the composition.

include haze penetration, reduction of reflections, and reduction of all light of all colors reaching the film.

CORRECTION FILTERS

Because of film's excessive sensitivity to blue, it often gives us a print in which blue tones, such as the sky, are reproduced as too light a tone of gray—too light, that is, in terms of the way the actual scene looks to the eye. In addition, the tone difference between a blue and a white in the original scene is often lost in the print, again because the film is virtually as sensitive to blue as it is to white. White clouds against a blue sky do not appear in the print as separate gray tones; they merge in one single tone. Similarly, the black-and-white image of a baby dressed in a white dress and lying on a blue blanket will quite probably show little or no contrast, and thus no separation, between dress and blanket.

To change the response of the film so that the subject will be recorded in the black-and-white print in gray scale brightness values approximately as it appeared to the eye, in color, we turn to the so-called correction filter. The troubles described in the previous paragraph can be overcome by using a yellow filter, which absorbs the ultraviolet and enough of the blue to separate white from blue in the scene and record them in approximately correct values. A green or yellowish-green colored filter is also often used as a correction filter. It gives much the same control over the blue light reflected from the subject as the yellow filter gives, but in addition the green filter absorbs some of the red. The green filter is, for example, useful in recording approximately correct tones in outdoor portraits, especially of suntanned faces, against blue sky.

CONTRAST FILTERS

Filters that carry the modification of brightness values beyond correct reproduction are regarded as contrast filters. An orange or a red filter gives white cloud effects against dark, dramatic skies, a distortion of the brightness values in the actual subject. A red filter makes red apples stand out in bright relief against dark foliage. The decision to use a contrast filter is based on the desire to increase the tone contrast between colors that would, without a filter, photograph as similar tones of gray. Red and green look about the same if reproduced in their correct brightness on panchromatic film. We could, of course, use a green filter, instead of red, to photograph the apple tree to achieve contrast between light foliage and dark fruit, but this would be quite contrary to our normal view of such a subject.

The effect of contrast filters can be visualized by keeping in mind the principal colors of the visible spectrum, ranging from the short wavelengths to the long. The natural order of the colors is violet, blue, blue-green, green, yellow, orange, red. A filter of any one of these colors lightens the tone of objects matching its own color and lightens slightly the tone of objects of neighboring colors in the spectrum order. It darkens those objects with colors farthest away from the filter color in the spectrum order. A red filter darkens blue more than an orange filter does, and much more than a yellow filter. Green darkens both blue and red. Yellow darkens blue, but tends to lighten green, orange, and red.

The difference between a correction filter and a contrast filter is not always clear. Any given filter will serve as one or the other, according to

FIGURE 24

Filter effects. Photographs were taken on panchromatic film, through filters indicated, of blocks of pure color. The colors are labeled at the top.

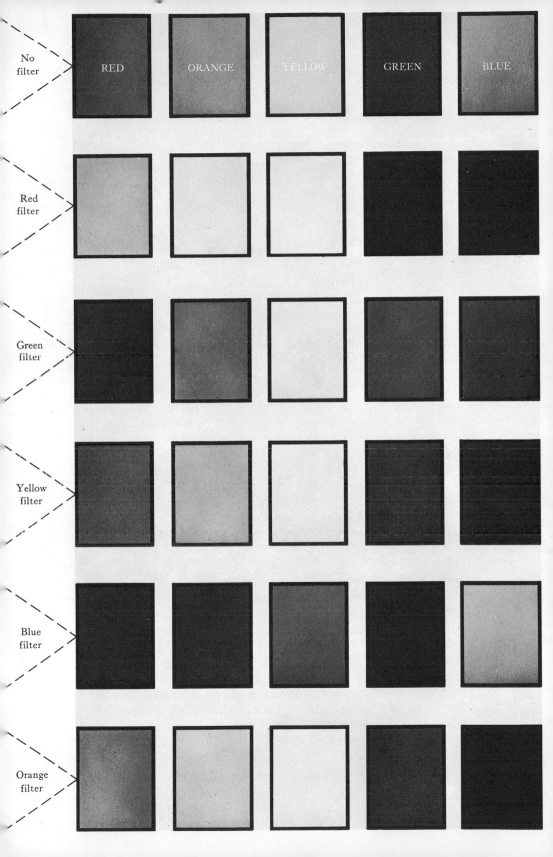

If the photographer visualizes a print to emphasize tone contrasts, he will often turn to filters before he makes the exposure in the camera.

the intent of the photographer. And the intent of the photographer must be related to the three factors that control the effect created by any filter: the color of the filter itself, the color of the light, and the color sensitivity of the film. The light is a factor primarily in terms of whether it is daylight, which has a high percentage of blue wavelengths, or tungsten light, which has a high percentage of yellow and red. As for the color sensitivity of the film, we have assumed for purposes of this discussion that the film is panchromatic; orthochromatic and blue-sensitive or color-blind films are rarely used.

If the photographer's intent is to get natural rendition of the subject, he is seeking a correction filter. If he wants to heighten the difference in brightness values between two colors, his intent is one of contrast. A single filter may be a correction filter at one time and a contrast filter at another.

HAZE FILTERS

Filters can be used for reducing the effect of natural, atmospheric haze, but not for penetrating smoke, fog, or smog. Normal atmospheric haze is caused by microscopic dust particles and water droplets in the earth's atmosphere. These minute particles interfere with the passage of light reflected from distant objects, especially in landscape scenes the photographer may find attractive as photographic subjects. This is the aerial perspective discussed in Chapter 3. The greater the distance between observer and the mountain or building, the greater the haze effect. The haze effect manifests itself in three ways: overall tones become lighter, contrast between elements within the scene decreases, and the overall color of the scene is distorted toward the blue.

The dust and water droplets in the air scatter the short wavelengths (ultraviolet, violet, and blue rays) the most. The result is that photographic film records more haze in the image than the eye sees in the actual scene because of the film's excessive sensitivity to these short wavelengths. If we can filter out these haze-creating wavelengths we can reduce and even eliminate the haze effect in the photograph. A medium yellow filter records haze approximately as the eye sees it; an orange filter reduces the haze effect on the film, and a red filter (especially if used with infrared-sensitive film) practically eliminates it.

Total elimination of haze may not, however, be desirable, depending upon the photographic purpose. Total haze elimination also means partial destruction of the illusion of the third dimension, since aerial perspective plays a strong role in creating that illusion. On the other hand, if the purpose is to show detail in a distant view, a haze-penetrating filter may be essential.

POLARIZING FILTERS

Filters that can cut out light that has undergone the change known as polarization are called polarizing filters. Reflections and glare (a special kind of reflection) from nonmetallic surfaces, such as glass, water, polished wood, a waxed floor, consist of polarized light, which means, you will recall from Chapter 6 on the nature of light, visible radiation that is vibrating, not in all directions at right angles to the ray, but in only one such direction. The polarizing filter eliminates this one remaining plane of vibration and, of course, eliminates the light, since if light cannot vibrate it cannot exist.

A polarizing filter is a sort of screen, or picket fence. A normal light ray, which is vibrating in all directions perpendicular to the ray, strikes the filter on one side, but it emerges on the other side vibrating in only the one direction which corresponds to the lines of the pickets in a picket fence. But what about the light ray that is already polarized by reflection? If the direction of vibration in the ray does not correspond to the polarizer's pickets, it will not be able to get through the fence. The ray will be stopped by the filter; thus the reflected light never reaches the film if the filter is placed over the camera lens.

The picket of the polarizer's fence—or its vibration plane—is in line with an indicator handle that projects from the mount of most of these filters specifically made for photographic use. Thus a ray of light will pass through the filter if its vibration is in line with the indicator handle. A normal ray that is vibrating in all possible directions has, of course, one vibration plane, which matches that of the filter. But an already polarized ray may be stopped or absorbed, depending upon the position of the filter. You can determine the relative positions of the polarized ray's vibration and the polarizer's pickets by looking at the photographic subject through the filter as you rotate it. Gradually, as you rotate the filter, the glare or reflected light is reduced until it finally disappears. This is the position, as indicated by the handle, in which the filter should be placed over the lens to eliminate the reflection.

Our discussion of the polarizing filter is not intended to imply that photographers should always attempt to eliminate all reflections and glare. Reflections may add highlights and sparkle to a picture, and glare may sometimes be a necessary part of the photographic interpretation. The use of the polarizer is indicated if reflections and glare are obscuring important texture and detail. This is often true when the photographer is attempting to shoot through glass; for example, through the glass of a store window to picture the window display. However, the camera's angle of view must be about 35 degrees from the surface of the window for the polarizer to subdue the reflections effectively. The same is true in eliminating reflections from water and other nonmetallic surfaces.

Don't expect to control reflections from shiny metal surfaces with this polarizing filter; it won't work. Light reflected from metal is not polarized, nor is the light reflected from paintings, murals, photographs, and other objects you may wish to copy photographically. A polarizing filter over the camera is of little help. Control of reflections from metal or from pictures to be copied requires polarizing filters over the lights as well as over the lens.

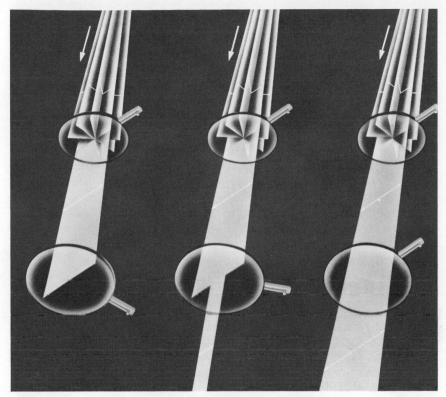

FIGURE 25

The polarizing filter. This drawing of the Kodak Pola Screen illustrates how light vibrating in only one direction can pass through the polarizing filter. When a second filter is placed below the first, with the handles of both in line, the polarized light passes through both (right). As the handle of the second filter is rotated to left or right, the light passing through it is gradually reduced (center). When the handle of the second filter reaches a position at right angles to the handle of the first, no light passes through the second filter (left).

The polarizing filter also darkens a blue sky, because light from the sky is reflected light, reflected or scattered by the atmosphere. Much of this reflected light is polarized. To use the filter to darken a blue sky, look at the sky through the filter as you rotate it. As the filter is turned, the sky darkens, and then gets lighter again as the filter is rotated further. You will note that the sky appears darkest when the indicator handle on the filter points at the sun. Place the filter over the lens in this same position, with the handle pointing as nearly as possible toward the sun. This means that the polarizing filter gives maximum effect when the sun's rays come from a 90-degree angle to the line of direction between camera and subject.

185

Filtering the exposing light improves many scenic shots. (Dr. Roy F. Wilcox, Carbondale, Pa.)

Vibrations are filtered by the polarizer, and not wavelengths; it has no effect on colors. It darkens a blue sky only because part of the light from the sky is already polarized. Because it has no selective effect on colors, the polarizer is an excellent filter for use with color films, as well as with black-and-white. The polarizing filter is the only known way of darkening the sky in color photography without altering the rendition of other colors in the scene. This filter does not work well, however, with hazy skies, and has no effect at all on overcast days.

About one half the light reflected from the subject is absorbed by the polarizing filter and, for this filter to be effective in darkening a blue sky, the camera must point at right angles to the direct rays of the sun. This means the subject will be side-lighted or top-lighted and this usually calls for an increase in exposure of one half to one full stop in addition to the increase necessary to compensate for the light absorbed by the filter.

NEUTRAL DENSITY FILTERS

These filters reduce the amount of light transmitted to the negative without selective filtering of any particular wavelengths, and they make no distinction between polarized and unpolarized light. These filters are neutral in the sense that they transmit and absorb equal amounts of all visible colors, and the relative brightness values in the subject remain unaltered. Neutral density filters have their primary application in shooting in bright sunlight with high-speed films, color or black-and-white. Some cameras cannot be stopped down enough to avoid overexposure with such a combination of intense light and fast film. In addition, even if the camera provides a shutter speed and f/number combination for correct exposure, the depth of field may be so great as to include a sharply defined and distracting background. The neutral density filter provides the answer, cutting the light reaching the film to a level that makes a correct exposure possible, or permitting a large aperture for depth-of-field shallowness.

FILTER MOUNTS AND SIZES

The most practical filters for general use are made of thin pieces of dyed gelatin, dyed cellulose sheets, or other transparent substances that have been mounted between two pieces of optical glass. Lacquered gelatin film squares are also available, and they are less expensive, but they are also easily scratched or marred by dirt, dust, grease, or moisture. A fingerprint on the surface of such a filter is almost impossible to remove. Filters mounted between glass are less easily damaged, and the glass surfaces can be cleaned successfully if the same care and techniques are used as in cleaning a lens.

Mounted filters are usually attached to camera lenses in one of two ways. On most cameras they are screwed directly to the lens, but on others they must be placed in an adapter ring, which slips over the lens and is held in place by friction. The filter is held within the adapter by a retaining ring or a lens shade screwed into the adapter ring. Adapter rings and filters come in various sizes to fit different lenses. Sizes are expressed in series numbers and in millimeter measurements.

FILTER FACTORS

Since filters absorb some of the light, less light is reaching the film and exposure must be increased, either with a slower shutter speed or larger

A red filter enhanced the silhouette effect in this backlighted scene. (John Suhay, Pueblo, Colo.)

aperture or both, to compensate for the light loss. The corrected exposure is determined by multiplying the no-filter exposure by a filter factor.

The filter factor is not a constant number. It depends not alone upon the amount of light the filter absorbs, but also upon the color sensitivity of the film and the color of the light. Generally, the deeper the color of the filter, the more light it absorbs and the higher the filter factor. The filter factor must be related to the useful light transmitted by the filter, and the useful light depends upon the color sensitivity of the film. Orthochromatic film, which is insensitive to red light, can be used with some filters, such as the polarizers, neutral density filters, and yellow, orange, and blue filters—but obviously not with red. But the filter factor is different from that for panchromatic films for all except the polarizers and the neutral density filters. In addition, the filter factor is nearly always less with tungsten light than with sunlight because tungsten light from photofloods, flashbulbs, and other incandescent sources contains a higher proportion of the long (yellow, orange, and red) wavelengths. The notable exception is the seldom used blue filter, which requires a higher factor with tungsten light to compensate for the relatively small amount of blue wavelengths in the light.

If the filter factor is two, the shutter speed must be halved or the lens aperture opened one full stop. Either will double the exposure, or, in effect, multiply the no-filter exposure by two. For example, if the no-filter exposure is 1/125 at f/16, for a filter with a factor of two, correct exposure would be 1/60 at f/16, or 1/125 at f/11. If the filter factor is three, then correction can be accomplished by opening the lens one and one-half stops or by halving the shutter speed and opening the aperture one-half stop.

More than one filter can be used over the lens at one time, as, for example, a polarizer and a colored filter. But then the two filter factors must be multiplied, not added, to get the correct factor for increasing exposure.

If exposures are determined with the guidance of a meter, the filter factor can be applied to the film speed setting for the meter. Simply divide the factor into the normal film speed and set the meter for this new exposure index.

Recommended filter factors are given in the following table, or factors can be found in instruction sheets packed with film or in the instruction sheets that come with the filters. Factors are also engraved with the markings on the rims of some mounted filters. However, all these factors apply to average conditions and average subjects, and they should not be regarded as absolutes. Some deliberate underexposure with a filter may result in enhancing the filter's effect. On the other hand, overexposures can destroy the effect of the filters with black-and-white film.

SUMMARY OF FILTER EFFECTS
With Panchromatic Film

Filters	Characteristics and Uses	Filter Factor
Medium Yellow	Absorbs ultraviolet, some violet, and blue. A correction filter in daylight. Useful in photographing scenery; darkens blue sky for cloud effects.	Sunlight 2 Tungsten 1.5
Orange or Deep Yellow	Absorbs ultraviolet, violet, and most blue rays. Contrast filter indoors and out. Darkens blue sky and blue water; enhances texture in outdoor subjects photographed under blue sky; some haze penetration.	Sunlight 3 Tungsten 2
Light Green	Absorbs ultraviolet, violet, some blue, some red. Correction filter under both sunlight and tungsten light. Excellent for outdoor portraits with sky as background, for landscapes and flowers.	Sunlight 4 Tungsten 3
Medium Red	Absorbs ultraviolet, violet, blue, and green. Contrast filter. Spectacular effects with clouds, buildings, other objects against almost black sky; haze penetration; moonlight effects with slight underexposure; excellent for sunsets. Used with infrared sensitive film.	Sunlight 8 Tungsten 4
Polarizer	Neutral gray in color, transmits rays of all visible colors; absorbs ultraviolet. Darkens blue sky; subdues reflections from glass or water, other nonmetallic surfaces to show texture and detail. Can be used with color film.	3

Filter factors given here are only approximate. Refer to the instruction sheet packed with the film for more precise factors or to instructions supplied by the filter manufacturer.

FILTER USE GUIDE CHART

Subject	Filter	Effect
Clouds, Blue Sky	Medium Yellow	Natural
	Orange	Sky darker than natural
	Red	Very dark sky
	Red plus Polarizer	Night effect

Subject	*Filter*	*Effect*
Marine Scenes (boat, beach)	Medium Yellow Orange Polarizer	Natural Dark water Cuts reflections
Sunsets	Medium Yellow Orange or Red	Natural Brilliant contrast
Landscapes	Blue Medium Yellow Orange Red Red with Infrared Film	Adds haze Natural Haze reduction Greater haze penetration Haze eliminated
Landscapes from Airplane	Yellow Orange or Red	Natural Haze penetration
Outdoor Portraits	Light Green	Natural
Dark Wood (like mahogany)	Red	Emphasis on grain pattern
Yellow Wood (like oak, maple, walnut)	Orange	Emphasis on grain pattern
Light, Blonde Wood Finishes	Medium Yellow	Natural
Polished Surfaces	Polarizer	Subdues reflections, detail revealed
Printed Signs	Complementary color to lettering	Increased contrast
Floral Displays	Green Close to color of flower	Lightens foliage, accents flowers Light blossom against dark foliage
Fall Foliage	Yellow Red	Lightens yellow leaves Strong contrast of red leaves against blue sky
Copying Stained Documents	Color matching stain	Subdues or eliminates stain
Blueprints	Red	Strong contrast
Glass Objects (pottery, china)	Polarizer Complementary color	Subdues reflections Increased contrast to emphasize design or patterns

Chapter 11

THE CHEMISTRY OF THE PHOTOGRAPHIC EMULSION

When we were considering the problems in creating an image we became involved in an aspect of physics: geometrical optics, the geometry involved when light, considered as moving in waves, is refracted by the lens. Having created the image with the lens and light, we must then deal with the recording of that image, and here we become involved with photochemistry: the transformation of radiant energy (light) into chemical energy. Thus we are dealing again with light, but now, instead of thinking of light as a wave motion, we had best think of it as being composed of tiny bundles of energy, the quanta or photons. It is the quanta absorbed by a substance that brings about a chemical change in that substance.

Examples of photochemical reactions include the production of vitamin D in the tissues of living animals, the tanning (or in the case of an overdose of light's energy, the sunburning) of skin, the fading of dyes in the covering of the living-room couch where sunlight strikes it regularly. Living plants combine the energy (the quanta) from sunlight with chlorophyll to make carbohydrates (sugar and starches) from carbon dioxide and water, a process known as photosynthesis. The photochemical reaction important in recording the optical image is the opposite of synthesis; it is a decomposition.

A photochemical reaction is one that involves the absorption of light energy, but not all such reactions are of any value in photography. For photography we must have a system with a predictable response to the impact of light; a system that reacts in direct proportion to the amount of light absorbed; a system that provides a result that can be made permanent, so that it will not fade or decompose under further exposure to light energy; and a system of extreme sensitivity to light.

Of the few compounds and elements that can make use of the energy of light, certain compounds of silver meet the demands of photography. These silver salts are unstable—that is, they decompose rather readily under the impact of light energy, and in decomposing they form finely divided metallic silver, jet black in color. This decomposition is, under normal circumstances, proportional to the amount of light absorbed, and

Photographic film, properly exposed, has amazing ability to record detail and texture. Put it to work.

the silver is a relatively stable product, giving a permanent or fixed account of the reaction.

The silver compounds will thus satisfy three fourths of the requirements for a photochemical process usable in photography. The only requirement remaining is that the compounds be exceptionally sensitive to light. At first glance it may appear that the silver compounds fail to pass this fourth test. They must be exposed to strong light for a long time before their decomposition becomes visible in the form of a deposit of metallic silver. (This process has, in fact, sometimes been utilized by portrait studios in so-called printing-out papers to supply proof prints to customers.) But we do not need to rely solely on a photochemical reaction to supply the image-forming silver. In the normal photographic process this photochemical reaction is merely the first stage of recording the image. A small amount of light begins the decomposition of the silver salts. This beginning is so small we cannot detect it even under the most powerful of microscopes, but later developments prove that the change, however small, does in fact exist. Since it does exist, we need a name for it, and it is traditionally called the *latent* (that is, invisible) *image*.

To get a visible result we must move on to the second stage in the process of recording the image. This second stage is called development of the latent image and is a purely chemical reaction in which light energy plays no further part. During development the latent image, or the initial decomposition of the silver salts caused by light, is built upon and greatly magnified until it does become visible.

THE HALIDES

Most silver compounds are photosensitive, but for photographic purposes the ones of transcendent importance are those compounds in which silver combines with one of the *halogens,* a family of very active chemical elements. The family includes fluorine, chlorine, bromine, and iodine. When any member of this family combines with silver the result is a *silver halide,* and the silver halides are among the rare compounds that form a latent image. Only three of the silver halides are in general use in photography: silver chloride, used for slow (contact) printing papers; silver bromide, used for films and fast (enlarging) papers; silver iodide, used in small amounts (seldom more than five per cent) with silver bromide in fast film emulsions. As we noted in Chapter 5, many enlarging papers contain a mixture of silver chloride and silver bromide.

Of the three halides used in photography, by far the most important is silver bromide. The silver bromide grains take various sizes and shapes, but most of them are hexagons or triangles that measure 1/1000 to 4/1000 of a millimeter (one to four microns) in width. Now, obviously, these grains or crystals are composed of the two elements, silver and bromine, but we need to know a bit more about the structure of the individual crystal if we are to understand why it reacts to light.

Nearly everyone today knows about atoms, the smallest particles of elements such as silver and bromine. For our purposes we may consider that each atom consists of a nucleus or center surrounded by a sort of solar system of electrons. The nucleus carries a positive electrical charge, which

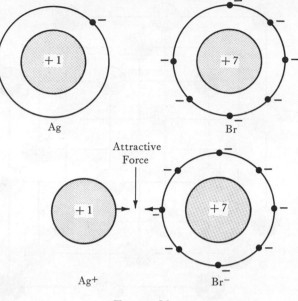

FIGURE 26

Silver bromide.

is balanced by the negative charge of the electrons. Sometimes this balance
of electrical charges is upset; the atoms of some elements are philanthropic
by nature and donate one or more electrons with little protest to their more
greedy fellow elements. When this happens neither the philanthropic
atoms or their greedy counterparts can any longer be electrically neutral
once a shift of electrons has been completed. Both now become electrically
charged atoms or *ions*. The atom that gave up one or more electrons is now
a positively charged ion (there are not enough electrons left to balance the
positive charge of the nucleus) and the atom that accepted the electron
donation must then be a negatively charged ion (having more electrons
than its normal complement). So, the atoms of two elements that have
completed this shift of electrons are mutually attracted by their opposite
electrical charges and form what is called an ionic compound. Such a compound is common table salt, chemically identified as sodium chloride or,
in the abbreviated form of chemical symbols, NaCl. In this compound there
is a multitude of positive sodium ions (sodium atoms minus one electron)
given the chemical symbol of Na^+ and an equal number of negative
chlorine ions (chlorine atoms plus one electron), Cl^-.

The same thing happens when silver bromide is formed: each silver
atom gives up an electron; each bromine atom gains an electron. Silver
bromide (AgBr) then is a combination of silver ions (Ag^+) and **bromine**

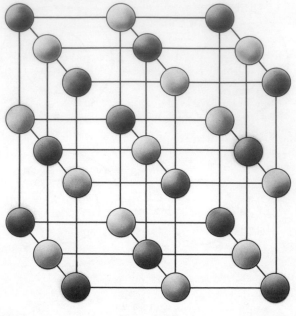

FIGURE 27

Silver halide crystal lattice.

ions (Br^-). The silver bromide grain or crystal is made up of the ions that form a three-dimensional lattice structure, so that no single silver ion is the particular partner of any bromine ion; rather, the two sorts of ions arrange themselves alternately in every direction, with the result that each silver ion is surrounded by six bromine ions and each bromine ion is surrounded by six silver ions. (See Figure 27) Each silver bromide crystal, so tiny that it can be seen only under a powerful microscope, contains one billion or more silver ions and an equal number of bromine ions. It should also be noted that the crystal lattice of the halide grain is not perfect. It has irregularities or cracks in it where one sort of ion or the other should be but is not, and some of these cracks are on the surface of the grain.

THE EMULSION

To be useful in photography, the silver halides must be suspended in some sort of medium that will keep each crystal or grain separate from its neighbors. Each grain must act as an individual; each is a unit for recording the latent image; each is a unit for development of the visible image. In addition, the medium in which the halides are suspended must be durable under handling and processing without presenting any obstacles to the penetration of either light or the processing solutions, which must reach the embedded halide crystals. Finally, it must be available in large quantities at reasonable cost.

The medium that satisfies all these requirements and adds a few useful extras is gelatin, a colloid extracted by boiling animal bones, hooves, horns, and hides. The gelatin used in photography generally comes from the ear and cheek sections of calf hides. Gelatin made from the hides of calves or cows is especially useful in photography because cows like a bit of spice in their diet; they eat hot-tasting plants, such as mustard, which contain sulphur compounds, and these sulphur compounds aid in the photochemical reaction that creates the latent image.

In addition to providing minute amounts of sulphur compounds, which act as sensitizing agents, gelatin is the ideal medium for preparing the photographic emulsion, because it is liquid when warm but sets to a gel when cool; it dries to a hard, compact, uniform layer; it swells in water or processing solutions but does not dissolve or disintegrate at temperatures normally used in photographic processes; it holds both the silver halide crystals and the developed silver image firmly in place; it is insoluble in cold water but absorbs up to ten times its weight in water; it can be hardened with such agents as formaldehyde or alum; it is a bromine acceptor—that is, it combines readily with small quantities of bromine freed from the halide crystal during the photochemical reaction that creates the latent image.

Manufacturers of today's films quite understandably keep the details of their methods of emulsion preparation shrouded by trade secrets, but the general procedures are known. They can be conveniently divided into five basic steps.

PRECIPITATION

First the silver halide is precipitated in a dilute gelatin solution. This is accomplished by adding silver nitrate ($AgNO_3$) to a solution of a soluble halide, such as potassium bromide (KBr). The reaction is a simple double decomposition that produces silver bromide (AgBr) and potassium nitrate (KNO_3)

$$AgNO_3 + KBr \longrightarrow AgBr + KNO_3$$

The silver bromide is almost insoluble, so it separates out, or precipitates. All other compounds involved on both sides of the equation are soluble, but because the silver bromide is not, it will coagulate or clot into a pale yellow mass or curd and settle to the bottom.

This coagulation and settling of the silver bromide can be prevented by letting this reaction take place in the presence of gelatin. The gelatin and

Selective lighting and selective focus isolated the center of interest. (John Middents, Lakeland, Fla.)

the potassium bromide are dissolved together in water before the silver nitrate is added. Then each grain of silver bromide formed by the chemical reaction is held in suspension by the gelatin. In this way the emulsion of light-sensitive silver halides is formed, each halide crystal cushioned by the gelatin and prevented from coagulating with its neighbors and prevented from settling out. The silver halides at this point in the process are not very sensitive to light. The precipitation stage of emulsion making is usually performed under a dim red light.

The method of mixing the silver nitrate and potassium bromide solutions is important. If the nitrate solution is dumped quickly into the potassium bromide-gelatin solution, many small crystals of silver bromide will be formed. If the silver nitrate is added very slowly, the first few crystals of silver bromide will act as collection centers for further crystals, and the result is larger and fewer crystals. Many small crystals give an emulsion of low sensitivity but high contrast; fewer but larger crystals mean high sensitivity but relatively low contrast.

Other controls are also available during the precipitation stage. Still finer grain emulsions are usually prepared by increasing the quantity of gelatin involved. Varying the concentrations of silver nitrate and potassium bromide will also alter the grain size. Potassium bromide is generally in excess, that is, present in quantities larger than necessary to react with all the available silver nitrates, and we shall see why when we reach the next stage of emulsion-making. For high-speed emulsions some iodide is added. This changes the size and shape of the crystal grains of silver bromide and boosts their sensitivity to light, probably because it affects the nature of the cracks or imperfections on the surface of the crystal lattice. The importance of this will become clearer during the discussion of the latent image theory in the next chapter.

RIPENING

This second stage in emulsion-making, which may, in practice, be combined with the first stage, simply involves heating the gelatin solution to 90° F or perhaps higher and keeping it at this high temperature for from 30 minutes to several hours. During this process the silver halide grains decrease in number but increase in size, and in light sensitivity as well, since large grains are more sensitive than small ones. Silver bromide is slightly soluble when an excess of the alkali halide (potassium bromide in this case) is present in the solution. The solubility of the silver bromide can also be increased somewhat by the addition of ammonia. Small silver halide grains dissolve but then recrystallize out on the large grains; the large grains grow larger at the expense of the smaller ones. In addition, the ripening process may be increased by two or more adjacent grains overcoming the cushioning effect of the gelatin under the influence of the heat. In that case they may get together to form a single large crystal.

Stages one and two in emulsion-making, taken together, help explain how manufacturers achieve a variety of emulsions. If rapid precipitation and short ripening are combined, the result will be many small silver halide grains distributed throughout the emulsion. If slow precipitation is combined with a long ripening period under high heat, the result must be larger grains but significantly fewer of them in any given area of the emulsion.

WASHING

Near the end of the ripening period more gelatin is usually added, and then the solution is allowed to cool so that it will set or gel. Next it is shredded into noodles and washed to eliminate the soluble potassium nitrate, the excess potassium bromide, which is also soluble, and any other unwanted elements or compounds, such as ammonia, added to aid ripening. Sometimes the manufacturer skips the washing stage, because it is not always essential. If the emulsion is being made for coating on a paper base to be used for making photographic prints, there may be no need to wash out these soluble compounds. This is so because these compounds migrate from the emulsion to the paper base. But if the emulsion is to be coated on a base impervious to these compounds, such as the base or support normally used for films, the emulsion must be washed, because these soluble compounds would prevent light from reaching the silver bromide crystals.

DIGESTION

During digestion, also called after-ripening, the emulsion is remelted and kept at 90° F or higher again for perhaps several hours. The compounds that made the silver bromide soluble during the first ripening period are now gone, so there is no further growth in the size of the grains but there is an increase in sensitivity and contrast, which is largely controlled by the nature of the particular gelatin added at the end of the first ripening period. This change comes about because chemical sensitizers added with the additional gelatin attach themselves to the surface of the halide crystals. It is here that the sulphur compounds, which occur naturally in some gelatin—that from cows, for example—or which have been added by the manufacturer, play their role. Gold compounds and even silver may also be added as chemical sensitizers. These sensitizers produce specks of silver sulfide, or of gold or silver, or a mixture of these on the surface of the silver halide crystals. These specks, or sensitivity centers, tend to form at the breaks or cracks in the crystal lattice. It is generally agreed that these specks play an important role in the formation of the latent image, although there is some disagreement on precisely what this role is.

After digestion is complete, hardening agents may be added to the emulsion to increase the gelatin's resistance to stress and strain caused by the swelling it undergoes during developing, fixing, and washing. Hardeners are usually salts of aluminum or chromium (alum or chrome alum) or formaldehyde.

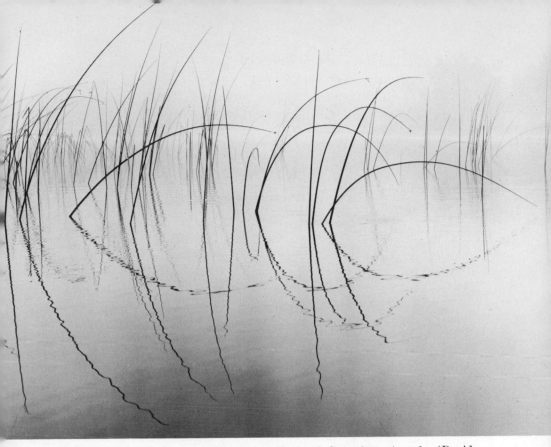

A prizewinner in the Annual Newspaper National Snapshots Awards. (David H. Stone, Sarnia, Ontario)

At this stage further chemicals are often added to achieve an emulsion of the desired characteristics. Among the most important of these for modern-day films are the *optical sensitizers*. These are dyes to extend the color sensitivity of the silver halides, which are normally sensitive only to the radiation energy of ultraviolet, violet, and blue, with some small sensitivity in the case of silver bromide into the green range of the spectrum. Dyes added to the emulsion in extremely small amounts stick to the surface of the halide grains and then sensitize the grain to all the wavelengths the dyes absorb. A red dye, for example, absorbs green light and thus sensitizes the halide crystals to green. A dye that absorbs red light sensitizes the halides to red. Thus we have three general classifications of emulsions according to their spectral sensitivity: an emulsion (on film or paper) that has not been optically sensitized (no dyes added) is a blue-sensitive (or ordinary or color-blind) emulsion. Printing papers may be coated with this type of emulsion, but only a very few films, designed for special purposes such as copying, have this undyed emulsion. An emulsion that has been dyed for sensitivity to green light is called *orthochromatic;* it is also sensitive to ultraviolet, violet, and blue. The third type, *panchromatic*, is sensitive to all colors of the visible spectrum, including red, and also to ultraviolet; most films used in ordinary photography today are panchromatic.

Doctoring the emulsion may also include the addition of glycerin to give pliability, or various compounds to reduce the danger of fog (unwanted decomposition of the halides to produce silver), and perhaps other additives for special purposes.

COATING

Only one process is now left: coating the emulsion on a suitable support —paper, celluloid or plastic film base, or glass. The liquid emulsion is fed onto the support to give a layer about 1/1000 of an inch thick, although this may vary according to the use for which the emulsion is intended. In some cases a double coating of emulsion is used. A top dressing of super-coating may also be added; this is a thin layer of plain gelatin to protect the silver halide emulsion from scratches and bruises. In the case of printing papers, a substratum coating may be put on the paper base first. Usually this is a layer of barium sulphate (often called baryta), an inert, intensely white substance that forms an excellent reflecting surface. This sub-layer can be modified to give the matte, semimatte, or glossy effects.

Still another coating is often applied to the rear surface of films. This is to prevent halation and is called the antihalation backing. Light from a bright source often penetrates emulsion and support but is scattered by deflection off the halide grains; some of these rays strike the back surface of the film at more than the critical angle (see Chapter 6) and thus are totally reflected. This means they return through the support and reach the emulsion again to expose more halide crystals. The result is a ring or halo effect around the original image of the bright light source. This is halation. This effect commonly occurs in night photographs when street lights or other bright point sources of light are included in the picture. Because these bright image spots are overexposed, there are enough light rays involved to create the halo effect; with weak light sources this effect does not occur, because the halo image is sublatent, that is, so weak it does not cause enough photochemical change in the silver halide crystals to make them developable. The antihalation layer contains a dye that absorbs the light that penetrates and prevents it from returning to the emulsion layer. The effect of halation can also be reduced by using a very thick film base or by using a gray base to absorb much of the halo reflection.

The antihalation backing is incorporated in a gelatin layer, which also helps keep the film from curling toward the emulsion side. The dye disappears during processing of the film because its color is destroyed by one of the chemicals in the developer solution.

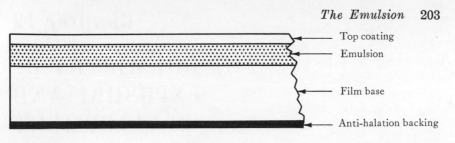

Top coating

Emulsion

Film base

Anti-halation backing

FIGURE 28

Cross section of photographic film.

Once all necessary layers have been coated on the emulsion support it is ready to be chilled to set the emulsion, dried, and cut to whatever size is wanted. Billions of silver halide crystals wind up in the emulsion of each sheet of film or paper, and they make up 30 to 40 per cent of the weight of the emulsion layer itself, although individually they are extremely small. If the silver bromide crystals were approximately the size of your little fingernail, the emulsion would be a foot thick.

Chapter 12

THE CHEMISTRY OF EXPOSURE AND DEVELOPMENT

We have seen in the previous chapter that photography depends upon the light sensitivity of silver halides. The light that surges through the lens for the fraction of a moment the shutter is open is enough to alter some of the billions of silver halide crystals in the emulsion of the film, and each crystal is altered in proportion to the amount of light it absorbs. The grains hit by light can then be converted, partially or completely, to metallic silver by development. The unexposed grains can also be converted to silver if we prolong development to at least ten—or it may take as much as one hundred—times the normal development period. What has happened that makes the exposed grains so much more susceptible to development than the unexposed grains? The same question can be posed in photographic terms by asking, What is the latent image?

LATENT IMAGE THEORY

It is known that when the exposed grain of silver halide is developed tiny specks of metallic silver appear at one or more isolated points on the surface of the grain. If development is carried far enough the whole grain is converted (or in chemical terms, reduced) to silver. It appears to be a reasonable assumption that submicroscopic specks of something must be present on some of the silver halide crystals before development starts, that these specks of something must provide a point of attack for the developer, and that at least one such speck must be present on each silver halide crystal that develops. As an experiment, remove a piece of film from its box and wrapping. Lay it emulsion side up on a table or desk directly under a light. Now place a small object, a coin or a pencil, on the film and leave both there for several hours. When you lift the coin or other object you have placed on the film, you will see it has left its mark; the area of the film that was under the coin will be lighter in color than the rest of the film emulsion. What caused the area of the emulsion that was exposed to light to darken? By chemical tests and X-ray crystallography we could establish that this darkening was caused by the formation of metallic silver. It is then logical to assume that the specks of something, the development centers, where the developer begins its attack, are also tiny specks of metallic silver. These invisible specks, each containing four to a dozen, perhaps more, atoms of silver, constitute the latent image, a change in the silver halides so permanent that photographs can be made from film developed days, months, even years after the film is exposed. Photographs have been made from film developed fifty years after it was exposed by Arctic explorers.

A satisfactory theory of the latent image must explain how these tiny colonies of silver atoms come about. Endless theorizing and experimentation have gone into the search for this explanation, but no one has yet come up with a theory that has won universal acceptance; no theory has yet been proven by empirical evidence. But the most likely theory seems to be one that divides latent-image formation into two general parts: the electronic stage and the ionic stage. This is based on the Gurney-Mott theory, advanced in 1938 by R. W. Gurney and N. F. Mott of Bristol University. This theory has since been modified in details, but it has been the launching pad for further hypotheses.

It appears rather well established that the quanta or packets of radiant energy in light knock electrons loose from the bromide ions in the crystal lattice. These bromide ions each have an extra electron anyway. These electrons thus turned loose are free to roam about in the crystal at a speed of about five miles per second at room temperature, a tremendous speed relative to the size of the crystal in which they move. But the departure of each such electron has left a state of disorder, for when the electron, energized by light, took off it left a bromine atom that is not at home in the lattice structure of the silver bromide crystal. It would be natural, it appears, for the electron to recombine with the bromine atom to reform a bromide ion. Perhaps this does happen in some cases; but if it were to happen always photography would not be possible; we need those electrons to join up with the silver ions of the crystal, if we are to have the silver specks of the latent image.

The bromine atom, created by the loss of an electron, must find some way to solve its problem other than by recapturing an electron. At the site of the bromine atom in the crystal lattice we have what is called a *positive hole*, which is not a name of a kind of matter, but rather a name for a state of matter: a bromine atom, electrically neutral, is surrounded by six positively charged silver ions. But this hole is mobile. An electron from a neighboring bromide ion jumps to the bromine atom in an effort to reestablish a normal state of crystal affairs, but this, of course, leaves another positive hole. Another electron jumps; the hole moves again. And so it goes until the positive hole reaches the surface of the crystal. There it can be trapped and held, because the last bromine atom formed reacts with one of those silver sulfide specks or other sensitivity compounds we read about in the previous chapter. The result is some such chemical reaction as

$$Bromine + silver\ sulfide \longrightarrow silver + sulfur\ bromide$$

It is probable that the sulfur bromide is absorbed by the gelatin, while the silver may help form the development centers, tiny deposits of silver on the surface of the crystal.

Meanwhile, what has happened to the runaway electron? It winds up getting trapped also, perhaps by silver ions located at the cracks or breaks in the lattice structure. These silver ions can accept the electrons and form an atom of silver, because the imperfections in the lattice allow room for this to happen. Some electrons and silver ions may join at interior cracks; others get together on the surface of the crystal. It is the ones that form on the surface that are important latent-image specks, because they are the ones that provide the points for attack by the developer.

This summary involves only one set of agents: one bromide ion, one quantum, one electron, one silver ion. Actually, of course, many of each must be involved in the activity inside each light-struck silver halide crystal. Studies have indicated that a crystal must absorb, on the average, 10 to 15 quanta to be developable. Each quantum may or may not initiate the series of reactions summarized above. But certainly many of them must start such activity, or we could not take photographs.

This completes the electronic stage of latent-image formation. Now the ionic stage begins. This consists of the migration of silver ions to the points where electrons have collected. We assume some silver ions are able to move about within the crystal. They are called interstitial ions. Perhaps some of these are formed when bromine frees silver from its combination with sulfur at sensitivity specks. The interstitial silver ions are repelled by the like charge of the positive holes gathering at the sensitivity specks but are attracted by the opposite charge at the point where the electrons have been trapped. Of course, as silver and electrons arrive at the same point they join hands and form more silver atoms. Soon, enough have formed to establish a stable colony of metallic silver: the latent image. The sensitivity compounds formed by the natural sulfur in the gelatin or by chemicals added in emulsion-making may aid in trapping electrons and silver ions, in addition to forming surface traps for positive holes.

A good sense of timing and a high shutter speed to immobilize the image will catch rapidly moving subject. The shutter speed for this shot was 1/500 of a second. (Herbert A. Gustin, Jr., Aurora, Ill.)

All of this, beginning with the exposure to light, apparently takes place in the smallest possible fraction of a second. It is virtually instantaneous. Positive holes and electrons, moving at tremendous speeds by our normal methods of reckoning, will travel less than 1/1000 of a millimeter before they are trapped.

The larger the silver halide grain, the more likely it is to have lattice cracks and sensitivity centers that form effective traps for electrons and positive holes. Therefore, the larger the grain, the more likely the formation of a latent image with a minimum of energy supplied by light. This appears to be the reason grain size and emulsion speed increase together.

Much of this theory of the latent image is still open to debate. It is being subjected constantly to further tests and experiments that may eventually alter its details considerably. These tests and experiments in research laboratories quite probably will also result in better films, as scientists learn more about the silver halides, the gelatin, and the various compounds used as sensitizers—and the various interactions of this whole complex procedure. It is possible that a clearer understanding of latent-image formation will result in the discovery of better ways of increasing the light sensitivity of silver halides.

DEVELOPMENT THEORY

Once the latent image has been formed, we can proceed to development of the visible record of the exposure. But here again we are involved with a process that is not completely understood. We do know that the essential function of a developing solution is to convert to metallic silver those silver halide grains that were partly decomposed by exposure to light. The essential process involved in development is relatively simple: it merely amplifies the latent image by depositing more silver upon it. This amplification is of major proportions. If we assume that the latent-image center on a single halide crystal contains perhaps ten atoms of silver, then development increases this amount at least one hundred million times, and perhaps as much as a billion times.

To magnify the latent-image silver we need, obviously, a source of additional silver. There are two sources available. One is the developer solution, which can be concocted so that it contains silver in the form of ions. The other source is the silver bromide crystals of the emulsion. Using the first source is called physical development; using the second, chemical development—although the process is really a chemical reaction in either case. A so-called physical developer contains silver ions in solution that, during development, form atoms of silver; these atoms precipitate out of solution onto the silver of the latent image. But this form of development is of little practical value to the average photographer; he uses the second

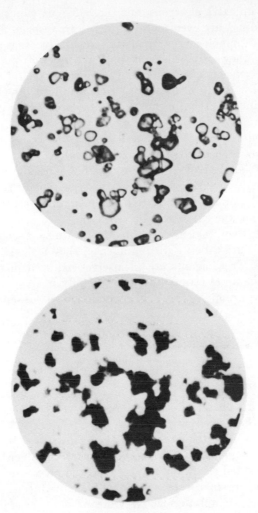

FIGURE 29

Photomicrographs of undeveloped (top) and developed (bottom) grains.

method—chemical development. But to understand this method we must know something about what the chemist calls reduction.

REDUCTION

As we have seen, the atoms of some elements, including silver, rather readily give up one or more of their outer electrons, and in doing so form a combination, or compound, with another element (or group of elements), which acquired the electrons. Oxygen is the prototype of the elements eager to lap up extra electrons, but the halogens (fluorine, chlorine, bromine, and iodine) are even more eager in this respect. The chemists have developed a terminology for discussing such a reaction or interchange of electrons, and they say the element that gave up electrons has been oxidized (a victim of oxygen's or some similar element's electron greed), while the element (or group of elements) that acquired the electrons has been reduced. Reduction, then, means electrons gained; oxidation means electrons lost.

If we bring silver and bromine together, the result is silver bromide. The silver has been oxidized (lost electrons) and the bromine has been reduced (gained electrons), leaving silver ions linked with bromide ions in a compound. Now, if we can get this reaction to reverse itself, each silver ion will gain an electron, to become again an atom of silver. In this reverse reaction the silver will be reduced.

Substances, then, that are capable of breaking up such combinations as silver bromide are called reducing agents; they make silver take back its lost electrons. These agents are themselves oxidized in the process, since they must give up electrons to reduce the silver.

For clarity we might think of development as, essentially, a two-step process:

1. Developer $\longrightarrow$ oxidized developer + free electron
2. Free electron + silver ion $\longrightarrow$ silver atom

The actual development reaction is much more complex than this, but it is essentially a transfer of electrons from developer to silver.

The strength of any reducing agent is its tendency to give up electrons; the greater this urge, the more active the agent as a reducer. A large number of reducing agents extract metallic silver from silver halides, but many of them cannot tell the difference between the unexposed and the exposed silver bromide crystals; they are too active as reducers. What we want is an agent strong enough to push electrons off onto the exposed halides, but not strong enough to force them onto the unexposed in a relatively short development period.

This, of course, raises the question of why some developers (reducing agents) make this distinction at all. A precise answer to this question cannot be given, for the simple reason that no single explanation has yet been advanced that agrees with all the known data. The laws of chemical reactions presently known do not seem to fit photographic development completely, although experiments have produced a number of theories.

It appears that the latent image, that speck of silver on an exposed crystal, in some way acts as a catalyst; that is, it speeds up the chemical reaction but does not itself take part in the reaction in any way that would change it from being metallic silver. It is possible that the reducing agent finds that the easiest place to push off its electrons is at the point on the silver halide crystal where this tiny deposit of latent-image silver exists. Perhaps the electrons move through the silver, a conductor of electricity, and find silver ions to join at the interface between latent-image silver and silver halide crystal. Thus, more silver is formed. This process could continue, accelerating as more silver is formed, until all the silver ions in the crystal are reduced, or until development is stopped by pulling the film out of the developing solution. The bromide ions, freed as the silver ions become atoms of silver, diffuse out into solution joining up with hydrogen, supplied by the water in the solution, to form hydrobromic acid.

REDUCING AGENTS

Among the reducing agents that have just the right energy level for photography are a number of organic compounds, compounds containing carbon. The photographic reducing agents in general use are almost all derivatives of benzene, a compound of carbon and hydrogen.

To obtain the derivatives of benzene that are useful photographic reducing agents, we need only replace one or more of the hydrogen atoms with groups of elements. If two hydrogen atoms are replaced by two hydroxyl groups (a combination of oxygen and hydrogen), we get a very common photographic reducing agent known as hydroquinone. If the so-called amino group (a combination of nitrogen and two atoms of hydrogen) is involved, we get para-aminophenol, sometimes given the trade name of Rodinal. If still a third group of elements is added, the methyl group (carbon plus three atoms of hydrogen), we get methyl para-aminophenol, often called metol; in Eastman Kodak developers it occurs in somewhat altered form, to improve its stability, as Elon. There are a number of other derivatives of benzene that are reducing agents, but there is no need to describe them all. A fairly common developer that is not a benzene derivative is Phenidone, a concoction introduced and protected under that trademarked name by Ilford, Ltd., of Great Britain.

Dissolve any one, or even two, of these agents in water, place exposed film in the solution, and you will very probably be disappointed; nothing much will happen. Reducing agents are essential, but other ingredients are needed, too, for a photographic developing soup effective under ordinary conditions.

THE DEVELOPING SOLUTION

Photographers may, and often do, prepare their own developing solutions, and these mixtures sometimes contain almost everything short of eye of frog and ear of newt. Ready-made developers are also available in

A $1000 prizewinner in the Annual Newspaper National Snapshot Awards. (Mrs. Cecile Briggs, Brattleboro, Vt.)

packages and cans containing all the necessary ingredients, usually in granulated form. Dissolving the powder in water is all that is necessary in the darkroom. Whether a do-it-yourself or a ready-made product, the photographic developer generally contains five basic ingredients, basic because each is added to perform a basic function regardless of the details of the solution formula. Quantities and individual chemicals may vary, but the classification of ingredients based on function remains the same. The five basic components of a developer solution include, of course, the developing or reducing agent, which has already been discussed in general terms. The four others are the solvent, the activator, the preservative, and the restrainer.

SOLVENT

Essential, of course, is a solvent in which the chemicals can dissolve, and this is nearly always plain water. It is seldom necessary to use distilled or chemically pure water, although occasionally impurities can cause trouble. In some special cases small amounts of other solvents may be needed in addition to water to get seldom used chemicals to go into and stay in solution; diethyleneglycol, the chemical used in many antifreeze mixtures, is sometimes used as a solvent.

The water, in addition to acting as a solvent, has other uses in photographic development. It penetrates and swells the gelatin of the emulsion. In penetrating the gelatin, the water carries the other chemicals of the developing solution to the silver halide crystals; no reaction can take place, of course, unless the silver halides and the developer come into actual contact.

ACTIVATOR

Most photographic reducing agents perform their appointed task promptly and efficiently only if they are in an alkaline solution. This means we must add an alkali to the developing solution to activate the reducer. The alkali, in effect, encourages the reducing agent to ionize or dissociate, that is, to split in solution into positive and negative ions. When this happens, the negative ions have electrons available that they readily donate to the positive silver ions of the silver halide crystals, and in the process, of course, are themselves oxidized. The actual chemical reaction that takes place while the exposed film is in the developer solution is very complicated, but it is essentially a shift of electrons from reducing agent to silver ions.

The type of alkali used and the amount used to a large extent control the activity of the developer. A strong alkali produces a rapid-acting developer that also produces high contrast; a weak alkali gives a relatively slow developer and less contrast. Alkalies used most often as activators in photographic developers, listed in order of increasing activity, are

Borax or sodium tetraborate
Kodalk Balanced Alkali
Sodium carbonate
Sodium hydroxide

Why not always use a strong alkali such as sodium hydroxide, since it means rapid development? The alkali, in addition to promoting ionization of the reducing agent, also softens the gelatin of the emulsion, and the stronger the alkali the greater this softening effect. If this is carried too far it may result in damage to the emulsion during processing. Also, a strong alkali can result in the reducing agent attacking the unexposed silver halide crystals, producing fog. The strongest alkalies are usually avoided, except when the objective is a high-contrast negative.

PRESERVATIVE

In a solution of reducing agent and alkali, the reducer is not particularly selective about the elements with which it reacts. In fact, it reacts very readily with the oxygen from the air and in the process is oxidized, and as a consequence is no longer an agent for reducing the silver halides. To preserve the reduction potential of the agent until it can reach silver halides, a preservative is added to the developing solution. Almost without exception this is sodium sulfite.

The reaction of the reducing agent with oxygen from the air is another extremely complex one, and just how the sulfite inhibits this reaction is not precisely known in the case of every developer with which it is used. The sulfite itself has an affinity for oxygen, but this alone does not satisfactorily explain its functions as a preservative. Apparently the reducing agent, in reacting with the oxygen, forms intermediate compounds such as quinone. These intermediate compounds act as catalysts that encourage further reaction between reducer and oxygen. It is believed that the sulfite puts a stop to this catalytic action by reacting with and thus canceling out the intermediate compounds.

Sodium sulfite is also a mild alkali and as such can act as a very mild activator; in a few developing solutions the sulfite is permitted to play both roles, activator and preservative, and no additional alkali is added.

RESTRAINER

Sometimes a mixture of the various developer solution ingredients results in just what is wanted except that the reducing agent displays a tendency to reduce the unexposed silver halides as well as the exposed ones. This obviously undesirable lack of discrimination needs to be checked, so a fifth ingredient is added to the solution, the restrainer. This is usually potassium bromide. The action of the potassium bromide is still another of those complex and not fully understood processes in photo-

The decisive moment is fleeting; the photographer must work quickly. (Lowell Georgia, Staff Photographer, Denver *Post*)

graphic chemistry. It appears, however, that the compound ionizes in solution and the bromide ions that carry a negative charge attach themselves (the chemical term is *adsorb*—note this is not the same as *absorb*) to the silver halide grains. This forms a barrier of negatively charged ions, which the electrons of the reducing agent find difficult to penetrate, except, apparently, at points on exposed grains where latent-image specks exist. The bromide retards reduction of the silver halides in general, but its effect is greatest on the unexposed crystals. Thus it restrains the formation of fog, which is nonimage silver.

Tossing all these ingredients into a single pot will produce not, as it might seem, a noxious witch's brew, but an effective photographic developer. Actually, some additional chemicals may be added or one or more of the so-called basics may be omitted, all for special purposes. Potassium bromide is most often left out of today's developers because it does have a tendency to reduce the effective speed of the film emulsion; that is, the bromide tends to restrain the reducing agent's attack on silver halide crystals that received a marginal exposure—just barely enough exposure to form the minimum in developable latent-image silver. Sodium sulfate can be added when the developer must be used at high temperatures, since it prevents the gelatin from swelling too much. Formulas for fine-grain developers sometimes include a silver halide solvent, such as sodium thiocyanate. Other antifoggants may be added in addition to or as substitutes for potassium bromide. The formulas for many developers sold in packaged form under trade names are not published, and they may contain chemicals other than those mentioned here.

The formulas for many standard soups are known, however, and two may be mentioned here as examples. A standard of longstanding, often copied with slight variations, is Eastman Kodak's D-76 film developer. D-76 contains both Elon and hydroquinone as reducing agents and thus is one of the general family known as MQ developers, the M referring to metol, another name for Elon, and the Q standing for the quinone of hydroquinone. Also in D-76 are sodium sulfite and borax, but no potassium bromide or other restrainer, ordinarily. From the list of ingredients it is obvious that D-76 is a relatively slow-acting developer, which produces a relatively low contrast. Average development time is about 11 minutes. Kodak Developer D-8 contains only hydroquinone as reducing agent; it has the usual sodium sulfite, and potassium bromide. The alkali in D-8 is strong and vigorous sodium hydroxide. Here is a fast-acting developer (average development time about 2 minutes), which produces high contrast.

FIXING THE IMAGE

After development is complete, the image-forming silver is present in the emulsion layer, but so are the unexposed and undeveloped silver halides that were not needed to form the image. These residual halide crystals, if left in the emulsion, would darken on exposure to light and spoil the image, so they must be eliminated. This is the purpose of fixing—making the image permanent.

Since the silver halides are insoluble, they must be converted to other chemical compounds or salts that can be dissolved and washed out of the emulsion. This is the basic purpose of fixation, accomplished usually by a chemical that has been in use since the first successful daguerreotype—sodium thiosulfate, once called sodium hyposulfite, from which came the commonly used term *hypo*.

In solution the sodium thiosulfate dissociates into sodium and thiosulfate ions. The thiosulfate ions combine with silver ions from the silver bromide to form a series of complex compounds that are soluble. The halide ions thus freed from the silver halide lattice structure also move into the general solution.

The thiosulfate ions must get into the gelatin layer of the emulsion, and after reacting with the silver ions the combination must move out of the gelatin. This means there is a need for agitation during the fixing period if this two-way movement into and out of the emulsion layer is to occur with maximum effectiveness.

Ingredients other than the sodium thiosulfate are usually added to the fixing bath. These include an acid to neutralize any of the alkaline developing solution that might still be present in the emulsion by the time it reaches the fixer. Actually, it is not a good idea to transfer the film directly from the developer to the fix, because stain or fog may result. This is why a rinse of plain water or weak solution of acetic acid is generally used between developer and fix. The acid in the fixing bath is merely added insurance that the developer will be effectively neutralized, but a strong acid cannot be used because it would decompose the hypo to form a fine suspension of sulfur, which, if it enters the emulsion, cannot be washed out. A weak acid, such as acetic acid, can be used if a preservative is added to the solution to restrain the slight tendency for this acid to form sulfur. The preservative usually used is again sodium sulfite, the same compound used as a preservative in developers, but the chemical reaction involved is not the same in the two cases. The sulfite in the hypo solution reacts with any sulfur formed to give another soluble compound.

Hypo solutions also frequently contain a hardener, which prevents excessive swelling and softening of the gelatin. This is usually potassium aluminum sulfate (usually called potassium alum or simply alum), or in a few cases, potassium chromium sulfate (chrom alum).

Boric acid is another common additive for fixing baths, since it helps buffer the solution—that is, it helps counteract the tendency of the alkaline developing solution carried into the fixer to reduce the acidity of the fixing solution.

Many darkroom workers prefer what is called a rapid fix—a hypo solution that effectively shortens the time in the fixing bath without endangering the permanence of the silver image. These solutions usually contain ammonium thiosulfate, which reacts faster with the silver ions of the halide crystals than does sodium thiosulfate. With any fixing bath there is some danger that the thiosulfate may dissolve some of the silver image if negative or print is left in the bath for too long a time. This is especially true of the rapid fixers, so care should be taken not to exceed the maximum recommended time in such solutions.

An alternative to fixation is a process called stabilization, often used in rapid processing of papers, for example in document-copying machines. It is also applicable, however, to processing regular photographs, but the resulting prints are generally more susceptible to fading and discoloration than are prints that have been fixed. Fixing, followed by washing, removes the unstable residual silver halides. Stabilization converts the silver halides into comparatively stable, colorless compounds that are simply left in the emulsion. Regular hypo can, as a matter of fact, be used as a stabilizer rather than as a fixer.

WASHING

After fixation, if hypo and the compounds it has formed with the unexposed silver halides are left in the gelatin emulsion, and in the case of prints in the paper base, a reaction can occur between these compounds and the silver of the image that produces a yellowish-brown silver sulfide. This reaction is similar to the production of tarnish on table silverware. When it appears in old photographs it is generally referred to as fading. High temperatures and moisture speed up this reaction, and eventually the silver sulfide may be oxidized slowly to silver sulfate, which is both white and soluble. Thus, the image actually disappears, beginning with the lowest densities, the highlight areas of a print.

Both the hypo and the soluble compounds that were formed by the combination of silver and hypo during fixation must be removed. This is the purpose of washing. Actually, washing cannot eliminate all of these salts left over from fixation. If each wash period reduces the salt content by one half, then one half is always left. However, washing can cut the amount of the salts to such a low value that prints and negatives will not stain or fade for many years and perhaps not to any significant degree ever, if they are protected from air, heat, and moisture.

Washing aids are available: the hypo-clearing agents mentioned in Chapters 4 and 5. Experiments conducted for the United States armed services disclosed that processed films and prints could be washed more rapidly in sea water than in fresh water. Sea water is a 2.6 per cent solution of sodium chloride. Why such a solution should increase the efficiency

Camera on tripod, aimed at the area in which explosions will occur, the film will catch the fireworks if the shutter is left open, recording the scene in the dramatic extremes of black and white.

of washing is not definitely known, but the presence of the salt—sodium chloride—was apparently the key factor, since adding table salt to fresh water produced the same results. But sodium chloride proved to be harmful to the permanence of the photographic image, so although sea water got rid of the fixation residue rapidly, no time was saved, because then the sodium chloride had to be washed out with fresh water. But an avenue for investigation had been opened, and soon other salts were discovered that proved to be harmless to image permanence. The result has been such washing aids as hypo neutralizers or clearing agents.

When extreme permanence—archival quality—is needed, the answer is the hypo eliminator. This oxidizes the residual hypo and other fixation salts to sodium and ammonium sulphate, stable compounds that will not cause trouble even many years later because they do not react with the image silver, with oxygen of the air, or with anything else. A typical hypo eliminator is a mixture of hydrogen peroxide and ammonia. Use of a hypo eliminator is not entirely free of risk, however, and it is a special purpose practice, not a normal one.

DEVELOPING 35-MM FILM

The 35-mm black-and-white films, increasingly used in recent years because of the increasing popularity of the 35-mm cameras, pose some additional problems in development and printing because of the small size of the negative. The clumps of metallic silver in the negative image must be kept as fine as possible to avoid a grainy appearance in the print. But at the same time photographers frequently prefer to shoot under the existing light, adding no light from flood lamps or flash, thus retaining the natural and realistic appearance of the original lighting in the image. This is quite feasible with today's high-speed films and the high-speed lenses on 35-mm cameras. To obtain high-quality images under these conditions, however, exposure and development must be accurately matched.

The authors have found wide divergence among professional newspaper photographers on techniques for developing 35-mm film. However, one consistent principle is followed: development is invariably based on the exposure index used with the film, which means that professional photographers are frequently using an index other than the standard ASA film speed. The exposure index varies as subject and lighting vary.

For example, 500 is a fairly common exposure index for Kodak Tri-X 35-mm film with development planned for two and one-quarter minutes at 80 degrees in Acufine, one of many developers packaged as a single-mix, dry powder. Acufine is designed for getting relatively fine-grain negatives from film exposed at high exposure indices. Some photographers use the same exposure index for Tri-X but develop for three minutes in Acufine at 70 degrees, or in Ethol UFG developer for three and one-half minutes at 75 degrees.

Agitation also varies. Some photographers agitate only for a few seconds at the beginning of the development period; others agitate very gently every 30 seconds. Variations in agitation can be used to control contrast, since contrast increases with agitation. Vigorous and frequent agitation gives greatly increased contrast and increased grain. If the lighting of the subject was flat, some increase in agitation to boost image contrast may be advisable.

For indoor situations, without flash, press photographers frequently boost the exposure index used with Tri-X 35-mm film to 1200 or even higher. A popular developer for the film exposed at this rating is again

Acufine—for three and one-half minutes at 75 degrees or three minutes at 80 degrees, with little and very gentle agitation.

For higher image quality, photographers frequently turn to Kodak Plus-X 35-mm film, exposed at indices of 200 or 300 and developed in D-76 (diluted one part regular mixture to one part water, or 1–1) for six to eight minutes at 70 degrees, with agitation for five seconds out of every 30 seconds. Ethol UFG is also a popular developer with Plus-X film.

Still higher quality can result from Kodak Panatomic-X film exposed at 80 to 100 and developed in D-76 for eight minutes at 70 degrees, or in Selectol Soft developer for two minutes at 75 degrees, with agitation every 30 seconds.

The number of variations in techniques almost match the number of photographers. Some develop all negatives at 80 degrees all the time. Some use the same time period consistently, but vary the temperature for different exposure ratings.

In the future new and different developers are certainties, so each photographer must begin with one film and decide by experience just which developer and time and temperature give him the best results, with the most positive control of negative density and contrast. There are many variables in film, film speed, developers, and subject-lighting contrast. Experience only teaches control.

Chapter 13

COLOR AS WE SEE IT

More than half the photographic film being exposed today is color film. One of the major reasons for this is the popularity of color with the amateur weekend and vacation-time snapshooter, who appears to be loading his camera with two basic assumptions in mind. He assumes that color added to his pictures will make them at least twice as good as they would be in black and white. And he also assumes that color will give the most lifelike records of birthday parties, vacation trips, and family activities. While the second of these assumptions is, in general, true, the first one is just as generally false.

Color pictures are not necessarily better than black-and-white pictures; they are merely different. Color may be an advantage or a disadvantage, depending upon the effect the photographer wants to produce. Black-and-white photographs are, by their very nature, abstractions, since they do not include the color of the actual world. For this reason, the photographer often finds it easier to emphasize and convey his own particular viewpoint, his own particular way of seeing a subject, with black-and-white film. Black-and-white prints can be starkly straightforward and uncompromising, literally forcing the viewer, through their delineation of form by black-and-white tones alone, to accept the photographer's point of view. But in pictures of family, friends, and of remembered vacation scenes we are often seeking not an abstraction but the illusion of reality recreated—with rich emotional overtones. The added dimension of color extends our reach for this goal.

In fact, we may overreach. Color may add a dimension that only gets in the way of the photograph's intent. Color is not an undiluted blessing; if it extends our reach in photography, it also expands our problems. Color photography retains all the demands of black-and-white photography and adds a goodly number of its own. The added problems build wider and deeper pitfalls, and we must acquire greater and more exact technical knowledge if we are to keep our failures and successes in the same proportion as they have been with black-and-white photography. We need, to begin with, an understanding of color, in general, and of its application to photography in particular.

Color is a property of light, that is, it can be described in purely physical terms as electromagnetic waves of varying lengths, as we have already

Autumn leaves are often best recorded in black-and-white or color with back-lighting. Translucent leaves stand out beautifully against a backdrop of clear water or sky.

seen in Chapter 6. This is color as the science of physics regards it. But color is also—and this is most fundamental—a property of vision. It is only because the retina of the eye responds in different ways to the stimulation of different wavelengths that our concept of color exists at all. And the concept of color does not end with this retinal stimulation; it must also include the necessary interpretation by the brain of that stimulation.

This pulls color out of the realm of pure physics and into that of psychology. The subjective aspects take on greatly increased importance in color photography; if we are to gain any understanding at all of color photography, we must never lose sight of this fundamental fact. We must make a clear distinction between the physical nature of colors and our mental perception of them. These are two quite different, although of course related, aspects of color.

From Chapter 6 we know that light constitutes part of the radiant energy spectrum, a part the human observer is aware of because the radiation within that comparatively narrow band can be received by his eyes, much as the radio station's broadcast radiations are received by the radio set in your home. However, the eye, unlike the radio set, does not sort out one particular wavelength and ignore all others; the eye receives and responds to all wavelengths ranging from 400 to 700 millimicrons, with nerve messages to the brain. If the stimulation presented to the eye includes all or nearly all the wavelengths between these two extremes in approximately equal amounts, the brain makes the interpretation of white or colorless light.

In this connection, it should be kept in mind that there is no absolute standard for white light, because the eye adapts to changing conditions. The most common example of this is the fact that we see both sunlight and tungsten light from a reading lamp as white, even though the energy distribution (the quantities of the various visible wavelengths) contained in the two kinds of light are not identical. This adaptability of the eye, which color film of necessity cannot share, poses one of the major problems in color photography. We shall need to refer to this point frequently.

If the radiation stimulus received by the eye is not a fairly uniform distribution of all wavelengths, but rather one single wavelength (*monochromatic*), we see color. The range of colors in the visible spectrum is, of course, familiar to everyone. If we describe color in the physicist's terms, as wavelengths, there are hundreds of different colors in the visible spectrum; but each slight change caused by a minute difference in wavelengths cannot be detected by the normal eye. Actually, the spectrum colors we normally see are, roughly, violet, blue, green, yellow, orange, and red.

But the colors we are concerned with are not those spread out for us by a prism that has dispersed the wavelengths of white light. The colors we deal with in everyday life, and in photography, are those reflected to our eyes by objects around us and, less frequently, those transmitted directly to our eyes from a light source or through a transparent medium. Never does reflected light contain only one wavelength, and rarely do we encounter monochromatic light from a direct source. Outside of the laboratory the only monochromatic light commonly seen is the yellow radiation of sodium vapor street lamps.

All the reflected light our eyes receive is a mixture of wavelengths, but usually some part of the spectrum is suppressed or even missing. The result is the sensation of color. The missing wavelengths have been absorbed by the object that reflected (or transmitted) the light. Thus, we say: "The grass is green." In truth, the greenness is not a physical characteristic of the grass; it has absorbed many of the wavelengths in white light and reflected mostly the green rays. It is these reflected rays that stimulate our eyes in such a way as to create the sensation we have labeled green. The color is the result of the interaction between the reflected radiation, our eyes, and our brain, which all together form our vision.

COLOR VISION

Not all the details of the mechanism with which eye and brain together distinguish colors are known. We do know that the retina is equipped with millions of light-sensitive cells of two distinct shapes: the *rods* and the *cones.* The impulses these cells send along the optic nerve cause the sensations the brain sorts out and interprets as sight. The brain interprets impulses from the rods simply as more or less light; the rods are color-blind. It is the impulses from the cones that create color sensations. And it is known that if three separate and limited bands of wavelengths from the visible spectrum are used in varying proportions to excite these cone cells, sensations can be created that the brain interprets as matching almost all colors. It is only necessary that the three wavelength bands not overlap, and a combination of any two must not produce a sensation matching the color of the third. Three such independent colors form a set of *primaries*. No unique set of primary colors exists, but the three commonly used in physics are red, green, and blue.

One theory of color vision holds that the cone cells form three separate systems for light reception, each of the three responding to about one third of the visible spectrum with, probably, some overlap. Thus, if light of 600 to 700 millimicrons strikes the eye, only one of these color-reception systems is stimulated and the brain sees red. If the light is reflected from an object that has absorbed the short (violet and blue) wavelengths but reflected wavelengths ranging from 500 to 700 millimicrons in approximately equal proportions, two reception systems in the eye are stimulated and the brain interprets this combined message to mean yellow. In fact, we can form yellow with a mixture of green and red light or by subtracting the blue wavelengths from white light, leaving green and red. It is the simultaneous stimulation of all three of the receptor systems that produces the sensation of white light, and stimulation of two or unequal stimulation of all three produces the sensations of various colors. Any color, then, can be produced with the three primaries—red, green, and blue—as the raw

Simple subjects can be effective in color as well as in black-and-white.

materials, and it has been upon this fundamental theory that color photography has been constructed.

THE PRIMARIES

Red, green, and blue are the primaries of physics because to work with these colors to produce all other colors we must work with beams of light.

If we set up three slide projectors to project round spots of light on a white screen we can demonstrate the way in which these primaries function. We will put a red filter over one projector lens, a green filter over the second, and a blue filter over the third. When the light beams from each are projected separately on the white screen we see spots of red, green, and blue color. If we superimpose the spots, new colors appear. Overlapping blue and green produces, quite understandably, a blue-green we call *cyan;* overlapping blue and red produces a purplish red we call *magenta.* Red and green superimposed produce yellow. All three primary colors superimposed on the same spot give white. This, we can see, is addition of two or all three colors, so red, green, and blue are sometimes referred to as the *additive primaries.* It will be by this term that we will refer to them for the remainder of our discussion of color and color photography.

It should be noted that we have found it is not necessary to reproduce a given radiation wavelength (or mixture of wavelengths) to reproduce a given color. All we need do is produce an effect on the receptor systems of the eye that will match the effect created by another set of wavelengths; the two appear the same to the eye-brain color analyzer even though the

Good lighting is needed for the illusion of a third dimension. Two lights were used to illuminate both the model and her painting.

component radiation energies are quite different. It is only because this type of color matching is possible that color photography is possible.

Color addition with three primaries is not the only way to arrive at all other colors. We can accomplish the same thing by subtraction, a much more familiar form of color mathematics. Color subtraction is nature's system, and it is the system we use when mixing paints or inks. A green leaf looks green because other colors of the white light that struck the leaf have been subtracted before the light is reflected to our eyes. In the fall an aspen leaf looks yellow not because it reflects only the yellow light of the spectrum; if this were true the leaf would look not yellow but almost black. The yellow band of the spectrum extends from 575 to 590 millimicrons, and that is such a small proportion of the light that it would create very little stimulation of the eye's sensitive cells. The aspen leaf looks yellow because it has absorbed the blue wavelengths and reflected red and green, and we already know that these two combined create the sensation of yellow.

We can, and often do, copy nature's system with a set of water colors. Using just three colors, which are commonly referred to as red, blue, and yellow, we can mix up a wide variety of other colors. This, too, is color subtraction. However, for best results we need a blue-red and a blue-green plus yellow, which is actually a mixture of red-green. What we need, in fact, are the cyan, magenta, and yellow produced by additive synthesis. Thus, cyan, magenta, and yellow are the *subtractive primaries*.

The fundamentals of subtractive colors can be summarized as follows:

$$\text{White} - \text{Blue} = \text{Green} + \text{Red} \ (\text{Yellow})$$
$$\text{White} - \text{Red} = \text{Blue} + \text{Green} \ (\text{Cyan})$$
$$\text{White} - \text{Green} = \text{Blue} + \text{Red} \ (\text{Magenta})$$

Note that in each case approximately one third of the light has been subtracted, leaving two thirds to form each of the subtractive primaries. Note also that the subtractive primaries are the *complementary colors* to the additive primaries, since any one of the subtractive primaries plus its missing color (magenta plus green, for example) will give white. It will help in understanding color photography if we think of the subtractive primaries in the following way:

$$\text{Yellow} = \text{minus Blue}$$
$$\text{Cyan} = \text{minus Red}$$
$$\text{Magenta} = \text{minus Green}$$

Combining the subtractive effects, we then get

Yellow and Magenta	= Red
Yellow and Cyan	= Green
Cyan and Magenta	= Blue
Cyan, Magenta, and Yellow	= Black

We can produce other, intermediate colors by varying the relative strengths of the subtractive primaries. Color films depend on the subtractive system. A color transparency or color print, viewed in white light, must permit just the right amount of blue, green, and red light to reach the eye if it is to look like the original subject. This is accomplished by forming in the emulsion layers during processing a yellow dye to absorb blue where the subject did not reflect blue, magenta to absorb green where there was no green, and cyan to absorb red where there was no red. Varying amounts of each of the subtractive color dyes will, of course, give varying control over the additive colors reaching the eye.

Additive mixture and subtractive effects are fundamentally different phenomena, but remember the eye is not concerned with how the radiation energies are produced, only with the effects created by sensations reaching the brain. A purple is a purple, as far as the eye and brain are concerned, and it makes no difference whether it was produced by addition or subtraction. We will see in the next chapter how color film is made and processed to produce the color-controlling subtractive primaries. Meanwhile, we need to consider some further general principles involved in understanding color as we see it.

COLOR ATTRIBUTES

For any intelligible discussion of color we must have a minimum number of terms with which to describe colors. We must, however, keep clearly in mind what we are describing. Color is not a physical characteristic of an object, but of the light reflected from it. Our problem is not solved by describing the physical nature of the light either. What we are really attempting to describe are sensations.

Sensations that give rise to the perception of color are affected by the three main attributes of color: *hue, saturation,* and *brightness.*

Hue is the principal attribute of color and the most obvious. Hue changes as the wavelength of the light changes. If we describe a color as red or yellow or blue, we are identifying it by hue. We can identify about 200 different hues.

Yet two sweaters may give rise to the same hue sensation—both may be red, for example—while their colors appear quite different to the eye. One sweater may be a brilliant red, a scarlet, while the other is a pale red, a pink. They are the same hue but they differ in saturation, the degree of concentration of the hue. The stronger the saturation the more obvious the hue; if saturation is zero there is, of course, no hue. (Saturation is sometimes referred to as *chroma*.)

Our mental image of a color may vary still further in terms of its apparent amount. Two sweaters may be of the same hue and saturation, yet we may describe one as a light red and the other as dark red. Our mental image of one has greater luminance than the other, and when we describe it as light red we are evaluating its brightness. Zero brightness means absolute darkness. (Brightness is sometimes referred to as *value*.)

Any color is a combination of the three color attributes. For example, the light from a tungsten lamp is yellow in hue (although it may look white because of the color adaptation of the eye), weak in saturation, high in brightness. The usual darkroom safelight used with printing papers is also yellow in hue, stronger in saturation, but weaker in brightness. A banana is yellow in hue, moderate in saturation, and weak in brightness.

Mixing a color with white desaturates that color; diluting it with black (or gray) degrades (darkens) it. A mahogany brown is a degraded red; a pale pink is a desaturated red.

EFFECT OF VIEWING CONDITIONS

The colors we see in an object depend not only upon the light absorption and reflection characteristics of that object, but upon two other factors as well: lighting conditions and surroundings.

Lighting conditions can vary quite widely and in a number of ways. First, and most important, variations exist in the energy distribution of light sources; that is, they vary in the proportional amounts of the different wavelengths they contain. Light sources that depart markedly from sunlight, for example, are the sodium vapor and mercury vapor street lights. Sodium lamps radiate energy almost entirely confined to the narrow yellow band of the spectrum, while mercury lamps give off a decided blue-green illumination. A blue coat under a sodium lamp tends to look black because there are relatively few blue wavelengths to be reflected to the eye. A red coat under a mercury lamp is also degraded toward black. Actually, two other factors play a considerable role in determining what color changes either coat undergoes. In ordinary circumstances some additional light sources are present to add some blue and red light to the general illumination, and rarely will a dyed fabric reflect only blue or only red light.

Less obvious examples of color distortion created by a light source occur under fluorescent lights, some of which are relatively rich in some wavelengths and poor in others. Their energy distribution is not a full contin-

The relationship of elements within the picture frame tell the story.

uous spectrum but a mixture of separated bands of wavelengths. This is why dress or suit buyers often take the clothing to a store window or even outside to check the fabric colors. One or more of the dyes used may fall within a gap in the indoor lighting's spectrum, and thus the colors appear darker or may even exhibit a shift in hue.

Differences we notice still less frequently occur under illumination from

231

a clear blue north sky, under direct sunlight, and under indoor tungsten lighting. The proportion of blue wavelengths is highest in the sky light, least in the tungsten light. This is, in effect, a fall in color temperature (see page 156), which alters colors; blues tend to decrease in saturation and brightness under tungsten light, while yellows and reds tend to increase in the same attributes. The eye adapts itself quickly to relatively minor changes in illumination, with the result that we may notice a yellow tone to tungsten light as we step inside from the sunlight, but after a few moments the indoor lighting seems a normal white. It is important that the photographer remember his color film is quite incapable of any similar automatic adaptation.

Intensity of the illumination also affects the colors we see. The cone cells of the retina, the color receptors, are relatively inactive in dim light, when most of our vision results from the messages sent by the color-blind rods. This explains why colors seem desaturated and dull at night. Color photographs that are dark, with desaturated colors, look as if they were taken at night even though they may have been taken in full sunlight. Also, if lighting is diffuse, as it is outdoors under an overcast sky, colors look desaturated and dull. If lighting is direct, such as full sunshine, colors look bright and strong.

Surroundings affect the quality of colors in two ways, through the reflected light coming from nearby colored surfaces and through contrast between neighboring colors.

Obviously under normal lighting circumstances objects are not illuminated solely by direct rays from a light source, but by reflected light as well, and this reflected light is often colored by the reflecting surfaces. Strongly colored reflected light, such as that coming from the painted side of a red barn, changes the color of objects near it. This factor of reflected light from surroundings is a very important one in color photography. Skin tones in outdoor portraits may be noticeably altered by reflected light from green foliage or from a blue sky. Our vision, strongly guided by what we know to be true, often fails to notice these green or blue flesh tones, but color film sees things as they are, not as the brain believes they should be. These color shifts can be quite obvious in a color photograph even though to the eye at the original scene they went completely unnoticed. Color shifts may occur from light reflected from surfaces not even included in the pictures.

The second factor created by surroundings, color contrast, is only important if the surrounding color is included in the picture. Colors change in hue, saturation, and brightness with a change in surroundings. A blue-green looks blue against a green background, but the same hue looks green against a blue background. Colors also take on greater saturation and a higher brightness level against a dark background. A color also appears brighter when viewed against a background of its complementary color. There is even some hue shift when two adjacent colors are not complementary; the eye tends to see them as if they were. Gray tends to shift toward blue when viewed simultaneously with a bright red.

All of the foregoing leads to the conclusion that much of our puzzlement over the apparently unreal results we sometimes get with color films is created by our own failure to look critically at the colors of the original scene, to force our brain to edit preconceptions and color memory. The eye tends to see what its partner in vision, the brain, wants it to see. We see shadows in a snow scene under a cloudless sky as normal shadows, when in fact they are more than likely strongly tinted with blue, reflected from the sky. We know a white house at sunset to be the same white house we saw at noon; but color film sees it as rosy pink at sunset.

This brings us to the admonition that cannot be repeated too often: the photographer must learn to see what is really there, not what he wants to be there or what memory tells him should be there.

COLOR COMPOSITION

Color photography increases our problems not only because we must learn to see color in all its physical and psychological aspects, but also because it poses new problems in composition. In black-and-white photography only variations in a single-tone scale affect our composition. By altering exposure (using filters if necessary) and development we can assign values of the brightness scale from black to white to any object imaged in the print. In color photography we must deal with a bewildering variety of visual values, and this variety often makes it difficult to achieve a unified composition. Color magnifies errors in judgment, vision, and technique. Viewers of the final print or transparency are much more critical of discrepancies between the colors of the photograph and the colors of actuality as they remember them. This is not to condemn deliberate distortions of values in a color photograph, since such distortion may contribute to purpose, but it is only a warning that such distortion is often challenged in color pictures but seldom challenged in black-and-white pictures.

Composition in color requires attention to all the general principles discussed in Chapter 3 in connection with black-and-white photography. Still important are subject matter and meaning. Color does not automatically confer additional impact or message-carrying power; color may, in fact, detract. Absence of color makes many subjects more powerful and meaningful in photographic reproduction, as such masters as Edward Weston, Paul Strand, and Henri Cartier-Bresson have demonstrated. A meaningless photograph is still meaningless after color has been added.

Color composition depends to a great extent on personal taste. We can

Wide-angle lens and a high viewpoint provide a different view of a city. (David Mathias, Staff Photographer, Denver *Post*)

only suggest general principles, and even these may be—often have been —violated with good reason.

Each color, of course, is only a part of the overall composition and has significance only in relation to other elements and other colors. We use color to help knit the composition into a unit, not to tear it into isolated bits. In this connection, it is well to remember that isolated areas of strong color near a border of the picture tend to lead the eye out of the frame.

A harmonious arrangement of colors is simply one that is pleasing, so there can be no absolute standards. Harmony increases with increased hue difference; thus, complementary colors generally harmonize well. But if both are high in either saturation or brightness, the result is likely to be a harsh clash. One should be unsaturated or of a low brightness level. Most colors have a certain natural brightness level and are usually best used at this level. For example, yellow is normally bright, while blue and purple are normally rather dark.

The temptation to include a wide-ranging gamut of colors should be resisted, usually. Unity in color can be aided by including, if possible, a relatively small number of hues and by letting one hue dominate through its repetition; or either the warm colors (red, orange, and to some extent yellow) or the cool colors (blues and greens) should dominate. Study of fine color photographs and paintings will reveal this as a common principle in color composition.

Contrasting colors can accentuate and thus draw attention to centers of interest or, contrarywise, draw attention away, thus working against the photographer's purpose.

Color can contribute to mood, suggesting warmth, coolness, weight or lack of weight, and size. These emotional effects of color are the result of psychological associations and literary allusions made familiar and convincing through repetition, but the associations can vary with circumstances and with geography and culture. Red is not only warm, but the symbol of danger, courage, passion. Orange, also warm, is associated with the annual harvest and can convey a sense of well-being and happiness. Yellow and green are somewhat ambiguous because of conflicting associations; yellow, in general a warm color, can suggest cowardice but is often pleasing and exciting in association with red and orange. Green can suggest tranquillity and safety, but is also associated with sickness and envy. Blues give an impression of coolness and, like violet and purple, may suggest dignity, richness, royalty.

Both colors and lighting affect the illusion of the third dimension in a photograph. Red is an advancing color; that is, it tends to stand out against the background, while blue is receding. Light colors against dark strengthen the illusion of depth. Diffuse lighting reduces depth; direct, side light deepens it.

Brilliantly colored objects should usually be sharply focused, but de-saturated hues, pastel shades, can be effective in blurred shapes. Dark colors suggest weight, while pastel shades indicate lightness and large size. In general, the larger the area, the weaker the color should be; the smaller the area, the stronger the color can be, and large areas of weak saturation balance small areas of strong saturation.

One of the best ways to develop an understanding of and personal feeling for color composition is to experiment. A variety of experiments and therefore experience can usually be accomplished with still life setups. A wide range of objects of various colors can be secured easily and they can be moved about at will, or they can remain fixed while lighting and background are changed. In experimenting with still life setups it is best to begin with simple arrangements of a few items; additional ones can be added as experimenting proceeds. Later experiments can be planned on the basis of what has been learned in previous ones, thus developing cumulative experience difficult to duplicate with random selection of subjects that just happen to present themselves.

This sort of planned study is best done with a camera that permits examination of composition on a ground glass. However, a large format camera is not necessary; a single-lens reflex, such as the Pentax, or a twin-lens reflex, such as the Rolleiflex, will serve admirably, and the cost of each exposure will be significantly less than with a large view camera.

Chapter 14

COLOR AS WE PHOTOGRAPH IT

With the fundamentals of color as seen behind us we can turn to the problems of color as photographed. Fortunately, researchers, who began their work almost with the beginning of black-and-white photography, have found the basic answers through long and complex research. We need only survey their answers to learn how best to use color films for reproduction of images.

Once upon a time, not really so very long ago, color photography was discouragingly expensive and difficult, requiring special cameras and knowledge of complex processing techniques that only the most determined had the patience to master. Today any camera is a color camera. The last remaining major obstacle to satisfactory color for the amateur—exposure calculation—is bowing to the assault of the automated camera. Progress since World War II has also included tremendous increases in the emulsion speeds of color materials, so that they now approach the speeds of the commonly used black-and-white films. And the end is by no means in sight.

The camera user, if he prefers, need do little more than push a button; the color lab will do the rest. Casual photography with color film has become as simple as black-and-white photography. But serious color photography has never been simple and probably never will be. The serious photographer wants consistent, predictable results, and planning based on knowledge always produces a higher percentage of successes than the law of averages. Consistent success with color film demands an understanding of at least the basic structure and processing of the film.

EARLY COLOR PROCESSES

Two routes to color photography appear to be available. The first and most obvious, because it is the most direct, is duplication in the picture of the spectral composition (the various wavelengths of light) reflected by the original subject. This was the approach on which much of the research and experimentation in the nineteenth century was based, resulting in color photographs made by Gabriel Lippmann in 1891 in Paris. The Lippmann process relies upon the phenomenon of interference in light waves reflected from a supporting layer underneath the emulsion. The silver halides in the emulsion are exposed and developed in layers separated by a distance equal to one half the wavelength of the light that caused the exposure. These layers of developed silver set up interference patterns in the light used to view the picture and thus reproduce the colors (wavelengths) of the original image. The principal involved is a familiar one; the colors we see in an oily film on the surface of water are caused by interference. Excellent photographs have been made by the Lippmann process, but it never became a practical system because of formidable processing techniques involved, the necessarily extremely slow speed of the emulsion (requiring exposures of minutes even in bright sunlight), and the necessity of viewing the finished product from one direction only. The Lippmann process is only of historical interest, and any attempt at further explanation would require more information on light and mathematics than we have been able to encompass in this book.

While the experiments with the Lippmann process were going on, other researchers had taken the second, indirect route to color photography. This involves no effort to duplicate the physical makeup of the original light, but simply to match it with a sensation compounded of a mixture of color primaries. Such an approach divides itself naturally into two major parts: (1) extracting separate records of the primary colors in the light reflected from the subject, and (2) reassembling these records into a unified positive image that will match the subject in color as well as in form.

One line of research resulted in an interesting and, at least to some extent, practical color system early in the twentieth century. This has been given the general name of the *additive* process. The exposure was made through a mosaic screen consisting of a great many tiny and transparent red, green, and blue spots. These spots were the filters used to separate the three primaries in the exposing light. After the emulsion had been developed and reversed to a positive, the resulting transparency was viewed through the same or a duplicate grid of colored spots. The appropriate amount of each primary color was thus transmitted from each tiny section of the image. The system works because the color spots are too small to be seen separately by the eye. Instead, the sensation is one created by additive mixture; the colors are seen as though the source were a uniform color of the mixture.

Best remembered of these processes was the Lumière Autochrome plate, which used a mixture of red, green, and blue dyed potato starch grains to form the mosaic. Dyed globules of resin were used in later materials. A difficulty with the Lumière process lay in getting an even distribution of the dyed grains, so that grains of a single color would not be clumped together in one place. To avoid this problem a method was devised for making a mechanically ruled screen of red, green, and blue lines to use as

A color division winner in the Annual Newspaper National Snapshot Awards.
(Katherine L. Lass, San Pedro, Calif.)

the filter mosaic. This is the method used in Dufaycolor. But the additive system still had many disadvantages in lengthy exposures, lack of sharp definition, and cost.

SEPARATION TECHNIQUES

So the additive system, using the mosaic filter, did not satisfy everyone. The search for a better way continued, beginning at the first step again, with separation of the primary colors.

This first step, obtaining separate records of the red, green, and blue light reflected from a subject, is not so difficult. Almost any camera, firmly placed and focused on an immobile subject, will do this. We simply expose three sheets of black-and-white panchromatic film one at a time, one through a red filter, one through a green filter, and one through a blue filter. The three images thus obtained are called *separation negatives*. But this method is impractical for a subject that may move between exposures and obviously, then, would be impractical for general use.

We can overcome this difficulty with the one-shot color cameras, which split the beam of light from a single lens into three parts to form three images identical in form but varying in densities according to the primary color filter placed in front of each sheet of film. The light is split by using pellicle mirrors, very thin semitransparent sheets that reflect only part of the light and transmit the rest. The first mirror set at an angle behind the lens deflects roughly one third of the light to the blue record film. A second mirror divides the remaining light, deflecting approximately one half to the red record film and passing the other half to the green record. The camera, a necessarily bulky affair, is constructed so that each sheet of film is held at the correct focal distance and all three images are sharp and identical in size.

Thus we see that separation records are not difficult to get, but what of the second step, reassembling those records in one image? Separation negatives can be used in a number of ways. Let us briefly examine three of them.

We can use each negative to make a positive transparency on a second sheet of black-and-white film. Each transparency is then placed in its own projector. The positive red record is projected through a red filter, green through a green filter, and blue through a blue filter. Color addition gives colors matching the original when all three are projected on a white screen simultaneously and in accurate superimposition. But this is complicated and limited in practical use.

Well, then, we can make black-and-white prints from the separation negatives. The prints, in turn, can be used to make photoengravings for full color reproductions in books, magazines, and newspapers. The engravings are used to print colored inks onto paper. But that does not give us a colored photograph.

So we can try making photographic prints from the separation negatives. This requires that three dyed positive images be superimposed in exact register on a single sheet of white paper. A number of methods have been tried for making the color positives, but only two have had any widespread use. They are the *imbibition* process and the *carbro* process. Both involve *tanning* development, a process that hardens the gelatin of the emulsion to a depth proportional to the amount of silver developed. The gelatin relief images secured by washing away the unhardened gelatin is then dyed with the subtractive primaries and superimposed in register. The Technicolor process in cinematography and the Kodak Dye Transfer process are methods of this sort. All such methods demand a great deal of skill and usually require *masking* to correct for the fact that the dyes used do not work perfectly. Masking involves superimposition of one photographic image on another to modify the result in the reproduction. These are processes for the advanced worker and as such are beyond the scope of this book.

THE INTEGRAL TRIPACK

Let us go back to the first step once more and try another approach. Why not arrange the three emulsions into sort of a triple-decker sandwich so that one exposure will strike all three, with red light recording on one, green on another, and blue on the third? At first this seems like a good idea, but we soon encounter a problem: if each emulsion is coated on a separate base it is impossible to get all three into contact, so the image cannot be focused sharply on all three at the same time.

The answer to simplified color photography finally came from this sandwich idea, however, in the form of the *integral tripack,* three emulsions coated on the same base.

Two musicians—and amateur photographers—Leopold Mannes and Leopold Godowsky, were primarily responsible for the first practical application of the multilayer principle. They became interested in color photography when they were sixteen years old, conducting their first experiments in the bathrooms of their homes in New York City. They somehow found time to study physics and mathematics as well as music, and in 1930 they accepted an invitation to join Eastman Kodak in a concentrated attack on the problem. For five years the research and testing went on in Kodak's laboratories in Rochester, New York, with Mannes and Godowsky occasionally timing development in the darkroom by whistling classical music.

In 1935, Kodak announced the first integral tricolor film, Kodachrome, the film that became the standard by which all other color films were judged for many years. A year later Agfa in Germany announced a tripack film. The principal difference between the two involved the method of producing the color in the three separate emulsions. Kodachrome did not (and does not today) contain dye couplers, as they are called, within the emulsion layers; these were provided by the developing solutions. Agfa, however, had solved the problem of preventing the molecules of dye from wandering from one emulsion to another and so had placed the couplers in the emulsions along with the silver halides. Thirty years after these first practical color films were placed on the market, there were 30 different color films available, most of which included the color couplers in the emulsion layers, anchored there by being joined with giant molecules too big to meander about. We shall return to the problem of the dye couplers when we discuss processing principles, but first we must examine the basic structure of the integral tripack color film.

One basic structure is common to most of the current color films. A majority are designed for reversal processing; that is, the original film is first developed to a negative image and then the same material is reversed to a positive. These films almost universally are designated by the suffix *chrome*—for example, Kodachrome and Anscochrome. A minority of the current color films produce negatives intended for making color prints. These are generally designated by the suffix *color;* Kodacolor and Ekta-color are examples.

The three emulsion layers are coated on the film base one after the other. The bottom layer is sensitive to red light and the middle layer to green light. The top layer is sensitive to blue light only; green and red light pass through it without exposing the color-blind halides in this top emulsion. Since there is no way to make the silver bromide crystals in the middle and bottom layers insensitive to blue light, some way had to be found to prevent blue wavelengths from penetrating beyond the top emulsion. This was accomplished by coating a yellow filter layer above the green sensitive emulsion. This yellow filter, formed of finely divided silver known as Carey-Lea silver suspended in gelatin, absorbs any penetrating blue light but freely passes green and red. After exposure the yellow color of the filter layer is destroyed during processing.

The middle emulsion layer directly under the yellow filter is orthochro-

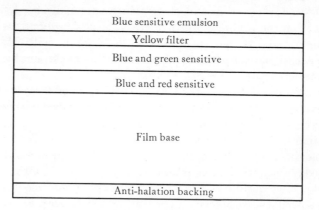

FIGURE 30

Cross section of color film.

matic, sensitive to blue (which cannot reach it) and green, but not to red. So the red light passes on to the bottom panchromatic emulsion, which is sensitive to blue (which cannot reach it) and red. Its sensitivity to green is so small as to be negligible. So the exposure is made simultaneously in the three extremely thin emulsions, each layer responding to one of the additive color primaries.

PROCESSING THE TRIPACK

The key to all tripack processes lies in *coupler* (color-forming) *development*. You will remember from Chapter 12 that during development, when the exposed silver halides are reduced to metallic silver, the developing agent is oxidized. The oxidation product is highly reactive and will immediately join in a chemical reaction with other substances incorporated either in the color film emulsions or in the color developer solutions. These substances that react with the oxidation product are the couplers. The reaction forms the dyes of the colored image. The insoluble dyes formed are the colors of the subtractive primaries, and they appear in the three emulsion layers in exact proportion to the amount of silver developed in each layer. The coupler in the top layer forms a yellow dye to subtract blue where there was no blue in the photographic subject; magenta is formed in the middle layer to subtract green, and cyan is formed in the bottom layer to subtract red.

It is in the processing that Kodachrome and a few other films depart from the majority of color materials. Kodachrome cannot be processed by the photographer because of the extreme complexity of the technique involved. Since the color couplers are not placed in the emulsions of Kodachrome, they must be supplied in the developing solutions. This means each emulsion layer must be given separate processing, a difficult technique requiring considerable training and extensive equipment. However, if the couplers are incorporated within the various emulsion layers, a single developer will reduce the exposed halides to silver and form the appropriate color in all three emulsions simultaneously. The dye color formed is controlled by the chemical structure of the couplers incorporated in each layer. This greatly simplifies the process and makes color developing in the home darkroom quite feasible.

In general, color developers are similar to black-and-white developers. They contain the same basic ingredients of developing agent, activator, preservative, and restrainer. However, proportions differ, the color-developing agent is a more complicated compound, and the solution contains additional special ingredients. Stronger alkalies, often two, are used as activators in color developers and, in addition, benzyl alcohol is frequently added as a booster to accelerate the penetration of the reducing agent into the three emulsion layers. A silver halide solvent is also included to help produce transparencies with clear whites by removing any excess silver halides. The concentration of the preservative (sodium sulfite) is much less than in black-and-white developers, because the oxidation products must be free to react with the couplers. A high concentration of sulfite would inhibit this; yet some preservative is necessary to curb aerial oxidation and to prevent stains. Citrazinic acid is sometimes added to color developers to control contrast by reacting with oxidation products to form colorless compounds.

REVERSAL FILMS

Whether couplers are incorporated in emulsions or in solutions, in either case the silver image must be removed by bleaching and the colored dye image left. Reversal films are first developed to a negative silver image in a developer that does not form any color, only the same sort of negative as black-and-white development produces. The film is then exposed to a strong, white light for a long enough time to form latent-image silver on all remaining halide crystals. Since the negative-image silver has already been exposed and developed, whatever silver we can develop from the remaining silver halides must form a positive image.

The light sensitivity of the wet emulsions is quite low, so the fogging exposure must be heavy. It is impossible to overexpose at this stage, because we want all the remaining silver halides to develop to give the full density of the positive image. The film is usually exposed by holding it about a foot away from a photoflood lamp for five to ten seconds.

After the second exposure the film goes into the second developer, a color coupler developer, which not only develops the positive silver image but the color image at the same time. Then all the silver is bleached out of the three emulsions and only the color image is left. The result is a positive transparency, which, when placed over a white light, will transmit the colors of the original subject by subtraction. Where cyan and magenta dyes appear in the transparency (the two dye images overlapping) only blue will be transmitted; yellow and cyan will transmit only green; yellow and magenta, only red. If there is a heavy dye deposit in all three layers, all light will be absorbed and black is the result; white appears if there is no dye in any of the layers. Colors other than blue, green, red, yellow, magenta, and cyan are produced by partial absorptions in various layers; orange will result from heavy absorption of blue light by yellow dye in the top layer, partial absorption of green light by some magenta dye in the middle layer, and no (or very little) absorption of red in the bottom layer.

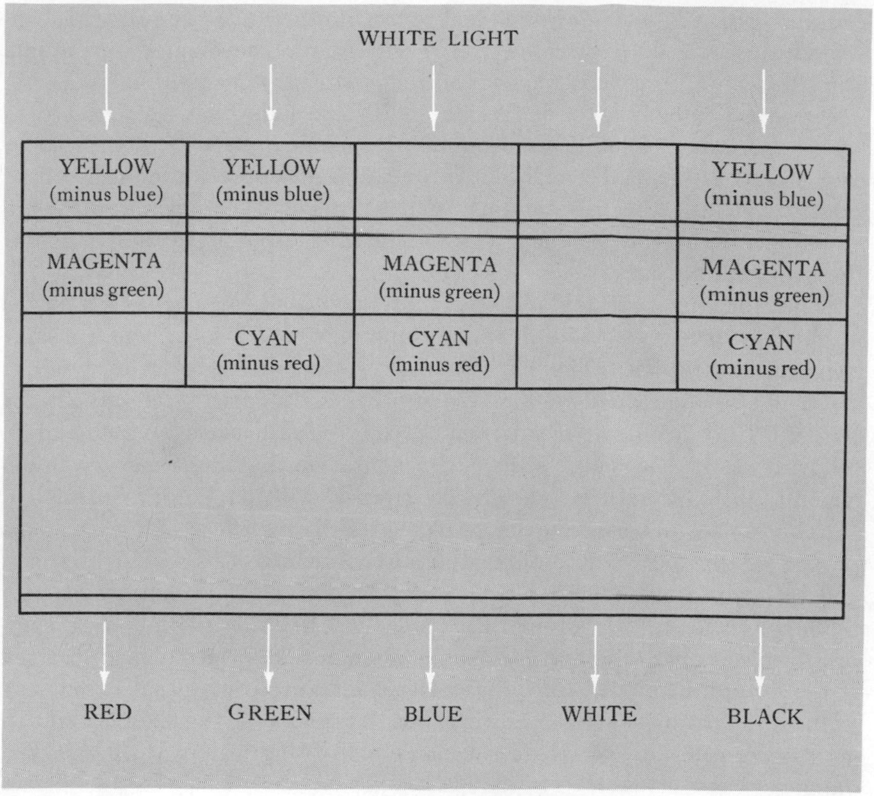

WHITE LIGHT

	RED	GREEN	BLUE	WHITE	BLACK
	YELLOW (minus blue)	YELLOW (minus blue)			YELLOW (minus blue)
	MAGENTA (minus green)		MAGENTA (minus green)		MAGENTA (minus green)
		CYAN (minus red)	CYAN (minus red)		CYAN (minus red)

RED   GREEN   BLUE   WHITE   BLACK

FIGURE 31

How color is reproduced in a positive transparency.

The essential steps of color reversal processing for films other than the Kodachrome type can be summarized as follows:

1. First development, to reduce exposed silver halides to the negative silver image.
2. Rinse and treatment in stop or hardening baths if recommended.
3. Reversal exposure for undeveloped silver halides.
4. Color development, to reduce all remaining silver halides to the positive silver image and, at the same time, to produce dyes in the three emulsions.
5. Another rinse, and clearing bath if recommended.
6. Bleaching, to convert all silver to soluble silver salts, leaving only dyes.
7. Rinse followed by fixing bath to dissolve silver salts.
8. Final wash.

The bleach used in color processing must remove the silver without affecting the dyes. A common bleach used after the second development contains potassium ferricyanide and potassium bromide. The silver is converted back to silver bromide, the reverse of the development reaction, and the silver bromide is removed in the customary fashion, in hypo.

Frequent rinsing, part of the reason for the lengthy time required in color processing, is vitally important. All chemicals left in the film after each treatment must be removed to prevent contamination of subsequent solutions. Plain running water is usually sufficient for rinsing, although sometimes chemicals may be added to neutralize or remove the residue of the previous bath.

Solutions cannot be used indiscriminately with all color materials. Baths in various processes perform similar functions but do not have the same chemical composition. The manufacturer works out a process in detail to match a specified product, then he supplies a prepared chemical kit for use with that product. Instructions for mixing and processing should be followed closely, although some experimentation may be necessary to determine slight variations that may be required with particular equipment.

Color materials must be processed carefully if the result is to be a proper balance between the three different emulsions. Temperatures, times, and agitation must be controlled accurately. The first development is particularly critical with reversal film, since too little or too much development leaves either too much or too little silver for the positive image formed in the second developer, thus giving either a transparency that is too dark or too light. In most steps following first development, the chemical action goes to completion; too little time or too little agitation is the greatest danger.

Whereas exposure and development latitude in negative materials is quite considerable, it is almost nonexistent with color reversal films because there is no printing stage when corrections and manipulations are possible. For a good quality image with reversal films, exposure and first development must be accurately balanced; any variation inevitably degrades picture quality.

From one viewpoint, reversal film can be regarded as the automatic film: if it is exposed correctly and processing instructions are followed closely, good results are virtually guaranteed. If processing is left to the film manufacturer or to any of the many reliable commercial laboratories, the photographer has only correct exposure as his responsibility, but this is a major one. Careful use of an exposure meter and accurate computations with flash are musts with color reversal film for consistent results. In addition, every color reversal film has a certain *color balance,* which is determined at time of manufacture. The colors of the image will accurately match the colors of the subject only if the illumination of the subject matches the color balance of the film. This subject is discussed more fully in the next chapter.

COLOR NEGATIVE FILMS

Color couplers are incorporated in the emulsion layers of all color negative films. After exposure these films are put through only one developer—a color developer, which produces a negative color image at the same time as it forms the negative silver in each layer. Blue skies are recorded as brownish-yellow in a color negative; greens appear as magenta, and yellow as blue. The silver image and undeveloped silver halides are removed by bleaching and fixing. The dye images are the same old friends, the subtractive primaries—yellow, magenta, and cyan, reading from the film's top emulsion layer to the bottom one. These colors are the negative or complementary colors to those of the subject that caused the exposure in each layer.

The color negative is used to expose three emulsions with incorporated color couplers that have been coated on paper. Processing of this material in a color developer, bleaching out the silver image and fixing out the undeveloped silver halides leaves a positive color image, formed again by the subtractive primaries. The negatives may also be used for exposing film for making color transparencies, or they may be used to expose a special panchromatic emulsion coated on paper to produce black-and-white prints.

The color negative system has been found to offer special advantages for reproduction of color photographs in newspapers. The negative is put in the enlarger in the usual way, but three black-and-white prints are made from the one negative on panchromatic paper. One print is made through a red filter; this makes the blue printer, the print from which a halftone engraving will be made to print the blue ink on the press. A green filter makes the red printer and a blue filter makes the yellow printer. The filters are complementary to the color being printed because we are making a positive from a negative. Masking is generally needed in this process, because the inks used on newspaper presses give unwanted undercolor: too much red under the blues and greens, too much yellow under the reds, blues, and violets. The masks subtract this unwanted color and also reduce the contrast in the separation prints. The prints are sent to the engraving department where the three printing plates are made.

Making color prints from color negatives has been greatly simplified for the photographer, since the manufacturer has built into the films—for instance, Eastman's Kodacolor—masks formed of color couplers. This is the reason Kodacolor negatives have a strong, overall orange cast. This built-in mask corrects for the imperfect functioning of the subtractive dyes.

In addition, the photographer can control color-rendering in the final

Simple in composition, but a prizewinner in the original color shot. (Austin D. Murray, Alexandria, Va.)

print, but he must use various filters in combinations to alter the light that reaches the emulsions of the printing paper. This is the reason one type of negative color film can be used for all subjects regardless of the nature of the illumination. Any distorted color values created by the illumination can be corrected during printing. Here, in fact, lies a major advantage of the color negative process. Just as in black-and-white processing, the negative and the positive are separate stages and can be separately controlled, permitting corrections. Dodging and fundamentally all the other controls available in black-and-white printing are also available in color printing from color negatives.

There appears to be no indication that reversal (positive transparency) color films will decrease in popularity, especially among amateur photographers, and we can see no reason why this popularity should decrease. However, it is quite possible that we will see significantly increased use of negative color films, at least among professional photographers shooting pictures for reproduction in newspapers, magazines, and books. Negative color is already the standard system with a great many newspapers because it is faster and cheaper when the end product is a full-color reproduction on a printing press.

Because the first color photographs were positive transparencies, this was the system to which engravers and printers geared their techniques for making color printing plates. Several different ways have been devised for producing the printing plates, but all of them necessitate the production of a negative from the positive.

With the color negative system, the negative is already available from the film exposed in the photographer's camera. It can be used to make a color-corrected print for the guidance of editors and engravers and to make the color separation prints on panchromatic paper, masked for color correction and improved with art work, ready for the engraver to screen and engrave. In general practice, the color negative system is faster and less expensive, because two steps have been eliminated. We do not have to reverse the original film image to a positive, nor do we have to turn the positive back into a negative for making color separations.

Chapter 15

COLOR EXPOSURE
AND FILTERING

For anyone who has taken even a few photographs with color film it will come as no surprise to be told that exposure is critical. Exposure is, in fact, the single greatest technical problem. In black-and-white photography, processing is normally divided into two stages, and shortcomings evident after the negative stage can often be corrected during the positive stage. The same is true, to a somewhat lesser degree, with color negative film since it, too, involves the two processing stages. But with color reversal films negative and positive are inextricably linked in a single series of processing steps. This means the original exposure of the film in the camera determines both negative and positive images.

The positive image is formed from the silver halides left in the three emulsions after the negative image is developed. For purposes of illustration, let us assume 100 silver halide grains are available for image formation in a small section of the film where an image highlight has been recorded. We shall further assume that we need a minimum of 20 of those grains to form adequate highlight detail and adequate color in the positive image. If exposure has produced latent-image silver on 90 of those grains, all 90 will be reduced in the first developer. We have only 10 left for reduction and color forming in the second development. The connection between cause and effect is obvious: too much exposure in the camera will produce a thin picture in pastel colors with highlight detail lost. The reverse will be true of shadow areas with too little exposure, leaving too many halides for second (color) development, resulting in dark, detail-less shadows.

In general, we assume the exposure latitude of color films to be only about a half-stop on either side of correct exposure. Actually, this is only true of subjects of average contrast. When the brightness range of the subject is short, exposure latitude with color film may be as much as two stops.

An exposure meter, properly used, will significantly increase the percentage of successful exposures with color film. Close-up meter readings are advisable, if feasible, of the lighter (but not the very lightest) areas of the subject. For most subjects correct rendition of the colors with light or medium brightness is most important. Even after exposure has been determined by the photographer's best judgment, based on an exposure meter's reading, it is often advisable to take three shots, bracketing the indicated exposure at one-stop or one-half stop intervals.

With reversal color films underexposure is generally preferable to overexposure. In fact, a slight underexposure may result in the most pleasing transparency, because it gives richly saturated colors. If there is a general rule on exposure with color film, it is just the opposite of the one often suggested for black-and-white film. With black-and-white film we expose for the shadows, favoring overexposure, but with color film we expose for the highlights, favoring underexposure.

A subject of high contrast (dense shadows and brilliant highlights) may be beyond the limited exposure range of color film. No exposure will be correct for all parts of the scene. This requires a decision favoring the most important part. Every photographer as he begins work with color film generally needs some experience with various subjects before he learns to recognize those with a brightness range exceeding film latitude. A major part of our difficulty stems from a remarkable characteristic of the mechanism with which we have been equipped for seeing, a characteristic that normally operates to our great advantage. It is only in photography that it becomes something of a handicap.

The eye adjusts in two ways to meet the fluctuations in illumination. Nearly everyone is familiar with the dilation and contraction of the iris of the eye. When the iris is wide open it admits about 16 times as much light to the retina as when it is fully stopped down. But in addition, the retina itself changes, automatically decreasing its sensitivity in bright light. By this system of *brightness adaptation* the eye maintains a relatively constant level of response, giving us approximately equal vision indoors and out. But this also means that our eyes are unreliable as instruments for estimating levels of illumination. Think for a moment of how bright the light from an incandescent lamp seems in a room at night, and then compare it in memory with how feeble the same lamp seems when the room is flooded by sunlight during the day.

In addition, the eye-brain assessment of the general level of illumination is strongly influenced by the contrast in the scene. We may decide that an indoor scene strongly lighted by a direct source is brighter than an outdoor scene under a cloudy sky. Actually the outdoor scene, though flatly lighted, has a much higher brightness level. Colors involved may also mislead us in visual estimations of brightness because highly saturated colors look brighter under relatively low lighting than colors of low saturation under strong lighting.

Brightness adaptation may take several seconds or even minutes to occur under conditions of extreme change. As you step from a brightly lighted

Humor is relatively rare in photography, but worth striving for. This was a prizewinning color shot in the original. (Mrs. Ann Minici, Douglas, Ariz.)

room into a photographic laboratory lighted only by safelights you find it almost impossible to see your way about for several seconds. But it is important to note that brightness adaptation occurs in less extreme situations and as the eye scans a limited scene, within one room or from one position outdoors. The eye changes its sensitivity, not only with the general illumination, but also with the particular area it is focused upon. As the eye moves from one part of the scene to another, brightness adaptation takes place very rapidly, requiring perhaps no longer than two tenths of a second, although this will vary greatly with conditions. Thus, we see detail in the highlights of a sunlight scene and detail in the shadows as well, with little or no apparent difficulty.

Still another characteristic of vision is involved here, a characteristic mentioned previously in Chapter 13 in connection with the way we see color. We tend to see objects as we know them to be, rather than as they actually are under a given light. Thus, a man's white shirt is still white, although he may be standing in a shadow, and looks brighter to us, perhaps, than another man's gray shirt in direct sunlight. Actually the gray shirt may be reflecting the most light. This characteristic of vision has been given the name of *brightness constancy*.

Brightness adaptation and brightness constancy are important in all photography, but they take on increased importance with color reversal films because of the short latitude of these films. Shadows always appear darker in the print or transparency than they did in the actual scene. This explains why flat lighting is so often recommended for color photography. The recommended lighting will look flat to the eye because of brightness adaptation and brightness constancy, but it will not be recorded as flat by the film.

Recommended lighting for color film gives only two or three times as much illumination to the highlights as to the shadows. All areas of the subject must be adequately lighted if we are to avoid shadow regions so dark that color and detail are lost. These areas will be obvious in the print or transparency, but don't blame the film. Brightness adaptation and brightness constancy kept those problem shadows from being evident to the eye you used to peer through the camera viewfinder.

Problem shadow areas confront the photographer both indoors and out. He can either sacrifice a part of the picture or throw some light into the shadows to get a closer balance between them and the highlights. Reflectors may serve the purpose—sometimes the natural reflecting surfaces inherent in the situation, such surfaces as sand or water. The use of reflectors mentioned in Chapter 9 will serve with color film as long as they do not change the color of the light. The flash fill technique discussed in the same chapter will work with color film, too, if the film and flash are properly matched in color temperature.

In lighting with artificial sources it is important to remember they provide a situation quite different from sunlight. Light falls off, we already know, at a rate roughly proportional to the square of the distance. The sun, however, is so tremendously far away that differences in distances from the sun to various objects on the earth are so small relative to the total distance involved that the effect is infinitesimal. But a light source we supply is relatively close to the objects to be photographed, and even two or three feet difference in distance from light to object can mean a significant difference in lighting. Brightness constancy may make it difficult for us to see this difference, but it will be strongly evident in the print or transparency.

COLOR BALANCE

An important factor in color photography is the color quality of the light illuminating the subject. Again, we are dealing here more with a characteristic of the mechanism of vision than we are with the idiosyncrasies of color film. Just as the eye is capable of brightness adaptation, so it is capable of *general color adaptation*. It seems that when our eyes are adapted to daylight the three receptor systems are about equal in sensitivity, and so the general illumination appears to be white or colorless. When we move indoors to a room illuminated by ordinary incandescent (tungsten) lamps we may at first notice a slight yellowish hue to the lighting. But soon this impression fades and the light indoors seems as white as the light we just left outdoors. The artificial lighting is yellower than daylight because tungsten light sources are weak in the blue end of the spectrum and somewhat weak in the green region. The eye, adjusting for this variation from the spectral-energy distribution of daylight, increases the sensitivity of the blue-light receptor system a good deal, and increases the sensitivity of the green-light receptor system somewhat. Thus, a sheet of white paper viewed outdoors in daylight and then taken indoors under tungsten light should look yellow, because the illumination indoors is definitely yellow compared with the daylight. But eye and brain report the paper is unchanged; it is still white. The color-receptor systems of the eye have adjusted to keep it so. Furthermore, there is another phenomenon involved that is known as *color constancy*. All normal colors tend to appear as they do in daylight regardless of the color quality of the illumination. Part of this is the result of general color adaptation, but part seems to be the result of color memory—our tendency to see colors as we know they should be.

Now, no color film as yet manufactured has either color adaptation or color memory. A film that correctly records a white sheet of paper as white in daylight records that same sheet of paper as a pale yellow in tungsten light. The film is given a particular color balance at the time it is made,

A *$1000 award winner in the Annual Newspaper National Snapshot Awards.* (Saunder Harris, Westport, Conn.)

and this cannot be altered. It is, however, possible to make changes in the color balance during the printing operation with color negative film.

There are basically two types of reversal films in terms of color balance: one type is balanced for daylight and the other is balanced for tungsten light.

Daylight-type films obviously cannot be manufactured to give equally accurate color rendition in all possible daylight situations. Color quality varies significantly between the time when the sun is shining directly on a subject and when the sun is momentarily obscured by a passing cloud. A radical difference occurs between sunrise and noon, and between noon and sunset. Daylight-type film is color balanced for use in sunlight on clear and hazy days between midmorning and midafternoon. These daylight-type films can be used for flash exposures with electronic flash or with blue flashbulbs. In effect, the blue tint in the lacquer covering the bulb's outside surface raises the color temperature of the light to approximately the level of daylight. The blue coating accomplishes this by filtering out some of the yellow, orange, and red wavelengths but letting all the blue rays pass.

Films for use with tungsten light are divided into three types. Type A films are balanced for the light from photoflood lamps rated at 3400 Kelvin. (See page 156 for explanation of Kelvin ratings.) Type B films are balanced for the light from 3200 K lamps. (This assumes that all lamps are used at rated voltage. If voltage falls below normal the Kelvin rating or color temperature of the light will also drop.) Type F films are balanced for use with clear flashbulbs. These tungsten-light films have increased sensitivity to blue and decreased sensitivity to red, thus compensating (as the eye does) for the difference in the color quality of the light.

Unless the photographer is seeking special effects he will not mix light sources of different spectral-energy distribution. No color film made can cope with a mixture of daylight and tungsten and give color rendition for both that will appear correct to the eye. If daylight films are used with tungsten light, the effect is an overall shift to the warm tones. A tungsten-balanced film used with daylight illumination will give an image with a shift to the cool tones; the picture will have an overall bluish cast. Such color shifts are not necessarily objectionable; it depends upon the photographer's objective. Sometimes a deliberate imbalance between film and illumination is chosen to achieve a certain effect. Actually, of course, color film gives, at best, only an approximation of true colors, no matter how ideal the conditions of exposure. But true rendition is only of great importance in scientific and medical photography; for the ordinary photographer the small color shifts that occur even when the film is used as the manufacturer intended will favor the photographic purpose more often than not.

In addition to balancing the sensitivities of the three emulsions to accommodate the type of illumination, the manufacturer of color materials also balances his films for either a short or a long exposure time. Reciprocity failures (see page 18) are much more frequent with color films than with black-and-white films, another aspect of the difference in exposure latitude. With color films, reciprocity failure is not simply a matter of loss of speed, compensated for by increasing exposure times, but it is also a matter of shifting color balance, since the effect of reciprocity failure varies between the three emulsions.

Most color films, of course, are intended for short exposures, since most pictures are taken with the shutter set between 1/25 and 1/200 of a second. A very few films, however, are intended for exposures of 1/5 of a second or longer. Kodak Ektacolor Type L is an example.

Color variations exist between the different brands of color film because of a difference in dyes employed. A quite noticeable difference exists, for example, in the colors recorded of the same subject by Kodachrome, Ektachrome, and Anscochrome. Some films favor the red end of the spectrum and tend to produce warm transparencies; others favor the blues and greens. The beginner should choose one kind of color film and use it regularly and exclusively until enough experience has accumulated to make changing films meaningful.

FILTERS FOR COLOR

Reversal color films that are balanced for one particular kind of light source can be used under other sources with the appropriate filter or filters over the camera lens. The filters alter the color quality of the light reaching the film and so alter the relative response from the three emulsion layers.

Whether or not you will wish to use filters extensively will depend primarily on how much control you want to exercise over color rendition. Full control with color reversal films is only possible with filters, so professional photographers often have an expensive kit full of filters. Others, who need to worry much less about color rendition, can get along quite comfortably with one to three filters.

Greater and more diverse needs exist for filters with color than with black-and-white, and as a result filters for color films seem to exist in prodigal profusion. To keep this from becoming mere confusion we should remember that filters for color films fall into three general classifications: (1) specific purpose conversion filters, (2) light-balancing filters, and (3) color-compensating filters.

A $500 prizewinner in the original color shot. (Louis L. Wood, Jr., Washington, D.C.)

SPECIAL PURPOSE FILTERS

The most commonly used filter in color work is the skylight or ultra-violet filter. The Kodak Skylight Filter (No. 1A) looks almost clear but has a slight pinkish cast. This is used to get rid of unwanted blue, which often appears in pictures of subjects in open shade, on rainy or overcast days, in distant scenic views, and in the shadows of snow scenes on bright days. The skylight filter is no longer essential with the new Kodachrome films, although it is still a help in some situations. Its benefits are most evident in close-up portraits made in the shade or on an overcast day. With Kodachrome II the skylight filter is not needed for subjects in bright sunlight or for brilliantly colored subjects in the shade. In some cases the distortion toward blue that daylight-type films give on a rainy, overcast day enhances the desired effect.

Ansco films require an ultraviolet filter, also almost colorless except for a slight yellowish tint, to accomplish the same purpose. The Kodak Skylight Filter and the ultraviolet filters designed for use with Ansco films are not interchangeable, however.

These filters require no increase in exposure. Some photographers leave one or the other on the lens all the time when shooting daylight-type film outdoors to protect the lens from dirt, sand, and water spray, and because they prefer the slight warming effect the filters give. Some camera lenses will affect color rendition, because some types of optical glass absorb ultraviolet rays. The need for a skylight filter, then, may vary with the lens.

Other special purpose filters are

> The Wratten 80B, a blue filter for daylight-type film with photoflood lighting.
> The Wratten 80C, for daylight-type film with photoflash lighting.
> The Wratten 85, a salmon-colored filter for Type A color films with daylight.
> The Wratten 85B, a salmon-colored filter for Type B color films with daylight.
> The Wratten 85C, for Type F color films with daylight.

In general, photographers have found converting tungsten film to daylight a much more successful procedure than the reverse. However, the best practice is to use the reversal film balanced for the particular light quality involved, whenever possible.

LIGHT-BALANCING FILTERS

Designed for changing the color quality of the light to match the color balance of tungsten-type films, light-balancing filters come in two series. The No. 82 (bluish) series raises the color temperature of a tungsten light source. The No. 81 (yellowish) series has the effect of lowering the temperature of the light.

Among the most useful of these filters are

> The 81A, used very much as the skylight filter with daylight emulsions to absorb ultraviolet and blue light and with Type B films (3200 K) for photoflood (3400 K) illumination.
> The 81D, for exposing tungsten film in daylight.
> The 82A, for exposing daylight film in sunlight before 9 A.M. and after 3 P.M. to reduce the warmish tone of the lighting, and for Type A film with 3200 K lamps.

Attempts to simplify the problem of calibrating light-balancing filters has resulted in the Decamired system. Mired stands for *micror*eciprocal *d*egrees, and Mireds are obtained by dividing color temperature into 1,000,000. The Decamired is 10 Mireds.

A Decamired system contains two sets of filters, one set of warming or reddish filters and one set of cooling or bluish filters. There will be three or four filters in each set. The Rolleiflex series of Decamired filters are numbered: R2, R5, and R11 in the red series, and B2, B5, and B11 in the blue series.

To use the DM filters the photographer subtracts the Decamired value of the light source from the Decamired value of the film. Manufacturers who furnish DM filters will also supply tables of these values, or the photographer can determine the DM value of the film by dividing its Kelvin rating (5500 K for most daylight-type films) into 1,000,000 and dividing again by 10. Color temperature meters are available, calibrated in Decamireds, for measuring the value of the light source.

Subtracting the DM value of the light source from the DM value of the film gives the required DM filter value. If it is a minus value, the need is a cooling or blue series filter; if a plus value, a warming or red series filter is required.

An example:

$$\text{Film rated at } 5500 \text{ K} = 18 \text{ DM}$$
$$\text{Light source is } 3400 \text{ K} = 29 \text{ DM}$$
$$\text{Then: } 18 - 29 = -11$$

We would need a B11 filter from the Rollei series.

COLOR-COMPENSATING FILTERS

To shift the color rendition either for effect or to correct for a given emulsion, color-compensating (CC) filters are used. These are aids for the professional photographer striving for precise color results. Color-compensating filters come in six colors—magenta, yellow, cyan, red, green, and blue—and in six or seven strengths (or densities) in each color, ranging from very light tints to those strongly colored. A filter in the CC series may be designated, for example, as a CC1OY, indicating it is a color-compensating filter with a density of .10 in yellow. The density is a measurement of the light-absorbing power of the filters. Each filter absorbs its complementary color or colors; in the case of the yellow filter, blue is absorbed. A red filter absorbs both blue and green (or cyan, red's complementary).

Professional photographers may run a series of exposure tests with a

The photographer held a piece of window screen over the lens to get the star burst effect on the sun and a piece of red cellophane (no filter at hand) to increase contrast. (Ed Maker, Staff Photographer, Denver *Post*)

new shipment of film to determine what CC filters must be used for critical studio work. Films occasionally vary slightly in color balance from one emulsion batch to the next, but this variation is so small it is of importance only to the professional worker who deals in critical color matching.

The same colors and values are used for color-printing (CP) filters made of acetate. They are designed for use in the color heads of enlargers and are more resistant to heat than CC filters.

FILTERS WITH NEGATIVE FILM

Filtering the light before it reaches the film can be ignored without heavy penalty in color rendering with negative films. The printing stage offers a supplementary control opportunity not available with reversal films. However, using a filter for the film exposing light may make printing easier in some cases, avoiding the necessity for extensive changes in the filter pack needed for color corrections at the printing stage. For example, an 81A (yellow) filter may help in photographing flowers in a shady area or in photographing snow scenes under a cloudless or nearly cloudless sky. An 82A (blue) filter helps in exposing Kodacolor and Ektacolor indoors with floodlights. If a single roll of Kodacolor film is to be exposed to both regular (clear) flashbulbs and daylight, the various negatives can be brought to approximately the same color balance by using the Kodak Wratten Filter No. 85C for the daylight shots. No filter is used with the flashbulb exposures. No filters are necessary with either daylight or flash if electronic flash is used instead of regular flashbulbs.

FILTER SUMMARY

The average photographer who is not intending to launch immediately into full-scale professional commercial or advertising photography will find the skylight (or ultraviolet) filter or the 81A filter (often recommended for use with new electronic flash units) the most useful. The second most useful filter for ordinary color photography is probably the polarizing filter, which will produce deep blue skies, increase color saturation, eliminate or subdue reflections in nonmetallic surfaces, and penetrate haze (when the camera axis is at right angles to the sun).

Another often useful filter is the 85C, since it will make it possible to take pictures outdoors with tungsten-balanced film. Or the choice may be the 85B filter, which works well with Kodak's High Speed Ektachrome film Type B. This film (ASA speed 125) is intended for shooting color transparencies indoors under existing light conditions, assuming the existing light comes from tungsten sources. (High Speed Ektachrome, Daylight Type, gives better results under fluorescent lighting.) The Type B film can be used outdoors with an 85B filter over the lens at an exposure index of 80. Thus, it is a fairly good all-around color film for transparencies.

Most of the filters for color film, with the exceptions of the skylight and ultraviolet filters, require an exposure correction to compensate for the light lost through filter absorption. The best procedure is to consult the film data sheet in each case for exposure factors or exposure recommendations with conversion filters. For light-balancing and CC filters, manufacturers furnish tables giving exposure data.

Although filters are ordinarily intended as tools for bringing exposing light into agreement with the color balance of the film, they can be used to do just the opposite: to introduce deliberate departures from normal color balance. Photographers do this to enhance the mood of the picture or to emphasize a personal interpretation.

CAMERAS FOR COLOR

Working with color reversal films puts a premium on correct composition in the camera viewfinder, since cropping is difficult with transparencies. This means a camera with interchangeable lenses is especially useful. Cameras that permit viewfinding on a ground glass also offer an advantage in color work. Offering both these features, plus relatively small cost per exposure, are the single-lens reflex (SLR) 35-mm cameras (such as the Honeywell Pentax) and the reflex cameras that take 120 size film, such as the single-lens Hasselblad and the twin-lens Rolleiflex. The ground-glass is ideal for color, because it helps the photographer really *see* his picture. This is important even with black-and-white film, but takes on added importance with color, because what might seem to be insignificant detail within the lens angle of view can have marked effect on the composition. An out-of-focus but bright and highly saturated spot of red in the background, for example, can easily throw a color composition out of balance. This spot of strong and distracting color will be quickly noticed in a ground-glass viewfinder.

With color reversal film all the work must be done before the shutter release is pressed. Once the exposure has been made, little can be done to alter the result.

BIBLIOGRAPHY

The literature of photography is extensive. Space does not permit an exhaustive listing here; the following is intended, rather, as a limited guide to further exploration of various topics in photography. The list does not include the more specialized books and manuals, nor does it include any selections from the vast periodical literature. For a much more exhaustive bibliography, see the one-volume *Photographic Literature* by Albert Boni (Morgan and Morgan, New York, 1962).

GENERAL

Among the general books the beginner will find helpful is the deservedly popular *This Is Photography* by Thomas H. Miller and Wyatt Brummitt (Garden City Books, Garden City, N.Y., 1959). An enduring standard reference book for the beginner, giving many detailed descriptions of techniques, is *The Amateur Photographer's Handbook* by Aaron Sussman, 6th edition (Crowell, New York, 1962).

Other excellent books for the beginner include

BOUCHER, Paul E., *Fundamentals of Photography,* D. Van Nostrand, New York, 1947.

DESCHIN, Jacob, *Say It with Your Camera, An Approach to Creative Photography,* Ziff-Davis, New York, 1960.

FEININGER, Andreas, *Feininger on Photography,* Crown, New York, 1953.

————, *Successful Photography,* Prentice-Hall, New York, 1954.

GOLDSMITH, Arthur A., Jr., *How to Take Better Pictures,* Bobbs-Merrill, New York, 1955.

HENLE, Fritz and H. M. Kinzer, *Photography for Everyone,* Viking, New York, 1959.

McCOY, Robert A., *Practical Photography,* McKnight and McKnight, Bloomington, Ill., 1950.

More advanced books covering photography in general, providing useful how-to-do-it helps, are

ABBOTT, Berenice, *New Guide to Better Photography,* Crown, New York, 1953.

FEININGER, Andreas, *Total Picture Control,* Crown, New York, 1961.

HALSMAN, Philippe, *Halsman on the Creation of Photographic Ideas,* Ziff-Davis, New York, 1961.

WHITING, John R., *Photography Is A Language,* Ziff-Davis, New York, 1946.

Strongly recommended are the Basic Photo Series books by Ansel Adams. The series includes separate books on *Camera and Lens, The Negative, The Print, Natural-Light Photography,* and *Artificial-Light Photography,* all published by Morgan and Morgan, New York. The Adams' Zone System of exposure is covered in *The Negative.* Also recommended for detailed explanation of the Zone System is *Zone System Manual* by Minor White (Morgan and Morgan, New York, 1961).

For intermediate and advanced level technical discussion and theory read

LARMORE, Lewis, *Introduction to Photographic Principles,* Prentice-Hall, Englewood Cliffs, N.J., 1958.
NEBLETTE, Carroll B. and others, *Photography, Its Materials and Processes,* D. Van Nostrand, New York, 1962.

PHOTOJOURNALISM

A beginner's guidebook with laboratory exercises is *Introductory and Publications Photography* by William C. Horrell (Kenilworth Press, Glen Ellyn, Ill., 1959). A similar basic manual is *Photographic Journalism, A Guide for Learning with the Graphic* by Truman Pouncey (William C. Brown, Dubuque, Iowa, 1952). *The Complete Book of Press Photography,* edited by Joseph Costa (New York, 1950), is a more advanced book, sponsored and published by the National Press Photographers Association. It is a collection of articles on special topics by experts. *Photojournalism, Pictures for Magazines and Newspapers* by Arthur Rothstein (Amphoto, New York, 1956) presumes some basic knowledge of photography and its techniques. *Graphic Graflex Photography* by Willard D. Morgan and Henry M. Lester (Morgan and Morgan, New York), frequently revised, is not basic, but offers numerous chapters on specialized techniques for publication photography. *Press Photography: Reporting with a Camera* by Robert B. Rhode and Floyd H. McCall (Macmillan, New York, 1961) treats newspaper photographers' camera and darkroom techniques. The book is illustrated with pictures taken by professional newspaper photographers. Illustrations are the strong feature of *1000 Ideas for Better News Pictures* by Hugh Sidey and Rodney Fox (Iowa State College Press, Ames, Iowa, 1956) and *Creative News Photography* by Rodney Fox and Robert Kerns (Iowa State University Press, Ames, Iowa, 1961). Theory and principles are emphasized in *Words and Pictures; An Introduction to Photojournalism* by Wilson Hicks (Harper, New York, 1952).

Those interested in free lancing in photography for newspapers and magazines should be acquainted with

ARNOLD, Edmund C., *Feature Photos that Sell,* Morgan and Morgan, New York, 1960.
GODSEY, Townsend, *Free Lance Photography,* Duell, Sloan and Pearce, New York, 1946.
ROSS, Kip, *Press Photography for the Free-Lance,* Ziff-Davis, New York, 1949.
SWEET, Ozzie, *My Camera Pays Off,* Amphoto, New York, 1958.

Legal problems in photography are discussed in *Photography and the Law* by George Chernoff and Hershel Sarbin (Amphoto, New York, 1958), useful for all photographers, but especially so for press photographers.

Student photographers, working for newspaper or yearbook, will find *Creative School Photography* by Irvin Lloyd (American Yearbook Co., Cambridge, Md., 1962) helpful, as well as *Better Pictures for a Better Yearbook* by Otha C. Spencer (Henington, Wolfe City, Texas, 1959).

Anyone interested in the available light techniques with the modern fast films and fast lenses will find specific and detailed suggestions by various professionals in *Available Light and Your Camera* (Amphoto, New York, 1956), edited by George B. Wright.

HISTORY OF PHOTOGRAPHY

Excellent and profusely illustrated are

POLLACK, Peter, *The Picture History of Photography,* Harry N. Abrams, New York, 1958.

GERNSHEIM, Helmut, *The History of Photography* [to 1914], Oxford University Press, London, 1955.

NEWHALL, Beaumont, *The History of Photography from 1839 to the Present Day,* revised and enlarged edition, Museum of Modern Art, New York, 1964.

NEWHALL, Beaumont and Nancy, *Masters of Photography,* George Braziller, New York, 1958.

Also historical in approach is *Creative Photography: Aesthetic Trends, 1839–1960* by Helmut Gernsheim (Boston Book and Art Shop, Boston, 1962). Less profusely illustrated but detailed in text is *History of Photography* by Joseph M. Eder (Columbia University Press, New York, 1945).

COLOR PHOTOGRAPHY

Fundamentals of color in general are covered thoroughly and understandably in *An Introduction to Color* by Ralph M. Evans (Wiley, New York, 1948). The book requires no particular background in the sciences or mathematics and gives extensive references to additional material. Another book by the same author, *Eye, Film, and Camera in Color Photography* (Wiley, New York, 1959), is an excellent guide to color photography as a creative medium. Also valuable is *Principles of Color Photography* by Ralph M. Evans, W. T. Hanson Jr., and W. Lyle Brewer (Wiley, New York, 1953). Neblette, *Photography, Its Materials and Processes* contains chapters on color photography by Howard C. Colton that cover some of the historically important processes.

Brief but useful are

Color as Seen and Photographed, 2nd edition, Eastman Kodak Co., Rochester, N.Y., 1962.

KRAMER, Arthur, *Color Photography Techniques,* Universal Photo Books, New York, 1958.

ROTHSTEIN, Arthur, *Creative Color in Photography,* Chilton, Philadelphia, 1963.

COMPOSITION

Provocative discussions, well illustrated, appear in

BARBER, E. Gordon, *Pictorial Composition in Monochrome and Colour,* Fountain Press, London, 1949.

BETHERS, Ray, *Composition in Pictures,* 2nd edition, Pitman, New York, 1956.
KEPES, Gyorgy, *Language of Vision,* Paul Theobold, Chicago, 1951.
WOLCHONOK, Louis, *The Art of Pictorial Composition,* Harper and Row, New York, 1961.

SCIENCE AND THEORY

A number of books explore the realm of light and its behavior. Among those the photographer who lacks an extensive background in science will find readable and informative are

COOK, J. Gordon, *We Live by the Sun,* Dial Press, New York, 1957.
LE GRAND, Yves, *Light, Colour and Vision,* Wiley, New York, 1957.
RUECHARDT, Eduard, *Light, Visible and Invisible,* University of Michigan Press, 1948.

Books on the science of photography, basic enough for the nonscientist, are

BAINES, H., *The Science of Photography,* Wiley, New York, 1958.
WALLS, H. J., *How Photography Works,* Macmillan, New York, 1959.

Requiring some background in science is *Fundamentals of Photographic Theory* by T. H. James and George C. Higgins, 2nd edition (Morgan and Morgan, New York, 1960). Quite difficult for the nonscientist but the classic treatise in the field of latent image and development theory is the work edited by C. E. Kenneth Mees, *The Theory of the Photographic Process,* revised edition (Macmillan, New York, 1954).

A valuable short work on the chemistry of photography is *Photo Chemistry in Black-and-White and Color Photography* by George T. Eaton (Eastman Kodak Co., Rochester, N.Y., 1957). This paperback is not excessively demanding for the nonchemist and is well worth careful study. Others on chemistry are

GLAFKIDES, Pierre, *Photographic Chemistry,* translated from the French by Keith M. Hornsby, two volumes, Macmillan, New York, 1958–60.
HORNSBY, K. M., *Basic Photo Chemistry,* Ziff-Davis, New York, 1956.

A classic reference on optics in photography is *Optics: The Technique of Definition* by Arthur Cox, 12th edition (Focal Press, London, 1961), part of the Manuals of Photo Technique series. Also valuable are

GREENLEAF, Allen R., *Photographic Optics,* Macmillan, New York, 1950.
LOCKETT, Arthur, *Camera Lenses,* 2nd edition, revised by H. W. Lee, Pitman, New York, 1947.

For the history of photographic research see *From Dry Plates to Ektachrome Film: A Story of Photographic Research* by Charles E. K. Mees (Ziff-Davis, New York, 1961).

PICTURES FOR STUDY

Books containing photographs worthy of study and analysis are many. Listed below are only a few, along with still fewer biographies of famous photographers.

ADAMS, Ansel, *Born Free and Equal,* U.S. Camera, New York, 1944.

———, *This Is the American Earth,* text by Nancy Newhall, Sierra Club, San Francisco, 1960.

AVEDON, Richard, *Observations,* text by Truman Capote, Simon and Schuster, New York, 1959.

BISCHOF, Werner, *Japan,* text by Robert Guillain, Simon and Schuster, New York, 1954.

———, *The World of Werner Bischof,* text by Manuel Gasser, Dutton, New York, 1959.

BOURKE-WHITE, Margaret, *Portrait of Myself,* Simon and Schuster, New York, 1963.

———, *Say, Is This the U.S.A.,* with Erskine Caldwell, Duell, Sloan and Pearce, New York, 1941.

———, *You Have Seen Their Faces,* with Erskine Caldwell, Modern Age Books, New York, 1934.

CAPA, Robert, *A Russian Journal,* with John Steinbeck, Viking Press, New York, 1948.

———, *Slightly Out of Focus,* Holt, Rinehart, and Winston, New York, 1947.

CARTIER-BRESSON, Henri, *The Decisive Moment,* Simon and Schuster, New York, 1952.

———, *The People of Moscow,* Simon and Schuster, New York, 1955.

———, *Photographs by Cartier-Bresson,* Grossman, New York, 1963.

EVANS, Walker, *American Photographs,* Museum of Modern Art, New York, 1938.

———, *Let Us Now Praise Famous Men,* with James Agee, Houghton Mifflin, Boston, 1960.

FABER, John, *Great Moments in News Photography,* T. Nelson, New York, 1960.

FEININGER, Andreas, *Changing America,* text by Patricia Dyett, Crown, New York, 1955.

FRANK, Robert, *The Americans,* Grove Press, New York, 1959.

KARSH, Yousuf, *Faces of Destiny,* Ziff-Davis, New York, 1946.

———, *In Search of Greatness,* Knopf, New York, 1962.

LANGE, Dorothea, *An American Exodus,* with Paul Taylor, Reynal Hitchcock, New York, 1939.

NATIONAL Association of Press Photographers, *Humor in News Photography,* T. Nelson, New York, 1961.

NEWHALL, Nancy, *Paul Strand Photographs 1915–1945,* Museum of Modern Art, New York, 1945.

NORMAN, Dorothy, *Alfred Stieglitz, Introduction to an American Seer,* Duell, Sloan and Pearce, New York, 1960.

PENN, Irving, *Moments Preserved,* Simon and Schuster, New York, 1960.

STEICHEN, Edward, *The Family of Man,* Simon and Schuster, New York, 1955.

———, *A Life in Photography,* Doubleday, New York, 1963.
WEEGEE (Arthur Fellig), *Naked City,* Essential Books, New York, 1945.
WESTON, Edward, *My Camera on Point Lobos,* Houghton Mifflin, Boston, 1950.

REFERENCE

An excellent one-volume work is the *Focal Encylopedia,* edited by Frederick Purves (Macmillan, New York, 1956). A special desk edition was published in 1960, containing all the text. but not all the illustrations.

INDEX

Index

Aberrations, 101, 104, 128
Accent light, 151, 162–163
Acceptance angle (exposure meters), 144, 146
Acetic acid, 62, 78, 217
Achromat lens, 128
Activator, in developers, 213–214
  (*See also* Alkali)
Adams, Ansel, 147
Additive (color) process, 238
Additive (exposure) system, 25–27
Aerial perspective, 37–40, 183
Agfa, 241
Agitation, in development, 59, 60, 220–221
  in fixer, 62
  in forced development, 64
Alkali, in developer, 62, 66, 213–214, 243
Alum, 197, 200, 217
Ammonium thiosulfate, 218
Angle of view, 109–113, 122–124
Angstrom unit, 88
Anscochrome, 242, 257
Antihalation backing, 202
Aperture, 11, 15, 19–22
  in additive system, 25
  in automatic cameras, 27–28
  and depth of field, 120, 125–127
  and diffraction, 98
Apochromat lens, 128

Background light, 152, 163
Back lighting, 134, 148, 151, 153, 162–163
Balance, in composition, 47–50, 52
Baryta, 202
Benzene, 211
Benzyl alcohol, 243
Bleach, in color processing, 244, 245–246
Blur (indicating time), 43
Borax, 214, 216
Boric acid, 217
Bounce light, 152, 161, 170

Bourke-White, Margaret, 4–6, 31
Brightness (color), 230, 251
Brightness adaptation, 251–253
Brightness constancy, 253
Bunsen, Robert, 18
Burning-in, 81–84

Callier effect, 72
Cameras, automatic, 27–28
  box, 11, 12
  color, 263
  Graflex, 13
  Graphic, 16
  Hasselblad, 263
  large format, 16
  one-shot color, 240
  pinhole, 11, 98, 100, 102
  reflex, 13–16, 113, 115, 116, 263
  35-mm, 12, 110–113, 114, 116, 144
  twin-lens, 16
  (*See also* Honeywell Pentax and Rolleiflex)
Carbro (color) process, 240
Carey-Lea silver, 242
Cartier-Bresson, Henri, 43, 233
Center of interest, 44–45, 52
Characteristic curve, 136–138
  of papers, 143
Chroma, 230
Chrome alum, 200, 217
Circle of confusion, 120–127
Citrazinic acid, 244
Clearing agent (*See* Hypo neutralizer)
Clearing time, 60
Color, added dimension in photography, 222
  attributes, 229–230
  distortion, 230–232
  in newspapers, 247–249
  property of vision, 223–224, 232, 233
  and wavelength, 88, 222–225, 231, 238
Color adaptation (of eye), 254
Color addition, 227, 240
Color balance (in film), 246, 254–257
Color composition, 233–235

Color constancy, 254
Color contrast, 232–233, 235, 251
Color correction, 128
Color couplers, 241–243
Color film, 222, 241–244
    classified by color balance, 254–257
    early types, 237–239, 241
    Kodachrome, 241, 243
    Kodacolor, 247
    negative, 247
    processing, 243–246
    reversal, 242, 244, 250
    transparencies, 244, 245
    tripack, 241–244
Color primaries, 225–229
Color prints, 240, 247–248
    carbro process, 240
    imbibition process, 240
Color separations, 239–243
Color subtraction, 228, 241, 244
Color temperature, 154, 156, 160
Color vision (theory), 225–226
Contact printing, 69, 71, 72
Contrast, 129–130, 139–141
    in average subject, 131
    and development, 59, 66, 141, 216,
        220–221
    and enlargers, 70–71
    in image sharpness, 36–38
    in negative, 74–75, 131–132, 135, 214
    in printing papers, 73–75, 81, 132
    (*See also* Color contrast)
Converging lens (*See* Positive lens)
Couplers, in color film, 241–242, 243
Critical angle, 95–96, 202
Cropping, 52–54, 80, 82–83

Daguerre, Louis J. M., 1, 4
Darkroom equipment, 56
Decamired system, 259–260
Densitometer, 135, 136
Density, 135–138
Depth illusion (*See* Third dimension)
Depth of field, 22, 120–127, 133, 187
Detergent (*See* Wetting agent)
Developers, Acufine, 220
    basic ingredients of, 211–216
    color, 243
    D-8, 216
    D-76, 216, 221
    Ethol UFG, 220, 221

Developers (*cont'd*)
    fine-grain, 216
    MQ, 216
    replenishing, 67–68
    Selectol Soft, 58, 160, 221
    storing, 67
Development, black-and-white film, 59–
        63
    color film, 243–246
    forced, 64
    monobath, 66–67
    35-mm film, 220–221
    theory, 208–211
    two-bath, 65–66
    water bath, 66
Development centers, 205, 206
Diaphragm (*See* Aperture)
Diffraction, 96–98
Digestion (emulsion making), 200
Dispersion, 94–95, 98
Diverging lens (*See* Negative lens)
Dodging, 83–84
Driffield, Vero C., 134
Drying, negatives, 63
    prints, 79
Dufacolor, 239
Dyes, as sensitizers, 201
    in color film, 243

Edgerton, Harold E., 158
Einstein, Albert, 86
Ektacolor, 242, 257, 262
Electronic flash, 158–160, 161–163, 172
Elon, 211, 216
Emulsion, 196–203
Enlargers, 70–72, 77
Enlarging procedure, 69, 75–78
    and depth of field, 125
EV (exposure value) system, 24–27
Exposure, 17–18, 133, 143–149
    additive system, 25–27
    automation, 27–28
    bracketing, 24
    bounce flash, 161, 170–171
    color film, 246, 250
    and development, 56–57
    with enlarger, 76–78, 79–80
    flash, 165–168, 170–171, 175
    with floodlights, 155
    with filters, 187–189
    multiple flash, 173

Exposure (*cont'd*)
    open flash, 173–174
    sensitometic test, 134–138
Exposure index, 138–139, 220
Exposure latitude, 133, 139
Exposure meters, 143–147, 189, 246, 250
Exposure table, 24

F/numbers, 19
    (*See also* Aperture)
Fading (prints), 218
Ferrotyping, 79
Fill light, 151, 152, 159, 162–163, 171, 174–175
Film, black-and-white, 222
    color sensitivity of, 177, 201–202
    orthochromatic, 189, 201, 242
    Panatomic-X, 58, 160, 221
    Panchromatic, 177, 189, 202, 243
    Plus-X, 221
    Tri-X, 220
    (*See also* color film)
Film latitude, 133, 139
Film speed, 22, 138–139
    in additive system, 25–27
    and filter factors, 189
    pushed, 64, 220
    safety factors, 138–139
Filters (for black-and-white film), 176–191
    correction, 179, 180, 183
    contrast, 180–183
    functions of, 178–187
    haze, 183
    neutral density, 187
    polarizing, 183–187, 190
    on sky, 179, 180, 185
Filters (for color film), 257–263
    polarizing, 186
    Decamired, 259–260
Filter absorption chart, 178
Filter effects table, 190
Filter factors, 187–190
Filter layer (color film), 242
Filter mounts, 187
Filter sizes, 187
Filter use guide chart, 190–191
Fixer, 62–63, 216–218
    in film processing, 60
    in print processing, 78–79
    rapid, 218

Flare, 105, 131–132
Flash (bulb), 155–158
    bare-bulb, 170
    synchronization, 160, 164–165
    exposure, 165–167
Flash (electronic), 158–160, 160–163, 172
    exposure, 167–168
    synchronization, 160, 164–165
    with sunlight, 175
Flash peak, 158
Flash techniques, 168–175
Flash with sunlight, 174–175, 253
Floodlights, 150, 154–155
Focal length, 20, 107–109, 110
    and angle of view, 109–113
    in composition, 42, 114, 122–124
    and depth of field, 125–126
    and image size, 109, 110
    and perspective, 113
    variable, 116–118
Footcandles, 25–26
Formaldehyde, 197, 200
Fox-Talbot, William Henry, 158
Front lighting, 150

Gamma, 140–143
Gelatin, 197
Glare, filtering of, 183–184
Glycerin, in print drying, 79
    in emulsion, 202
Godowsky, Leopold, 241
Grain, 58, 63, 64, 67, 208, 220
Guide numbers, for flash, 165–168
Gurney-Mott theory, 205
Gurney, R. W., 205

H & D Curve, 136
Halation, 202
Halides (*See* Silver halides)
Halo effect, 202
Halogens, 194, 210
Hardener, 62, 217
Hardening, 62, 200
Haze, 37, 183
Honeywell Pentax, 113, 116
    for color photography, 236, 263
    cutaway view of, 13
    photograph of, 20
    photographs taken with, 23, 42, 58, 112, 120, 122–124, 160–163, 172

Horizon, in photographs, 40
Hue, 229
Hurter, Ferdinand, 134
Huygens, Christian, 85
Hyperfocal distance, 127
Hypo (*See* Fixer)
Hypo eliminator, 219–220
Hypo neutralizer, 63, 79, 218–219
Hydroquinone, 211, 216

Imbibition (color process), 240
Induction period, 81
Intensity formula, 19
Interference, 107, 238
Ionic compounds, 195–196

Karsh, Yousuf, 129
Kelvin, 156
Key light, 151, 152, 162–163, 171
Kodachrome, 241, 243, 257, 258
Kodacolor, 247, 262
Kodak Dye Transfer, 241
Kodak Photo-Flo, 63
Kodak Pola Screen, 185
Kodalk Balanced Alkali, 214

Latent image, 194, 197, 204–208, 210, 216
Lens, 11
  aberrations, 101, 104
  angle of view, 109–113
  color correction, 128
  coating, 105–106
  distortions, 113–114
  flare, 105
  focal length, 107–109, 110, 113
  making, 104–105
  perspective, 113–114
Lenses, 11
  automatic, 15
  auxiliary, 118–119
  cleaning of, 128
  compound, 104–107
  interchangeable, 110–113, 122–124
  retrofocus, 115–116
  Rollei Mutar, 118–119
  semi-telephoto, 42
  simple, 102–103
  Takumar, 23, 42, 104, 116, 122–124
  telephoto, 110, 112, 114–115, 117, 124, 140

Lenses (*cont'd*)
  35-mm camera, 12, 110–113, 114
  wide-angle, 42, 51, 110–113, 121, 234
  zoom, 116–118
Light, as electromagnetic radiation, 85
  as energy, 192–194
  corpuscle theory, 85–86
  frequency, 88–89
  photons, 86, 89–90, 192
  rays, 89
  speed of, 89, 92–93
  wave theory, 85, 86–89
  wavelengths, 87–88, 95, 98, 177
Lighting, basic, 152–153
  color photography, 230, 253–254
  effects of, 150
  five functions of, 151–152
  flash, 168–175
  forms of, 150–151
  modeling, 152, 161–163
  texture, 153–154
  triangular, 162
Light values, 24–27
Linear perspective, 36–40
Lines, in composition, 36, 45–47, 49–50
Lippmann, Gabriel, 237
Lippmann process, 237–238
Log *e*, 136
Logarithms, 135–136
Lumen seconds, 157
Lumiere color process, 238–239

Magnification formula, 70
Mannes, Leopold, 241
Masking, in color photography, 241, 247
Maxwell, James Clerk, 85
Meters, exposure, 143–147, 189
Metol, 211, 216
Micron, 88
Millimicron, 88
Milliseconds, 158
Mired, 259
Monochromatic light, 224
Mott, N. F., 205
Multiple flash, 171–173

Negative lens, 103, 104, 114–115
Neutralizer (*See* Hypo neutralizer)
Newton, Sir Isaac, 85, 86
Niépce, Joseph-Nicéphore, 1, 4

Opacity, 135–136
Open-flash technique, 173–174
Optical glass, 105
Optics, 100–101
  geometrical, 91–98
  (*See also* Lens and Lenses)
Oxidation, 210, 214, 243

Pentax (*See* Honeywell Pentax)
Perspective, 36–40, 113–114, 122–124
Photochemistry, 192
Photoelectric cell, 90, 143
Photography, as art, 6–8
  defined, 1, 10, 17–18
  inspirational, 6
  recording process, 9
  and reality, 1–4, 9, 10
  utilitarian, 4–6
Photon, 86, 192
Pinholes, in film processing, 59–60, 62
Planck, Max, 86
Polarization, 98–99, 183 187
Positive hole, 205, 208
Positive lens, 101, 104, 114–115
Potassium bromide, 197, 199, 200, 214,
  216, 246
Potassium ferricyanide, 246
Preservative, 214, 217, 244
Primaries, additive, 227, 239, 242–
  243
  subtractive, 228, 241, 243, 244
  (*See also* Color)
Printing-out papers, 72, 194
Printing papers, 72–75, 202
  for color negatives, 247–248
  variable-contrast, 70, 75
Profile lighting, 153
Projection printing (*See* Enlarging)
Proximity, in composition, 47, 49

Quanta, 86, 90, 205, 206
Quantum theory, 86, 192

Radiation, 85, 86–87
Rapid fixer, 62
Reciprocity, 18, 257
Rectilinear propagation, 91, 94
Reducing agents, 210–211, 213
Reduction, 209, 210

Reflection, 91–92
  color, 232
  filtering of, 183, 184
  flash, 170
  total, 95
Reflectors, 150, 152, 253
Reflex (*See* Cameras)
Refraction, 92–94, 95
Refractive index, 94, 95, 107
Repetition, in composition, 44, 46, 47
Replenishment, 67–68
Restrainer, 214–216
Reticulation, 58
Reversal film (color), 242, 257
Rhythm, in composition, 44, 47
Ripening of emulsion, 199–200
Rodinal, 211
Rolleiflex, 118, 119, 160, 236, 260, 263
Rollei Mutars, 118–119
Roscoe, Sir Henry, 18
Rule of the thirds, 45, 53

Saturation (color), 230, 236
Scale, in photographs, 40–42
Selectol Soft developer, 58, 160, 221
Sensitivity centers, 200, 208
Sensitizers, 200, 201
Sensitometer, 135, 136–137
Sensitometry, 133–143
Separation negatives, 240
Sheet film, development of, 60
Shutter, 11, 18–19, 21–22
  in additive system, 25
  and flash synchronization, 160, 164–
  165
  focal-plane, 11–12, 15, 164–165
Side lighting, 151, 152, 153–154
Silhouette, 153
Silver, in development, 208–211
  image forming, 1, 197, 204–208
  in photochemistry, 192–196
Silver bromide, 194–199, 203, 210
Silver halides, 1, 194, 196, 197, 204,
  208, 216–217
  (*See also* Exposure and Develop-
  ment)
Silver iodide, 194, 199
Skylight filter, 258
Slave units, 173
Sodium carbonate, 214

Sodium hydroxide, 214, 216
Sodium sulfate, 216
Sodium sulfite, 214, 216, 217, 244
Sodium thiosulfate, 217
Solarization, 138
Space, and scale, 40
  in composition, 36–42
Spectrum, 86, 88, 180, 224, 225
Spot meters, 146
Spotlight, 150, 153, 154, 163
Stability, in composition, 47–50, 52
Stabilization, 218
Stop bath, in film processing, 62
  in print processing, 78
Stops, 19
  (*See also* Aperture)
Strand, Paul, 233
Sulphur, in emulsion, 197, 200
Synchronization, 160, 164–165

Technicolor process, 241
Telephoto lens (*See* Lens)
Temperature, in film development, 57–
  58, 66, 67, 220–221
  in print development, 80
Test strips, 76
Texture, lighting for, 153–154
Third dimension, 30, 36, 38, 235

Time, in composition, 42–44
  in film development, 58–59, 66, 67,
    141, 149
  in print development, 81
Timing (exposure), 43–44
Tone, in composition, 50–52
Top lighting, 151
Transmission, 135–136
Tripack (color film), 241–244

Ultraviolet filter, 259

Value (color), 230
Viewpoint, 9, 34
  and emphasis, 40–41
  and linear perspective, 39–40
Vision, and brightness, 251
  and color, 224–226, 232, 233, 254

Washing, 218–219
  negatives, 63
  prints, 79
Watt-second, 167
Weston, Edward, 233
Wetting agent, 63
Wide-angle lens (*See* Lens)
Wiping negatives, 63

Zone System (exposure), 147–149